York St John

Shakespeare's *Othello* has exercised a powerful fascination over audiences for centuries with its intense portrayal of passionate love and destructive jealousy. This study is a major exercise in the historicization of *Othello*. Initially the author examines the early Jacobean context of the play, and the discourses which formed its writing. Circulating simultaneously in late Renaissance London were accounts of Mediterranean clashes between Turks and Venetians, treatises on the professionalization of England's military forces, depictions of North Africans and blackamoors, and narratives of jealous husbands who murdered their wives. In the centuries after 1604, productions of *Othello* stressed the contextual discourse that best reflected current cultural concerns.

The first section examines these four sets of contemporary writings and demonstrates how they were embedded in the text of *Othello*. The following chapters trace *Othello*'s history on stage or in film in England and the United States from the Restoration to the late 1980s. Each chapter highlights particular productions or performers to demonstrate how and why elements from Shakespeare's text were emphasized or repressed. In the Restoration, for example, Othello was a gentleman and an officer, his characterization shaped by actors who had served in King Charles' army. During the Victorian period, in contrast, the Moor's private role of devoted husband was privileged over his occupation. When Paul Robeson performed Othello in 1930 and 1943–44, race was highlighted as the play's central issue. *Othello* is thus revealed as a significant shaper and major reflector of cultural meanings, as it participated in a complex negotiation between actors, critics, audiences, and the culture at large.

OTHELLO

OTHELLO

A contextual history

VIRGINIA MASON VAUGHAN

Professor of English, Clark University, Worcester, Massachusetts

CAMBRIDGE
UNIVERSITY PRESS

Published by the Press Syndicate of the University of Cambridge
The Pitt Building, Trumpington Street, Cambridge CB2 1RP, United Kingdom

Cambridge University Press
The Edinburgh Building, Cambridge CB2 2RU, United Kingdom
40 West 20th Street, New York, NY 10011-4211, USA
10 Stamford Road, Oakleigh, Melbourne 3166, Australia

First published 1994
First paperback edition 1996

Typeset in Monotype Baskerville

A catalogue record for this book is available from the British Library

Library of Congress cataloguing in publication data

Vaughan, Virginia Mason.
Othello: a contextual history / Virginia Mason Vaughan.
p.   cm.
Includes index.
ISBN 0 521 46069 7 (hardback)
1. Shakespeare, William, 1564–1616. Othello.   2. Shakespeare, William, 1564–1616
Contemporary England.   3. Literature and history – England – History – 17th century.
4. Shakespeare, William, 1564–1616 – Stage history.   I. Title.
PR2829.V38   1995
822.3'3 – dc20   93-50148   CIP

ISBN 0 521 46069 7 hardback
ISBN 0 521 58708 5 paperback

Transferred to digital printing 2000

For the Welsh boys
Where I have garnered up my heart

Contents

Illustrations

Acknowledgments

When a book takes several years to complete, especially when it has vied with other projects, the author cannot recall every conversational tip, friendly suggestion, or helpful critique. Many students, academic colleagues, friends, and librarians – more of each than I can remember by name – have contributed to the pages that follow; I am thankful to all who assisted and encouraged along the way. Here I gratefully acknowledge some specific debts. The largest is to those who critiqued the entire manuscript in its final stages: two anonymous readers for Cambridge University Press, and two better known but no less demanding critics, Kent Cartwright and Alden T. Vaughan. While I did not accept every single suggestion, this book is infinitely better because of their painstaking efforts. I also appreciate the patience of my editor, Sarah Stanton.

Others have helped with particular segments of the book. They include Dame Peggy Ashcroft, Leeds Barroll, Dana N. Benelli, Jaq Bessell, Christine Bolt, Marcia Butzel, John C. Conron, Peter Donaldson, Martin B. Duberman, Ron Engle, Werner Gundersheimer, Andrew Gurr, Kathy Howlett, Nancy Maguire, Margaret Mikesell, Harry Pedicord, John Pocock, Denis Salter, John Sena, Charles Shattuck, Ann Thompson, John Thompson, and F. Mary White.

I also owe a great debt to the institutions that supported my research. Foremost is the Folger Shakespeare Library in Washington DC, where this project began in 1987 when I was the proud recipient of an O. B. Hardison senior fellowship; in the spring of 1987 I read an early version of chapter 5 to the Folger Institute's Colloquium, where the feedback was generous and instructive. I am particularly grateful to the Folger's knowledgeable, efficient, and courteous staff, especially Julie Ainsworth, Jean Miller, and Betsy Walsh, and to my fellow readers who listened so patiently along the way.

I am also indebted to the Henry E. Huntington Library in San Marino, California, for awarding me an Andrew Mellon fellowship during the summer of 1989. Staff members of the British Library were also helpful on my sporadic trips to London. At the American Antiquarian Society in Worcester, Massachusetts, I was able to look at reviews from an unparalleled collection of nineteenth-century American newspapers. The staff at the Pusey Library of Harvard University assisted my reading of Henry Irving's study book, in the Harvard Theatre Collection. The curator at Smallhythe, Ellen Terry's home in Kent, England, kindly xeroxed Terry's notes on her text of *Othello*. The Shakespeare Centre Library at Stratford generously reproduced the promptbook of the Trevor Nunn 1989 Royal Shakespeare Company *Othello* so that I could work on it at home. The reference staff of the Robert Hutchings Goddard Library at Clark University – especially Mary Hartman and Irene Walsh – helped me fill in the remaining gaps. As I reflect back over the years I've been involved in the study of *Othello*, I am overwhelmed by how much I owe to dedicated librarians and archivists in the United States and England.

Earlier versions of chapters 5 and 7 appeared in article form, and I thank the editors of *Theatre History Studies* and *Shakespeare Worldwide* for permission to reuse the material that appeared in these journals.

I was also fortunate to be able to present chapters 6 and 9 as seminar papers at meetings of the Shakespeare Association of America and the Shakespeare Institute at Stratford. Cary Mazer and Peter Holland, my astute seminar leaders, led engaging discussions; these chapters are thereby clearer and sounder. I also shared part of chapter 8 with the Columbia University Shakespeare Seminar, and the ensuing spirited interchange helped shape my thinking.

Most of the illustrations in this book came from promptbooks, the art collection, or the rare books of the Folger Shakespeare Library, which has graciously given its permission to reproduce them. Figure 15 appears courtesy of the British Library, figure 17 by permission of Castle Hill Productions, Inc., while figures 18 and 19 are reproduced from the Joe Cocks Studio Collection at the Shakespeare Centre Library.

Finally, I must acknowledge the support I have received through the years from my colleagues at Clark University; special thanks are due to my department chair, Serena Sue Hilsinger, who has helped in hundreds of quiet ways, and to Edith Mathis, upon whom I depend more than I can say.

Introduction

O, who hath done this deed?
Nobody; I myself.

(Othello, 5.2.124–25)

Othello has been a central focus of my thinking, research, and writing for the past decade. My obsession with Shakespeare's tragedy started in 1982 when I joined forces with Margaret Lael Mikesell to compile the Garland Annotated Bibliography on *Othello*. For the next eight years, I culled innumerable libraries, reading and annotating all the relevant books, articles, dissertations, reviews, and notes I could find. In the process I encountered a broader range of critical and methodological approaches than I had known existed. I also began to have my own ideas about *Othello*.

A side adventure was a temporary stint as Associate Editor of the New Variorum *Othello*, then under the direction of John Hazel Smith, a man bent on collecting everything ever written on "his" play. In my New Variorum hat, I worked on *Othello*'s complicated stage history, devoting a six-month fellowship at the Folger Shakespeare Library to reading traditional sources – promptbooks, actors' memoirs, reviews. But I soon realized that the world did not need another comprehensive stage history of *Othello*; scholars, actors, and students could already turn to works by Marvin Rosenberg, Gino J. Matteo, and Julie Hankey for masterful overviews of the play's stage history and analyses of the most famous productions and best known actors.[1] In 1986, however, John Hazel Smith, a scholar beloved by

---

[1] See Marvin Rosenberg, *The Masks of Othello* (Berkeley: University of California Press, 1961); Gino J. Matteo, *Shakespeare's "Othello": The Study and the Stage, 1604–1904* (Salzburg: Institut für Englische Sprache und Literatur, 1974); and Julie Hankey, ed., *Othello* (Bristol: Bristol Classical Press, 1987). A more compact but no less helpful overview is provided by Carol Jones Carlisle in *Shakespeare from the Greenroom: Actors' Criticisms of Four Major Tragedies* (Chapel Hill: University of North Carolina Press, 1969), pp. 172–263.

students and professional colleagues alike, suddenly and tragically succumbed to cancer. Since the partnership I had embarked on was not to be, I resigned from the New Variorum project with great sadness.

Othello was not done with me yet. In 1988 the Trustees of the Shakespeare Association of America asked me to organize a seminar on "*Othello*: New Perspectives" for its annual conference in Boston. That seminar soon ballooned into two sessions, each devoted to a variety of critical perspectives and methodologies. In collaboration with Kent Cartwright, I selected eleven of the essays for an anthology published under the same title.[2]

The collaborations with Margaret Lael Mikesell, John Hazel Smith, and Kent Cartwright had been immensely rewarding and stimulating, yet most of my work on this magnificent play had involved the processing of other scholars' views. It was time to find my own voice. In 1989 I published an account of *Othello* on the Restoration stage in *Theatre History Studies*;[3] the same year I wrote an essay on William Charles Macready's *Othello* (not published until 1991) for the Japanese annual, *Shakespeare Worldwide*.[4] By 1990 I realized that I was well on my way toward my own book on *Othello*. In particular, I had compiled broad-ranging sources in two categories: the first, contexts from the early seventeenth century that would have been available to Shakespeare; the second, materials about subsequent theatrical representations.

As a result, this book is divided in two complementary sections. The first four chapters focus on *Othello* at the moment of production; they historicize major elements that have, in turn, influenced subsequent interpretations, performances, and adaptations. They provide contexts – the sort of things Shakespeare might have incorporated deliberately or osmotically.[5]

Shakespeare's sources for *Othello*'s plot, characterizations, and language are well known, particularly through the most widely used

---

[2] Virginia Mason Vaughan and Kent Cartwright, eds., *Othello: New Perspectives* (Cranbury, NJ: Fairleigh Dickinson University Press, 1991). We added a twelfth essay by a ringer – Barbara Hodgdon's discussion of *Othello* adaptations in opera and film.

[3] "Politics and Plagiarism: *Othello* in the Restoration," *Theatre History Studies*, 9 (1989): 1–21. This article has been revised and expanded in chapter 5.

[4] "The Road to Astor Place: The English and American Othellos of William Charles Macready," *Shakespeare Worldwide*, 13 (1991), pp. 99–115. Parts of this essay have been incorporated into chapter 7.

[5] I borrow the latter term from Margaret Loftus Ranald, *Shakespeare and His Social Context: Essays in Osmotic Knowledge and Literary Interpretation* (New York: AMS Press, 1987).

compendium, Geoffrey Bullough's *Narrative and Dramatic Sources of Shakespeare*. Scholars generally agree that Shakespeare took his plot from Giraldi Cinthio's *Gli Hecatommithi* (1566), Decade 3, Story 7, perhaps adding some psychological analysis from Geoffrey Fenton's tale of an "Albanoyse Captain" in *Certain Tragicall Discourses* (1567). Details about Moors were lifted from John Pory's translation of John Leo's *Geographical Historie of Africa* (1600), about Venice from Lewes Lewkenor's translation of Gaspar Contarini's *The Commonwealth and Gouernment of Venice* (1599), and about Turks from Richard Knolles' *Generall Historie of the Turkes* (1603). Shakespeare adapted Cinthio's spare narrative to the theatre by speeding up the action, adding the double time scheme, and deepening the hero's and villain's characterizations.[6]

The tactics of traditional source study have been to trace specific words, phrases, characters, and events that the dramatist must have borrowed from another text and to estimate each text's overall influence on Shakespeare's play by measuring the frequency of such details. Source studies have demonstrated the eclectic quality of Shakespeare's mind and his use of various texts during the process of composition, but they are limited by a narrow conception of "source." To qualify as a source, a text must have elements that are replicated in Shakespeare's play.

New Historicism and Cultural Materialism propose broader, more flexible discursive influences. In Stephen Greenblatt's words, "the work of art is the product of a negotiation between a creator or class of creators, equipped with a complex, communally shared repertoire of conventions, and the institutions and practices of society."[7] Greenblatt readily admits that it is impossible to identify such conventions and cultural practices in their entirety or with all certainty, yet cultural contexts are often as important as specific sources in the attempt to understand a particular work. They place the literary text – as closely as a late-twentieth-century reader can – within the cultural milieu of its production.

Despite some controversy over the authenticity of extant records,[8]

[6] Geoffrey Bullough, *Narrative and Dramatic Sources of Shakespeare* (New York: Columbia University Press, 1973), vol. VII, pp. 193–265.

[7] Stephen Greenblatt, "Toward a Poetics of Culture," in *New Historicism*, ed. H. Aram Veeser (New York: Routledge, 1989), pp. 1–14; quote from p. 12.

[8] Cf. Horace Howard Furness's discussion of *Othello*'s date in *A New Variorum Edition of Shakespeare: Othello* (New York: Dover, 1963; repr. of J. B. Lippincott's edition, 1886), pp. 344–57. E. A. J. Honigmann disputes the accepted 1604 date, arguing instead for late 1601

scholars accept 1604 as the year of *Othello*'s first performance and 1603–04 as the period of composition. Thus Shakespeare composed *Othello* during a crucial year for the British people and for his dramatic company. On 24 March 1603 Queen Elizabeth died; on 19 May, the Lord Chamberlain's Men were made into the King's Men; and on 3 August, James VI of Scotland was crowned King of England. Londoners were curious about their new king. Immediately after his accession, London presses began to publish panegyrics and descriptions of his journey south from Scotland; they also reissued his *Basilikon Doron*, *Daemonology*, and *Lepanto*. Shakespeare, presumably an avid reader of visual and verbal signs, was thus exposed to a host of new texts related to James and his interests. Some of these texts have been identified as direct sources for *Othello*; others are equally important as contexts. By examining sources and contexts together, we can learn about the contemporary concerns – domestic and global – that are refracted in the first tragedy Shakespeare wrote as a King's Man.

To bring some order out of this chaotic wealth of materials, I focus in the first half of my book on four discursive fields[9] that resonate through many late sixteenth and early seventeenth-century texts, including *Othello*. I begin with a nexus of global discourses. First, we find repeated expressions of concern about the Turkish threat to Europe: Christian "civility" opposes Islamic "barbarism." During the sixteenth century, Ottomite victories, including the 1572 capture of Cyprus from Venice, and travelers' tales of events "passing strange," persuaded Europeans that Christian civilization in Europe was in jeopardy. Superimposed onto the conception of a world divided between "them" and "us" were the discourses of "Orientalism" and colonialism.[10] The effort to maintain and expand European

or 1602. See "The First Quarto of *Hamlet* and the Date of *Othello*," *Review of English Studies*, 44 (1993): 211–19.

[9] By "discursive field," I mean a subset of what Michel Foucault described as a "discursive formation," defined by Annabel Patterson as "a horizontal system of interrelated institutions and the 'codes,' or discourses that made them work." (See her essay, "Historical Scholarship," in *Introduction to Scholarship in Modern Languages and Literatures*, ed. Joseph Gibaldi [New York: The Modern Language Association, 1992], pp. 183–200; quote from p. 185.) The discursive formation of Jacobean England circa 1604 would combine all of the institutions that existed and all discourses that were available at the time. A discursive field – tracts and treatises on marriage, for example – is but a small portion of a larger, complex web.

[10] For a pathbreaking outline of the concept of "Orientalism," see Edward W. Said, *Orientalism* (New York: Pantheon, 1978), esp. chapters 1–2.

civilization was furthered by repeated assertions of Europe's superiority over alien peoples.

A second discursive field resonating through *Othello* focuses on the military and its role in society. During the Renaissance the medieval image of the "parfit, gentil knight" who fought against the Saracen to regain the holy sepulchre (Chaucer's description) was gradually superseded by a new sense of professionalism. Military theorists argued that the art of war be a science, yet the old chivalric ideal held its power. Venice, as a city-state that needed to protect a vast overseas trading network, was caught between the old ideal and the new science; like England under Elizabeth and James, Venice needed military prowess but feared its subversive potential, disbanding its armies at each war's end. This ambivalence resulted in the Venetian practice of employing "strangers," *condottiere*, as a professional, standing army. The status of non-Venetian captains was necessarily ambiguous – vital to the state's safety, but seldom a fully accepted part of it. Othello is caught between the old ideals and the new professionalism; his adherence to a chivalric code of honor defines his sense of "occupation" and makes him more vulnerable to the wiles of Iago, a perversion of the new military man.

The concept of racial difference is a third major discursive field in *Othello*, cutting across other discourses as well. With the exploration and exploitation of Africa begun by the Portuguese in the fifteenth century, race became a global concept, though not as rigid as it was to become in the nineteenth century: European whites argued about the origins and humanity of Moors and East and West Indians, resting their cases on the ethnocentric certainty that their own selves and ways were central and superior. Race also affects the microcosm in *Othello*, for the marriage of a black man and a white woman is the emotional core of Shakespeare's play. And as recent commentators have shown, race was (and is) integrally tied to concepts of gender and sexuality.[11]

My fourth discursive field is therefore based on marital and sexual relations, the union of husband and wife, male and female.

[11] Cf. Ania Loomba's discussion of "Sexuality and Racial Difference" in *Gender, Race, Renaissance Drama* (Manchester: University of Manchester Press, 1989), pp. 38–64; Kim Hall's unpub. Ph.D. diss., "Acknowledging Things of Darkness" (University of Pennsylvania, 1990); and an anthology published too recently to be incorporated into my analysis, *Women, "Race," and Writing in the Early Modern Period*, ed. Patricia Parker and Margo Hendricks (London: Routledge, 1994).

Subjugation of the female Other is not simply a convenient domestic arrangement but a fundamental building block of the patriarchal state. Venice kept its aristocracy pure by rigid control over marriage; Desdemona's elopement is thus subversive of the state as well as the family.

Othello is, of course, multivocal, the issues it embodies complicated. Even the four fairly straightforward discursive fields I have selected here comprehend a wide array of views – some of them contradictory – that overlap and interpenetrate. To discuss them in terms of four categories is necessarily to oversimplify. At the same time, material so vast has to be focused if it is to be comprehended. Though the discussions that follow will show how these discursive fields resonate from global politics in the macrocosm to the microcosmic relations of husband and wife, for the sake of manageability, I will discuss them separately.

A not-so-hidden agenda in this study is to show that *Othello*, particularly when staged without drastic cuts in Act I, can be a profoundly political drama. Too often the play has been dismissed as domestic tragedy, lesser in some sense than *Macbeth* or *King Lear* because its hero is not a king, and its major action, suspected adultery, has no dynastic repercussions.[12] But Othello's loss, as I shall demonstrate, does have frightening consequences for Venice, a city precariously balanced on the frontiers of Christian civilization. That precariousness was a crucial ingredient in the "myth of Venice," a concept common in the texts published in 1603 and no less important to Shakespeare's drama. The first chapter begins, therefore, with sixteenth- and seventeenth-century global politics.

The book's second section traces *Othello*'s history in England and the United States from the Restoration to the late 1980s. It is not meant to be a comprehensive stage history; the chapters are more detailed than a survey allows, focusing on particular *epistemes* (the Restoration), actors (Macready, Salvini, Robeson), or productions (Delaval, Welles, Nunn). Here the effort is also to historicize, to place the *Othello* of a particular generation and culture within its historical

---

[12] For discussion of *Othello* as domestic tragedy, see Coppelia Kahn, *Man's Estate: Masculine Identity in Shakespeare* (Berkeley: University of California Press, 1981), pp. 140–50; Carol Thomas Neely, "Women and Men in *Othello*," in *Broken Nuptials in Shakespeare's Plays* (New Haven: Yale University Press, 1985), pp.105–35; and Marianne L. Novy, "Marriage and Mutuality in *Othello*," in *Love's Argument: Gender Relations in Shakespeare* (Chapel Hill: University of North Carolina Press, 1984), pp. 125–49.

framework and to demonstrate why elements from the original text(s) were emphasized or repressed. When I can, I try to show how the discursive fields outlined in Part I influenced, in turn, the thinking of actors and managers who presented *Othello* to public audiences. Sometimes one field will dominate: the Restoration, for example, was far more concerned with Othello's military prowess than his race, whereas some late twentieth-century productions emphasize the drama's racial overtones. My goal is to show *Othello* not simply as a product of a cultural milieu but also as a *maker* of cultural meanings, part of a complex negotiation between each episteme's cultural attitudes, its actors, and their audiences. Thus the second section of *Othello: A Contextual History* emphasizes decisions involved in production and tries, whenever possible, to assess what attitudes actors brought to performances and how audiences responded.

Such contextualization is important in understanding adaptations, productions that substantially alter Shakespeare's text. While *Othello* was not subject to the improvements of William Davenant or Nahum Tate, it has been adapted for opera and film.[13] It would take another book to discuss such adaptations in comprehensive detail; here the focus is on one cinematic version that stays comparatively close to Shakespeare's original: Orson Welles's 1955 film, which has recently been reedited and reissued.

My selections are admittedly different from those of traditional historians who wanted to discover the "best" Othellos, the "most fully realized" Iagos. I concede that there is a significant difference between good acting and bad (though what might please a Victorian could offend someone in the 1990s), but I am not concerned here with qualitative judgments about performance. Such judgments, I believe, are often based on the "essentialist" assumption that dramatic character is discrete, knowable, and clearly defined. Instead, I see Shakespeare's texts and the characters inscribed therein as open to a multiplicity of interpretations, some of them contradictory. Unlike earlier twentieth-century critics, we no longer have to decide if Othello is noble *or* barbaric, a hero *or* a sentimental fool. Generations of critics have argued that he can be either or both

---

[13] For an excellent discussion of Verdi's *Otello* and twentieth-century cinematic adaptations, see Barbara Hodgdon, "Kiss Me Deadly; or, the Des/demonized Spectacle," in *Othello: New Perspectives*, pp. 214–55. Film adaptations also include the western *Jubal* and the rock musical *Catch My Soul*.

– the text supports contradictory readings.[14] But how an actor or a particular production deals with those contradictory signals tells us much about assumptions and values – beliefs that necessarily involve issues about nationalism, militarism, race, and gender.

Although a few of the texts and events described in these pages have not been considered before in any great detail or in relation to *Othello*, most of the contexts provided are already familiar to Shakespearean scholars. This book's contribution, I believe, is to bring a broad range of texts *together* in an intertextual framework. The result is an historical contextualization within which (and against which) *Othello* can be read.

This is risky business. During 1991 I participated in a panel, "Historicizing *Othello*," at the Columbia University Shakespeare Seminar. During the discussion that followed, a distinguished member of the audience asked, "Why historicize?" That question has nagged me ever since. Why indeed? Part of my justification is self-serving; I enjoy primary texts and the creative pleasure of trying to fit bits and pieces of historical evidence into a larger, coherent pattern. I also believe that historicizing provides ways in and out of the text, bridging the gap between Shakespeare's age and our own. If we didn't know anything about Jacobean attitudes towards women and marriage, for example, wouldn't Emilia's speech about the double standard strike us as common sense – what every woman knows but does not say – rather than a subversive declaration to an audience in 1604? Historical contexts can serve as a means to the end of understanding. They remind us that no truth is absolute, that our own readings and hearings take place within a discrete historical epoch and are therefore subject to qualification and even dismissal by future generations. Historical contexts also mitigate Western culture's tendency toward bardolatry by situating Shakespeare's texts within a particular time and place. While the dramatist may, indeed, prove to be what Ben Jonson claimed, a writer "for all time," his words are consistently reencoded by succeeding generations.

One might also ask, why especially historicize *Othello*? The answer to this hypothetical question seems more obvious, for in *Othello* Shakespeare wove an intricate web that we still struggle to unravel. Scholars and audiences have been aware for decades (certainly since

---

[14] For a good overview of twentieth-century approaches to Othello's character, see Margaret Lael Mikesell's introduction to *Othello: An Annotated Bibliography* (New York: Garland, 1990), pp. xi–xxv.

Paul Robeson's performance in 1943) of *Othello* as a text about constructions of racial identity.[15] In the 1990s we are beginning to connect constructions of gender with racial attitudes and to place both within the contexts of colonialism, postcolonialism, and military interventionism. *Othello*, written at the beginning of England's overseas colonial enterprise, now seems strangely prescient because it probes all of these connections, attaching the private story of a husband and wife to the larger concerns of the Venetian Empire and even larger issues of cultural exchange and conflict that still plague us.

We are also learning to historicize the text itself. My stint on the New Variorum *Othello* taught me that *Othello*'s several texts are highly problematic. Because this volume is not primarily concerned with textual issues, I rely on a modern edition of *Othello*, but, in keeping with current trends in analytic bibliography, the choice of edition has not been casual. Except for chapter 11 (where I use M. R. Ridley's Arden edition because it served as promptcopy for the Trevor Nunn 1989 Royal Shakespeare Company production), quotations from *Othello* in this book are taken from Norman Sanders' 1984 New Cambridge edition, which conflates Q1 and the First Folio. Sanders argues that both are authoritative, reflecting "two stages of composition for both of which Shakespeare himself was responsible."[16] Sanders' recognition of both texts' validity makes his conflated version the best now available for my purposes.

[15] See, for example, Winthrop D. Jordan, *White Over Black: American Attitudes Toward the Negro, 1550–1812* (Chapel Hill: University of North Carolina Press, 1968), pp. 37–43, where Jordan uses *Othello* to demonstrate how entrenched color prejudice was in early modern English consciousness.

[16] Norman Sanders, ed., *Othello* (Cambridge: Cambridge University Press, 1984), p. 206.

PART I

Jacobean contexts

CHAPTER I

Global discourse: Venetians and Turks

This is Venice; / My house is not a grange.

(*Othello*, 1.1.106–07)

European distrust of alien cultures was nothing new in 1604. From the ancient Greeks to the present, Edward Said has shown, European culture partly defined itself in opposition to the Orient. Said traces the separation of East and West back as far as *The Iliad* and Aeschylus' *The Persians*. In such texts, he asserts, "A line is drawn between two continents. Europe is powerful and articulate; Asia is defeated and distant." Thus the "motif of the Orient as insinuating danger" was prevalent in Western thought long before the first Crusade,[1] but the rise of the Ottoman Empire turned a motif into an obsession. By Shakespeare's day "the Turk" represented all that was barbaric and demonic, in contrast to the Christian's civil and moral rightness.

Orientalism was not the only discourse that shaped world affairs during the Renaissance. With the exploration of Africa and Asia and the "discovery" of the New World, colonialism profoundly informed European attitudes toward foreign nations. Charles Verlinden explains that colonization derives from the Latin word "colere," – to cultivate or put to use. From the earliest times, he argues, societies customarily appropriated new territories for their own use.[2] Verlinden further defines colonization as "a process by which the frontier of a less technologically developed or less organized civilization – and organization is also a technique – yielded before a civilization whose technological equipment was superior."[3] Thus the ancient Greeks pushed into the Mediterranean perimeter; Rome reached as far as

---

[1] Edward W. Said, *Orientalism* (New York: Pantheon, 1978), p. 57.
[2] Charles Verlinden, *The Beginnings of Modern Colonization*, trans. Yvonne Freccero (Ithaca: Cornell University Press, 1970), p. ix.   [3] Ibid., p. xiv.

13

England; the Germanic tribes penetrated into Gaul; and William the Conqueror invaded England, changing its nature forever.

"Medieval colonization," observes Verlinden, "was primarily the work of the Italian city republics, which created colonies first in the Holy Land and then on the remains of the Byzantine Empire along the shores of the Aegean, the Ionian, and even the Black Sea."[4] Strategically located in the eastern Mediterranean, the island of Cyprus was a logical target for any power that wished to engage in trade between East and West. It is hardly surprising that Venice deemed it a crucial imperial possession.

The discourses of Orientalism and colonialism, which thrived in Italy, Spain, and France during the Middle Ages had moved to England by the Renaissance. When Shakespeare wrote *Othello*, both were lively issues in text and diplomacy. For example, during August 1600 a Moroccan envoy to Queen Elizabeth discussed trade relations and a potential joint effort against Spain. Reactions in England were mixed, ranging from the refusal of many mariners to transport the "infidels," to fascination with their exotic qualities. In his review of the extant records, Jack D'Amico found "not one image of the Moroccan, but many images, from the dangerously inscrutable alien to the exotically attractive ally."[5] English views of the Moroccan king El-Mansour were shaped partly by Orientalism (he and his court were seductive, different, and dangerous) and partly by colonialism (his kingdom might be of use to England in its global enterprises). But England's reactions were also animated by her traditional distrust of foreigners on the one hand and by the desire to find an ally against popish Spain on the other.[6] English ambivalence was thus multifaceted, charged with a variety of agendas both private and public.

Even more complicated was England's attitude toward Venice, which vacillated between assertions of similarity and insistence on difference. Like England, Venice was a Christian nation with a mercantile economy, an island that depended on its navy for financial and political security, and a mixed government with imperial

---

[4] Ibid., pp. xix–xx.
[5] Jack D'Amico, *The Moor in English Renaissance Drama* (Tampa, Florida: University of South Florida Press, 1991), p. 39. See his entire discussion in chapter 1.
[6] See G. K. Hunter, "Elizabethans and foreigners," in his collection of essays, *Dramatic Identities and Cultural Tradition: Studies in Shakespeare and His Contemporaries* (Liverpool: Liverpool University Press, 1978), throughout, but esp. p. 14.

aspirations. But Venice was also perceived as alien. As a Catholic, Italian city-state, it was subject to English prejudices and phobias.[7] Formal relations between England and Venice began soon after James I's accession. On 17 November 1603, Venetian ambassadors Piero Duodo and Nicolo Molin arrived in Southampton, the first ambassadors from the Republic of Venice to England in Shakespeare's lifetime. During Elizabeth's reign relations had been poor, and only after her death did the Venetian Senate vote to send formal emissaries to the English monarch. From Southampton Duodo and Molin were escorted by the newly knighted Sir Lewis Lewkenor to Salisbury, near the King's lodgings at Wilton House, and on 30 November, the ambassadors had their first audience with the King. At their second audience, they complained of pirated Venetian ships, a major bone of contention between Venice and England. King James promised to investigate.[8]

James was embroiled at the time in diplomatic maneuvers. Would he end the war with Spain? Would he support the Dutch? Would he successfully expand England's overseas empire? How would he respond to conspiracies against his power at home? He was also intrigued by Venice. Duodo and Molin reported after their audience of 9 December with James that, "with great affability, [he] spoke at length about the Government and the laws of the Republic, and about the splendour of Venice. He praised the wisdom of the Senate, which had preserved the State through so many centuries, and showed profound knowledge of our history."[9] Indeed, as Leeds Barroll observes of the ambassadors' reception, James went to great effort "in order to bestow special honor on these Venetian visitors."[10]

James probably meant to flatter the ambassadors, who were disgruntled over poor accommodations at their arrival and spent much of their energy competing with other European ambassadors for regal attention and precedence at court. But the King's remarks also reflect his familiarity with the "myth of Venice," a widespread Renaissance belief that Venice was the epitome of a rationally

---

[7] See G. K. Hunter, "English Folly and Italian Vice," in *Dramatic Identities*, pp. 103–32; repr. from *Jacobean Theatre*, ed. John Russell Brown and B. Harris (Stratford-upon-Avon Studies, I [1960]).

[8] See Horatio F. Brown, ed., *Calendar of State Papers and Manuscripts Relating to English Affairs, Existing in the Archives and Collections of Venice* (London: Kraus Reprint, 1970), vol. X, pp. 116–19. [9] Ibid., p. 122.

[10] Leeds Barroll, *Politics, Plague, and Shakespeare's Theater* (Ithaca: Cornell University Press, 1991), p. 61.

ordered and prosperous republic, its experience analogous in many ways to England's.)

The myth of Venice[11] had been widely disseminated in England through William Thomas' *Historie of Italie* (1549), and more importantly, Lewis Lewkenor's translation of Gaspar Contarini's *The Commonwealth and Gouernment of Venice* (1599). Thomas had likened Venice's system of government to England's; the Great Council, in particular, resembled Parliament, "for unto it manie matters of importance are appealed, and that [which] it doeth, is unreformable." Like England in the mid-sixteenth century, Venice feared "least ciuile sedicion might be the destruction of their common wealth."[12] Historian William Bouwsma observes that during the Renaissance, Europe believed "[t]he myth that Venice ideally combined freedom and order and was therefore durable beyond any polity previously known to man."[13] The Venetian Republic was perceived, Felix Gilbert explains, as an example of a society "in which justice ruled, where everyone could live according to his convictions and in which peace, not military expansion, was regarded as the highest good."[14] Many Englishmen of Shakespeare's day saw the Venetian republic as a government like their own – representing ideals of fairness and justice.[15] But although the Venetian Republic had come to stand for an ideally ordered state, a model of "civility," and a mirror of what England aspired to be under James, the Italian city was also a source of anxiety and tension.

If Venice was called a virgin city by many, she was judged a whore by others. To keep their daughters intact and their lineage pure, the city fathers not only condoned but promoted prostitution. In a popular pamphlet of 1611, for example, Thomas Coryat presents for his readers' delectation an engraving of a Venetian courtesan elaborately clothed except for naked and voluptuous breasts; his text explains that because "Venice is famoused ouer all Christendome"

---

[11] After I completed the primary research for this chapter, I discovered David C. McPherson's *Shakespeare, Jonson, and the Myth of Venice* (Newark, DE: University of Delaware Press, 1990). McPherson covers the same ground outlined here, dividing the Venetian image into four perspectives: Venice the Rich, Venice the Wise, Venice the Just, and Venice *città galante*.

[12] William Thomas, *Historie of Italie* (London: Thomas Bertelet, 1549), pp. 78v and 81v.

[13] William J. Bouwsma, *Venice and the Defense of Republican Liberty* (Berkeley: University of California Press, 1968), p. 162.

[14] Felix Gilbert, "Venetian Secrets," *New York Review of Books* (16 July 1987): 37–39; quote from 37.

[15] See Murray J. Levith, *Shakespeare's Italian Settings and Plays* (New York: St. Martins, 1989), p. 14 for a discussion of English perceptions of Venice.

for its courtesans, he deemed it appropriate to insert "a picture of one of their nobler Cortezans, according to her Venetian habites."[16]

In addition to its sexual corruption, Venice the whore was regarded as venal. Ben Jonson's *Volpone* (1606) depicts Venetian merchants and professionals as rapacious men who will sell anything, even their wives, for gain. "At the level of achievement," speculates G. K. Hunter, "they are Magnificos, Avvocatori, etc.; but beneath the Venetian robes lie the predatory fur and feather and membrane of fox and flesh-fly, raven, gor-crow, and vulture."[17] Venice's sophistication could also be read as a sign of its inherent corruption. In *Othello* Shakespeare would capitalize on the entire range of English attitudes toward the "Virgin" city inhabited by courtesans and con artists.

The positive side of the myth seems to be partially the result of Venetian propaganda. During the sixteenth century, after losing much of its power, Venice began an exercise in self-fashioning. It created a "glorifying picture of Venice's virtues and greatness" in the hopes of reestablishing itself as a great power.[18] Lewis Lewkenor was largely responsible for transmitting Venetian myth to England in his 1599 translation of Contarini's *Commonwealth and Government of Venice*, a text that Shakespeare knew and used when he crafted *Othello*.[19] A Cambridge Master of Arts, Lewkenor was fluent in languages. King James knighted him in April 1603 and later instituted a new court office for him, the Master of Ceremonies, "whose function was to look after the lodgings and the general well-being of ambassadors and to grapple with the knotty problems entailed by their inveterate stickling for precedence and etiquette."[20] Lewkenor was appointed to the post by letters patent on 7 November 1605, but it is clear from the Venetian Calendar of State papers that he had been filling this role ever since James arrived in England.

Lewkenor's translation of Contarini was intended to articulate the Venetian myth to an Elizabethan audience.[21] His dedicatory epistle to the Lady Anne, Countess of Warwick, exalts the "virgin city,"

[16] Thomas Coryat, *Coryat's Crudities* (London: Printed by W. S., 1611), pp. 260–62.

[17] Hunter, "Elizabethans and Foreigners," p. 23.

[18] Gilbert, "Venetian Secrets," 37.

[19] See Kenneth Muir, "Shakespeare and Lewkenor," *Review of English Studies*, NS 7 (1956): 182–83, and T. Sipahigil, "Lewkenor and *Othello*: An Addendum," *Notes and Queries*, NS 19 (1972): 127.

[20] E. K. Chambers, *The Elizabethan Stage* (Oxford: Clarendon Press, 1923), vol. I, p. 53.

[21] For an enlightening discussion of the myth of Venice especially as it relates to Ben Jonson's *Volpone*, see Jonathan Goldberg, *James I and the Politics of Literature* (Baltimore: The Johns Hopkins University Press, 1983), pp. 74–80.

Figure 1: A Venetian courtesan from Thomas Coryat's *Crudities* (1611).

which, unlike most Italian cities, had never been subject to foreign control. Venice, Lewkenor insisted, was a noble commonwealth, *"gloriously shining in the cleere knowledge of her owne incomparable worthinesse ... like a beautifull virgine."*[22] Following Lewkenor's Epistle are four poetic perspectives on Venice. Edmund Spenser lauds

> Fayre *Venice*, flower of the last worlds delight,
> And next to them in beauty draweth neare,
> But farre exceedes in policie of right. (A3v)

In another poem, Maurice Kissen asserts the Venetian myth at its most idealistic:

> *Venice* inuincible, the Adriatique wonder,
> Admirde of all the world for power and glorie,
> Whom no ambitious force could yet bring vnder,
> Is here presented in her States rare storye,
> Where all corrupt means to aspire are curbd,
> And Officers for vertues worth elected. (A4r)

More critical is I. Ashley's sonnet. Noting the Virgin's painted face, it predicts:

> In these pure colours coyest eyes to please,
> Then gazing in thy shadowes peereles eye,
> Enamour'd like *Narcissus* thou shalt dye. (A3v)

Ashley was addressing the underside of Venetian myth and articulating English fear of Venetian corruption, its reputation for vice, and the prominence of elaborately gowned and painted courtesans within Venetian polite society. This is not the perspective that Lewkenor wanted to reinforce, as his note "To the Reader" made clear:

Then what more perfect and liuely pattern of a well ordered Aristocraticall gouernment can there in the worlde bee expressed, then that of their Councell of Pregati or Senators, which being the onely chiefe and principall members of all supreame power; yet haue not any power, mean, or possibility at all to tyranize, or to peruert their Country lawes. (A2v)

The Senators, in Lewkenor's mind, were the ideal philosopher-rulers. They were *"unweaponed men in gownes"* who *"with such happinesse of success giue direction & law to many mightie and warlike armies both by sea and land."* These *"long robed citizens"* were honored by the greatest princes of Europe, yet there was *"not one among them to bee found that doth*

---

[22] [Gaspar Contarini], *The Commonwealth and Government of Venice*, trans. Lewis Lewkenor (London: Imprinted by Iohn Windet for Edmund Mattes, 1599), sig. A2r.

aspire to any greater appellation of honour, or higher tytle of dignitie then to be called a Gentleman of Venice" (A3r). Like Plato's philosopher-kings, the long-robed citizens ruled by setting aside their baser passions. For, as Contarini argued,

[E]vil shal that commonwealth be prouided for, that shal be committed to the gouernment of a man, whom many times those inferior and brutish powers doe perturbe, & call backe from the true path of reason … [T]his office of gouerning assemblings of men should be giuen to the minde and reason onely. (pp. 10–11)

Lewkenor's preface admonishes the reader to "*reade this discourse … with all friendlinesse and fauour*" because all "*the whole world honoreth her [Venice] with the name of a Virgin, a name though in all places most sacred & venerable, yet in no place more dearely and religiously to bee reuerenced, then with us, who have thence deriued our blessednesse*" (A4r). Venice's virginity shows not only that it has never been penetrated by foreign powers; it is the sign and semblance of value. Like the patriarch's control over a virgin daughter, the Venetian Senate (and by analogy the English Parliament) ruled its commonwealth by virtue and reason.

The dissemination of the myth of Venice was not confined to Lewkenor's translation. During England's year of dynastic transition and political uncertainty, several texts published in London, including Giovanni Botero's *An Historical Description of the Most Famous Kingdomes and Commonweales in the Worlde*, exploited the interest in global affairs. Giovanni Botero outlined the popular conception of the Venetian commonwealth as a system of checks and balances. These included "a prince of great maiestie sitting at the helme of the common wealth, yet both he and his authoritie subiected to the lawes, and therein an Idea of a most excellent monarchie." But Venice was also the "patterne of a well ordered Aristocracie" in the councils of the Pregati and a model of democracy in "their great councell, consisting at the least of three thousa[n]d gentlemen."[23]

There is no doubt that Shakespeare was familiar with the Venetian myth.[24] It's even possible that Shakespeare's interest in Venice extended beyond the curious and eclectic artist's search for authentic detail and colorful background. Two days after James first received the Venetian ambassadors, the Chamber Account records that while

[23] Giovanni Botero, *An Historical Description of the Most Famous Kingdomes and Commonweales in the Worlde* (London: Iohn Iaggard, 1603), p. 117.

[24] Violet M. Jefferey even goes so far as to argue that Shakespeare must have visited Venice. See "Shakespeare's Venice," *Modern Language Review*, 27 (1932): 24–35.

the King was at Wilton House: "John Hemyngs one of his Maiesties players" was paid "for the paynes and expences of himself and the rest of the company in comming from Mortelake in the countie of Surrie unto the courte aforesaid and there presenting before his Maiuestie one play."[25] This might have been a performance of Shakespeare's new play, *Othello*. Though the Venetian ambassadors were not able to attend, Shakespeare's representation of the Venetian Senate in Act I could have been a calculated appeal for their approbation.[26]

So much for wild surmise. We know that *Othello* was performed at Whitehall on 1 November 1604; we know that *The Merchant of Venice* was performed at court on 10 February 1605 and, "commaunded by the Kings Maiuesty," was repeated on 12 February;[27] we also know that the Venetian ambassadors attended two "masks" or masquerades at Court during the Christmas celebrations that winter.[28] The *Calendar of State Papers, Venetian* indicates that court productions had political ramifications. They were carefully planned, and those who did the planning knew who would attend and the sorts of plays that would be appropriate. And where the ambassador sat in relation to the King often became a major diplomatic issue. If the Venetian ambassadors had seen a court performance of *Othello*, they might have found Shakespeare's representation of the Venetian Senate and the myth of Venice strangely ambivalent, particularly in its depiction of vulnerability underlying the state's apparent strength.

*   *   *   *

Othello's first act displays Venetian "civilization" at a time of crisis, imperiled by a threat from the alien Other, the barbaric Turk. Roderigo, the epitome of Venice's "curled darlings," describes Othello in the opening scene as an "extravagant and wheeling stranger / Of here and everywhere." Without a city identification of his own, Othello's sense of self must come from his occupation – peripatetic mercenary, for it is a commonplace of *Othello* criticism that the hero is an alien in Venice and that his unfamiliarity with its

[25] E. K. Chambers, *William Shakespeare: A Study of Facts and Problems* (Oxford: Clarendon Press, 1930), vol. II, p. 329.
[26] See Barroll's revisionist account of the Venetian ambassadors' visit in *Politics, Plague*, pp. 61–67. Barroll argues that although the King's Men's first court performance is of great interest to us, it "could not possibly have been a central event at the time" (p. 66).
[27] Chambers, *William Shakespeare*, vol. II, p. 331.
[28] See Brown, *Calendar of State Papers*, vol. X, pp. 206–14.

customs contributes to his vulnerability. Set apart by his color and
life history, he can never be completely secure in the city he serves.

In contrast to Othello, Venice seems sure of its identity as the play
begins – urbane and civilized; as Brabantio exclaims, "This is
Venice; / My house is not a grange" (1.1.106–07). Centuries of legal
and governmental tradition have defined Venice as the locus of
rational judgment. Contarini, for example, claims a special virtue for
his city, arguing that "man is by nature made a ciuile creature." He
enters into civil society in order "to liue happily and commodiously
... [T]he whole reason of ciuil institution pertaineth, that by the
easiest way possible the citizens may be possessors of a happy life."
That happy life can only occur when "the whole commonwealth
may seeme accommodated to vertue."[29] But in the opening scenes of
Othello the virtuous commonwealth is threatened by the barbarous
Turk.

Caught in a liminal zone between Venice's Christian civility and
the Ottomite's pagan barbarism is Cyprus, a Venetian colony under
siege. Cyprus is the frontier, the uttermost edge of western civilization,
simultaneously vulnerable to attack from without and subversion
from within.[30] Even after the destruction of the Turkish fleet, it
remains "a town of war, / Yet wild, the people's hearts brimful of
fear" (2.3.194–95). Cyprus's geographical and political position
mirror Othello's psychic situation. Like Cyprus, Othello can be
colonized by Venice – he can be put to use. But he can never become
wholly Venetian. This liminal positioning makes him vulnerable to
Iago's wiles and, like Cyprus, if he is not fortified, he will "turn
Turk."

What enemy imperils the colonial outpost? Throughout *Othello*,
characters repeatedly refer to the Turkish threat as if the audience
knows just who that enemy is, but the concept of "the Turk" is a
good deal more complicated than a simple label indicates. The
Venetian ideal of a commonwealth composed of virtuous and happy
citizens is partly defined by the thing it is not.

Individuals achieve self-fashioning, in Stephen Greenblatt's words,
"in relation to something perceived as alien, strange or hostile. This
threatening other – heretic, savage, witch, adulteress, traitor, Anti-

---

[29] Lewkenor, trans., *Commonwealth of Venice*, pp. 8–9.

[30] McPherson argues that Shakespeare's audience was probably well aware that Cyprus had
been lost to the Turks thirty-two years earlier. Such knowledge would have cast the Senate
scene in an ironic light; it would also make Othello's death and the loss of his military
services a public disaster as well as a domestic tragedy. See *Shakespeare, Jonson*, pp. 79–81.

christ – must be discovered or reinvented in order to be attacked and destroyed."[31] So too with nations. "It is perfectly natural for the human mind," contends Edward Said, "to resist assaults on it of untreated strangeness; therefore cultures have always been inclined to impose complete transformations on other cultures, receiving these other cultures not as they are but as, for the benefit of the receiver, they ought to be."[32] While this phenomenon is apparent in all cultures, it is especially pervasive in Europe's view of the Orient. And in Shakespeare's day, the Eastern Other – the Turk – was not only transformed but demonized as well in a European frenzy of fear and hatred that indicate just how threatened the West really felt.

In 1603 the Ottoman Empire controlled most of Eastern Europe and one third of the known world.[33] Venice was a leading bastion of Christian civilization. As a nation of traders, it depended on open sea lanes; to preserve its shipping routes, Venice maintained garrisons throughout the Mediterranean. The security of Rhodes and Cyprus was precarious at best, and in 1572 Venice lost the latter island to the Turks. Not surprisingly, Venetians defined the Turk as irrational, deceitful, and cruel. Lozarro Soranzo's *The Ottoman*, published in our year of interest, 1603, is a clear example of an anti-Turk tract. According to an entry in Elizabethan handwriting on the Huntington Library copy, Soranzo was a Venetian Senator. The text makes clear that he was the son of Jacomo Soranzo, a Venetian general. His lengthy analysis of the Turkish threat describes Ottomite military strength and its tyrannical government and concludes with a call for Europe to unite its forces and take Constantinople.

Soranzo began his diatribe with a brief characterization of the present Ottomite emperor, Mahomet the Third:

he did there euerie day more and more discouer his fiercenesse and crueltie; by causing (sometimes in deed of an indignation and rage, but sometimes of a fantastical humour) the teates of women to bee pinched off with hote burning tongues, by putting to death, two thousand *Softi* (that is to say Schollers) onely because they had made a sign unto him of some vnchast cogitation, and by killing many other persons, vpon verie light and slender occasions.[34]

[31] Stephen Greenblatt, *Renaissance Self-Fashioning from More to Shakespeare* (Chicago: University of Chicago Press, 1980), p. 9.　　[32] Said, *Orientalism*, p. 67.
[33] I take this assessment from J. R. Hale, *War and Society in Renaissance Europe, 1450–1620* (New York: St. Martin's, 1985), p. 16.
[34] Lozarro Soranzo, *The Ottoman of Lazaro Soranzo*, trans. Abraham Hartwell (London: Imprinted by Iohn Windet, 1603), p. 2r.

The Turk was also deceitful. According to Soranzo, they "greatly practise militarie stratagemes, or wilie pollicies in warre, whereby they do vse to mingle deceite with force[;] ... and also because fraud and deceite is a thing most proper to a Turke."[35]

Another affront to Christian values lay in the Turk's devotion to war. Christians, argued Soranzo, wage war to attain peace, whereas the Turks "take the onely ende of warre to bee warre," whereby "they have enlarged their Empire."[36] They also are greedy for bribes and gifts; they are, in short, everything Venice prides itself in not being.

More startling still to a late twentieth-century reader, Soranzo expounds a sixteenth-century Venetian version of the domino theory. If the Turk moves against Venice, he argued, eventually all of Italy will fall. If the frontier is not supported by the united forces of Christendom, the Evil Empire will triumph.[37] Soranzo was not alone. Abraham Ortelius reiterates the domino sentiment in his *Epitome of the Theater of the Worlde*, published in London the same year. Like Soranzo, Ortelius fears Mahomet the Third, who took the city of Agria, "and threatens to doe wors if God inspire not the hartes of the Christian Princes vnitedlye to resiste him."[38]

Richard Knolles' preface to his 1603 folio, *The Generall Historie of the Turkes*, expressed the same fears:

[the Ottoman Empire,] drunk with the pleasant wine of perpetuall felicitie, holdeth all the rest of the world in scorne, thundering out nothing but still bloud and warre, with a full persuasion in time to rule ouer all, preferring unto it selfe no other limits than the vttermost bounds of the earth, from the rising of the Sunne unto the going downe of the same.

The Turk, claimed Knolles, is a greedy lion, "lurking in his den," ready to devour all. "So perished the kingdomes of Bulgaria, Seruia, Bosna, and Epirus, with the famous illands of Rhodes and Cyprus."[39] Knolles, like Soranzo, stressed the Turk's Otherness, embodied particularly in his Mahometan religion and his cruelty. At the siege of St. Elmo on Malta (1565), for example, "The Turks after they had taken the castle, finding certaine of the knights yet breathing, and but

---

[35] Ibid., p. 33v.   [36] Ibid., p. 41r.   [37] Ibid., pp. 75r–v.

[38] Abraham Ortelius, *His Epitome of the Theater of the Worlde* (London: Printed for Ieames Shawe, 1603), p. 102v.

[39] Richard Knolles, *The Generall Historie of the Turkes* (London: Printed by Adam Islip, 1603), sig. A5r. Italics removed.

halfe dead, first cut their hearts out of their breasts, and then their heads from their bodies; after that they hanged them vp by the heeles in their red cloakes with white crosses."[40]

Of more immediate relevance to *Othello*, Knolles provided a detailed account of the events leading up to the battle of Lepanto, including Selimus' decision to take Cyprus and the debate of the Venetian Senate as to whether their reports of Turkish intentions were reliable and whether they should prepare for war. He then vividly described the battle itself and the ensuing siege at Famagusta, concluding that the fall of the citadel "was the fatall ruine of CYPRUS, one of the most fruitfull and beautifull islands of the Mediterranean."[41]

Shakespeare must have read this portion of Knolles' 1,000-page folio, for as Geoffrey Bullough notes, he drew on Knolles for the description of Famagusta, "the glad news of the 'segregation of the Turkish fleet' (II.i.10), and the festivities proclaimed by the Herald in II.2."[42] But even if Shakespeare simply had thumbed through Knolles' volume, he would have seen engravings of vicious Ottoman emperors decked in elaborate turbans. He would also have sensed – by the bulk of the volume if by nothing else – Knolles' fear of Turkish threats to Christian civilization.

Knolles dedicated his tome to King James, praising the monarch's 1595 poem on the Battle of Lepanto, which "set forth the greatest and most glorious victorie that euer was by any of the Christian confederat princes obtained against these the *Othoman* Kings or Emperors."[43] *His Maiesties Lepanto, or, Heroicall Song* appears in the Stationer's Register immediately after James' accession on 12 April 1603; obviously the printers wasted no time in exploiting English curiosity about their new king. Printed by Simon Stafford and Henry Hook soon after, James' *Lepanto* (first printed in Edinburgh in 1591) is a short heroic poem that celebrates the Christian hero of Lepanto, Don John of Austria. The poem begins epically:

> I sing a wondrous worke of God,
> I sing his mercies great,
> I sing his justice heere-withall
> Pow'rd from his holy seat.

[40] Ibid., p. 803.   [41] Ibid., p. 867.
[42] Geoffrey Bullough, *Narrative and Dramatic Sources of Shakespeare* (London: Routledge and Kegan Paul, 1973), vol. VIII, p. 214.   [43] Knolles, *Generall Historie*, sig. A3r.

The heroic battle "fought in LEPANTOES gulfe," was, in James'
words, "Betwixt the baptiz'd race, / And circumsised Turband
Turkes."[44] The first scene occurs in Heaven, where Satan taunts God
with the Turk's potency. Jehovah responds by sending the angel
Gabriel to stir up Venetian resistance. As the Turkish forces mount
their attack, he finally succeeds in convincing Venice to act. The
poem then recounts the battle, focusing particularly on Don John's
personal heroism. James presents the battle of Lepanto as a chivalric
struggle between the forces of good and evil, the fight epitomized in
a hand-to-hand combat reminiscent of *The Song of Roland* or *The Cid*:

> A Turke on him doth with a darte,
>   Reuenge his fellowes death,
> Whill time a Turk with arrow doth,
>   Shoot through a Christians arme,
> A Christian with a Pike dooth pearce
>   The hand that did the harme.[45]

The closing Chorus of Venetians sings praises to God for the city's
miraculous deliverance:

> Sing praises then both young and olde,
>   That in this towne remaine,
> To him that hath releeued our necks,
>   From Turkish yoak prophaine.[46]

Thus in James' own literary discourse Lepanto was God's victory
over the Antichrist. And though his poem was written a decade
before his accession, in 1603 it was more topical than ever.

In his first year as king of England, James was forced to examine
the Venetian-Turkish conflict from a more practical perspective than
he had used in his youthful poem. The newly arrived Venetian
ambassadors sought trade agreements to protect their ships from
English pirates and Turkish depredations. They feared that the
English might negotiate successfully with the Turk and that the
English war with Spain would hamper their cause. On 25 December
1603, ambassador Molin wrote to reassure the Doge: "The King

---

[44] Quotations of *Lepanto* are from James Craigie, ed., *The Poems of James VI of Scotland*
(Edinburgh: William Blackwood and Sons for the Scottish Text Society, 3rd series, no.
XXII, 1955). The lines cited here are from p. 202.   [45] Ibid., pp. 238–40.
[46] Ibid., p. 248.

openly shows that he has no affection for the Turkish alliance, and that he thinks all Christian Princes ought to unite for the destruction of their common foe."[47]

As the documents surveyed here reveal, two types of discourse about the Venetian-Turkish confrontation circulated in early seventeenth-century London: on a mythic level, the conflict was Manichean, symbolic of the universal struggle between the forces of good and evil; on a political level, the conflict was practical, focusing on trade and the balance of power among European nations and allowing for changing alliances and even negotiations with the Ottomite Empire. Both discourses inform *Othello*.

Emrys Jones suggested in 1968 that James' *Lepanto* might have influenced Shakespeare's depiction of Venice and Cyprus. Details in the play, he proposes, "suggest that Shakespeare had the events of 1570–71 in mind," including the conflicting reports received by the Senators, the number of the galleys, and the movement of the Turkish fleet. Jones also noted that "Shakespeare could...have taken for granted a general interest in the Ottoman empire which is very remote from what a modern audience brings to *Othello*."[48] But in his final paragraph Jones backs off with a disclaimer: "it has to be admitted that Shakespeare seems to have no direct indebtedness to James."[49] What does direct indebtedness mean? If it depends only on specific verbal parallels, there is one relevant word cluster: James' "circumcised Turband Turkes" is echoed in Othello's final soliloquy when he describes the "turbaned Turk' as a "circumcised dog" (5.2.349–51), though, admittedly, such racial epithets were standard fare in contemporary discourse about Turks and Ottomites.[50]

More important than verbal parallels, Shakespeare exploits similar perceptions of a global struggle between the forces of good and evil, a seeming binary opposition that in reality is complex and multifaceted. Yet the dramatist undercuts simple categories by making the most deceitful character not a Turk but a Venetian. Just as England must have felt in 1603 that it was entering a new era, with all the anticipation, excitement, and anxiety of a dynastic transition, Shakespeare's Venice rests on a shaky foundation. *Othello* represents, in Nick Potter's words, an "attempt to negotiate the distance and

[47] Brown, *Calendar of State Papers*, vol. X, p. 125.
[48] Emrys Jones, "'Othello', 'Lepanto', and the Cyprus Wars," *Shakespeare Survey 21* (Cambridge: Cambridge University Press, 1968), pp. 47–52, esp. p. 51.   [49] Ibid., p. 52.
[50] McPherson also notes this verbal parallel. See *Shakespeare, Jonson*, p. 78.

tension between order and chaos." Act I "shows us the state
confronting a potentially shattering disruption, an apparently
irreconcilable conflict between one of its leading members and its
General, and yet absorbing this threat in the face of a larger threat,
the Turkish fleet."[51] When that larger threat disappears, the threat
from within surfaces.

*   *   *   *

The Variorum edition notes particular words and phrases used in
Othello's opening lines to convey the reality of Venice. Desdemona
escapes with a "gondolier"; Brabantio, a "Magnifico," calls for
"officers of night"; Iago has seen action at Rhodes and Cyprus; the
city is caught in a sudden crisis by the advent of the Turkish fleet.[52]
As one of the "wealthy curled darlings" of Venice, Roderigo speaks
for his class. Had Desdemona not made such a "gross revolt" with an
"extravagant and wheeling stranger," Roderigo would not veer
"from the sense of all civility" to trifle with Brabantio's reverence.
Though we may later adopt Desdemona's point of view, from
Roderigo's and Brabantio's perspective at least, she has violated
cultural taboos by marrying without her father's permission, and by
wedding a Moor. In the trial scene she shows further subversiveness,
asserting that she was "half the wooer" and insisting that she follow
Othello to Cyprus.

From one perspective, then, Desdemona and her lascivious Moor
have threatened not just Brabantio but the social order. Marriage
among the aristocracy of Venice was a carefully controlled political
ritual. Contarini reported that "The marriages among the nobility,
are for the most part alwaies treated of by a third person, the bride
being neuer suffered so much as to behold her future husband, nor he
her, till their marriage dower, and all thinges thereunto appertaining,
bee fully agreede vpon and concluded."[53] The Venetian aristocracy
tried to keep its blood lines pure. Dowers were large, in William
Thomas' words, because the nobility wanted "to encrease the
nobilitee of [their] owne bloude, and by meane of suche aliaunces to

---

[51] Graham Holderness, Nick Potter, and John Turner, *Shakespeare: The Play of History* (Iowa
City: University of Iowa Press, 1988), pp. 186–87.
[52] Furness's note on "officers of night" relates Shakespeare's text specifically to Lewkenor's
translation of Contarini. See Horace Howard Furness, ed., *A New Variorum Edition of
Shakespeare: Othello* (New York: Dover Publications, 1963; repr. of the 1886 Lippincott
edition), p. 28.   [53] Lewkenor, trans., *Commonwealth of Venice*, p. 194.

attein more habilitee to rule and reigne in [their] common wealth."[54] Desdemona's elopement with a wheeling stranger subverts this precarious balance. Brabantio warns:

> if such actions may have passage free,
> Bondslaves and pagans shall our statesmen be. (1.2.98–99)

The opposition between Venice and the Turk is foregrounded, as everyone knows, in the third scene of *Othello*. Though Shakespeare may have been confused (or indifferent) about distinctions between the Venetian Council of Ten and the Senate,[55] the dramatist makes clear that the leading rulers of the commonwealth are assembled on a matter of great urgency. The Quarto stage direction reads: "*Enter Duke and Senators, set at a Table with lights and attendants.*" The Duke and Senators immediately respond to varied reports concerning the Turkish fleet. Whether there are 107, 140, or 200 ships, their presence is a danger to Venice, their target more important than their number. The first Senator argues that the Turks' destination cannot be Rhodes; Cyprus is an easier target and more strategic. The preparation for Rhodes must be a diversion. A message from Montano on Cyprus confirms this deduction; the Senators conclude, "'Tis certain then for Cyprus" (1.3.43).

Though this part of Act 1, scene 3 is often cut in performance, it is important for several reasons. It establishes the Venetian Council with its presiding Duke as a thoughtful tribunal that weighs evidence and draws careful conclusions. Venice is the locus of rational deliberation. This scene also demonstrates the urgency of Council business and the realities of sixteenth-century global politics. The colonial outpost on Cyprus must be maintained at all costs; if it falls, the city itself is vulnerable.

The urgency of the crisis also assures the audience that Brabantio's charge against Othello is doomed. Iago has already warned in scene 1 that the state "Cannot with safety cast him" (1.1.148), and Othello has affirmed "My services which I have done the signiory / Shall out-tongue his complaints" (1.2.18–19). Scene 3's opening representation of the violent clash of Venetian forces and "the general enemy Ottoman" (49) makes even clearer that the state needs Othello. He is their chosen protector, the chivalric knight who will rescue Venice from a greedy dragon.

The threat posed by the Turkish fleet calls for extraordinary

---

[54] Thomas, *Historie of Italie*, p. 84r–v.   [55] See Levith, *Shakespeare's Italy*, pp. 14–15.

measures. Contarini described the Venetian response to naval crises in his *Commonwealth and Gouernment of Venice*:

[I]f the occasions of the commonwealth doe so require, and that there be a great nauie indeed to bee set out, then there is appointed & proposed over the whole nauie a Captaine generall with high and preheminent authoritie not onely ouer the same, but also ouer all maritime prouinces in manner as great, as that the Romain Dictator was wont to haue, saue onely that this in all things obeyeth the authority of the Senate, and the decrees of the commonwealth ... [W]hen the Captaine generall of the nauie shall come to any Citie, ... [t]he authoritie of all the other gouernors for that time ceaseth: and whosoeuer in whatsoeuer cause may appeal from any other magistrate to the Captaine generall: who onely if it shall so please him, may administer justice, dispose of the publike money, and alone himselfe exercise the office and authority of all the rest.[56]

The arrival of the Turkish fleet described in Act 1 is just this sort of threat, and the extraordinary power Contarini described is the authority the Senate proposes to give to Othello. Brabantio hasn't a chance.

It is a sign of Brabantio's prestige that the Duke is willing to interrupt state affairs and listen to his complaint. Confident of his position, Othello can speak with authority of his adventurous life, wooing the Senate with his exotic tales as he had wooed Desdemona. And she confirms his confidence, openly declaring her love. Admonished to be cheerful over the loss of Desdemona, Brabantio reminds the Senate of the relation between one subversion and another:

> So let the Turk of Cyprus us beguile,
> We lose it not so long as we can smile[.]   (1.3.208–09)

Even if the lovers had not won over the Duke and his Council, the dictates of realpolitik are pressing. The Duke turns from Brabantio to the affairs of state. His switch to prose marks the renewed urgency of his charge:

The Turk with a most mighty preparation makes for Cyprus. Othello, the fortitude of the place is best known to you; and though we have there a substitute of most allowed sufficiency, yet opinion, a more sovereign mistress of effects, throws a more safer voice on you. (1.3.219–23)

The domestic crisis is subsumed into the national interest.

Shakespeare uses the private conversation as a frame for Act 1, concluding, as he began, with Iago's attempt to gull Roderigo with

---

[56] Lewkenor, trans., *Commonwealth of Venice*, pp. 136–37.

specious reasoning. Like the Venetian state that sees itself as a model of reason, order, and clarity, Iago proclaims, "we have reason to cool our raging motions, our carnal stings, our unbitted lusts" (1.3.322–23). The Moor (like the Turk) is, in contrast, inconstant, changeable in his will. If he is an "erring barbarian" – the overt enemy to Venice – "super-subtle" Desdemona represents the enemy within (1.3.343–44).

Act 2 continues the opposition of Venetian and Turk, serving as a transition from the public emphasis of *Othello*'s opening scenes to the private sphere of the temptation scene in Act 3, scene 3. During the second act the Turk is transformed from a military object to a representation of the enemy within. The expression "to turn Turk" dated from the fourteenth century;[57] it could mean to turn into an inhabitant of Turkey, or to become a muslim, or, in a third sense, to be a "cruel, rigorous or tyrannical man; anyone behaving as a barbarian or savage; one who treats his wife hardly; a bad-tempered or unmanageable man."[58] In this sense, Othello does, in fact, "turn Turk."

Act 2 begins with the segregation of the Turkish fleet, a providential sign of God's blessing on the Venetian enterprise. Even so, Turks are on everyone's mind. Iago claims his slanderous badinage about women is true, "or else I am a Turk" (2.1.112). (His penchants for deceit and cruelty will later qualify him in Venetian eyes.) Othello announces that "The Turks are drowned." With the external enemy removed, his attention turns to Desdemona; so does Iago's.

Next, Cassio's drunken disorder disrupts the consummation of Othello's marriage, and, again the public subsumes the private. Angry at being roused from his bed, Othello demands:

> Are we turned Turks, and to ourselves do that
> Which heaven hath forbid the Ottomites?
> For Christian shame, put by this barbarous brawl. (2.3.151–53)

The antinomy is clear. If we are not Christians, we are Turkish barbarians. Heaven may have dispersed the Turkish fleet, but it cannot control the Turk within.

---

[57] See Norman Daniel, *The Arabs and Medieval Europe* (London: Longman, 1975), p. 302 for a discussion of the history of the expression.

[58] *OED* (1989 ed.), vol. XVIII, p. 689. *The Policy of the Turkish Empire*, anonymously published, defined "Turke" as "one that is accursed and a vagabond" (London: Printed for Iohn Windet, 1597), p. 7.

On Cyprus the real Venetian enemy is Iago. Nick Potter describes the Ensign as an individual alienated from his society.[59] His role as a critic of Venice turns him into a destroyer. On Cyprus, Venice's liminal outpost, Iago can operate without the checks and balances of Venetian government. On the frontier the underside of Venice can emerge and even dominate, destroying Venice's facade of rational order.

That Venice is the focus in Act 3, where we see an image counter to Contarini's rationally organized commonwealth. Iago plays upon Venice's reputation as the home of courtesans and forbidden lusts.[60] As a stranger to Venetian customs, Othello is moved rapidly from one myth of Venice to another. All Iago has to do is explain:

> I know our country disposition well:
> In Venice they do let God see the pranks
> They dare not show their husbands. Their best
>   conscience
> Is not to leav't undone, but keep't unknown.   (3.3.203–06)

Desdemona has rejected matches of "her own clime, complexion, and degree, / Whereto we see in all things nature tends" (3.3.232–33). Her marriage to Othello not only violates the state but the order of nature itself, demonstrating "a will most rank, / Foul disproportion, thoughts unnatural" (3.3.234–35).

As Iago toys with definitions established in the play's opening scenes, the terms "Venetian" and "Turk" become increasingly slippery. On the one hand, Desdemona is a true Venetian; true, that is, to the city's whore image by being unchaste, deceitful, and given to vice. On the other, she has violated the city's virgin image, disturbing Venetian order and degree and has shown herself to be un-Venetian. While Iago can describe Desdemona both ways, Othello admits that he is also un-Venetian. He has "not those soft parts of conversation / That chamberers have" (3.3.266–67). He doesn't understand Venetian ways and customs. But in the bifurcated world of the play, it is difficult to maintain liminality. According to the colonial paradigm, Cyprus must be possessed by Venice or the Turks – it can't be independent. If Othello is not Venetian, he must perforce be Turkish. His transformation into Turk begins when he tells Desdemona that an Egyptian charmer gave his father the

---

[59] Nick Potter in *Shakespeare: The Play of History*, p. 192.
[60] See Goldberg, *King James*, pp. 77–78.

missing handkerchief. "Dyed in mummy," this handkerchief denotes Othello's exotic otherness, his Orientalism, his alienation from Christian, hence Venetian, culture.[61]

Desdemona rejects Iago's view of Venice. To her, Venice continues to represent the body politic. Its affairs may have "puddled" Othello's clear spirits by their import, and she fears that the elopement may have affected Othello's career. She begs:

> If haply you my father do suspect
> An instrument of this your calling back,
> Lay not your blame on me. If you have lost him,
> I have lost him too. (4.2.43–46)

Desdemona is partly right. Lodovico's sudden appearance with messages from Venice directing that Cyprus be turned over to Cassio is in some sense a rejection of Othello. Now that the threat from the Turk has been destroyed, Venice, as Contarini tells us was customary, takes back the extraordinary powers she had thrust upon her Captain General. Othello is recalled to Venice until the next crisis.

Shakespeare continues to play with the categories he has established. When Othello accuses Desdemona of being a strumpet, she replies, "No, as I am a Christian," but Othello counters that if Desdemona is a Christian, she cannot be that "cunning whore of Venice / That married with Othello" (4.2.81–88). Venice is no longer Christian in Othello's mind; like the Turk, it is heathenish, deceitful, inconstant. Iago has confused the signifiers; words Othello took for granted no longer ring true.

Emilia ruefully observes that Desdemona forsook many noble marriages in favor of Othello, the outsider, the non-Venetian. Not a proper man like Lodovico, he is what Roderigo rightly called him, "an extravagant and wheeling stranger."

Act 5's fatal conclusion brings the Venetian/Turk confrontation to its disastrous closure, collapsing the global struggle of Act 1 into the psychomachic struggle for Othello's soul. Venice – with some help from heaven – can destroy the enemy without, but it can only contain the enemy within. Lodovico, the Act 5 spokesman for the Republic, judges Othello less harshly than the murderer judges himself, claiming that Othello, "that wert once so good," has

---

[61] Johnny Davis has discovered that the higher grades of mummy were always black. He also notes that betrothal gifts, such as handkerchiefs, were generally viewed as emblematic of the giver. I am grateful to him for sharing ideas from his forthcoming Ph.D. dissertation, "In and Out of Doors in *Othello*" (University of Maryland).

"Fallen in the practice of a damned slave" (5.2.288–89). That slave, unlike Othello and Cassio, is Venetian.

Othello's final speech and culminating suicide is civilization's last victory over the Turk. In those famous lines, Othello exhorts the Venetians who surround him:

> Set you down this;
> And say besides that in Aleppo once
> Where a malignant and a turbaned Turk
> Beat a Venetian and traduced the state,
> I took by th'throat the circumcised dog
> And smote him thus.   (5.2.347–52)

On the microcosmic level Othello reasserts the myth of Venice; his rational and virtuous self confronts and destroys the irrational and cruel Turk within.

It is not surprising that so many great actors – Kean, Salvini, Aldridge – ended the play with Othello's final words. The moral dichotomies aroused in Othello's psyche seem reconciled with his death. It is in some ways a more comfortable ending. But the other enemy within the city does not die. Though he is destined to be tortured, Iago remains on stage, silent and presumably un-repentant.[62] By destroying Venice's protector, he may have left the Republic vulnerable to external, military enemies. Even more terrifying, his relentless destruction of Othello has drastically undercut the myth of Venetian governance that Lodovico's final ordering of affairs seeks to reimpose. His silent presence reminds us that, whether societal or personal, human self-fashioning is fragile, that the constructs upon which we base our identity are precarious, that, in Greenblatt's words, "the chaotic can slide into the demonic."[63]

If Venice, the ideal commonwealth based on a rational govern-ment of checks and balances, could be subverted so easily, might not England in 1604, beginning a new dynasty with an unfamiliar Scottish king, be equally vulnerable? Few, perhaps, in *Othello*'s original audience would have grasped that thought, yet the pre-cariousness of a nation's identity – not just an individual's – lurks behind the tragedy of Othello and his wife, infusing the drama with much of its power.

---

[62] By costume and casting – doublets, facial hair, and build – Iago can be made to resemble the other Venetians, a visual similarity that emphasizes his evil as a symbol of the city's corruption.   [63] Greenblatt, *Renaissance Self-Fashioning*, p. 9.

CHAPTER 2

Military discourse: knights and mercenaries

> For I have served him, and the man commands
> Like a full soldier.
>
> (*Othello*, 2.1.35–36)

Global confrontation between Turk and Christian worried six-teenth- and seventeenth-century military theorists perhaps more than court politicians. The Turks were renowned for courage, skill, and cruelty on the battlefield. In 1578 Thomas Procter argued in his treatise, *Of the Knowledge and Conduct of Warres*, that by the exercise of arms and by virtue of "the huge monstrous multitudes of barbarous Scithyens, the Turkes in no longe time, haue subdued so many kinges and countreyes, and extended their Empyre so farre, into all the three partes of the worlde, & yet prosecuteth and thrusteth the same further daylie." To counter this threat, Procter admonished all noble Englishmen to renew their knowledge and practice of arms, "to be a wall and defence for their countrye."[1]

Procter's concern is symptomatic of Renaissance Europe's aware-ness of warfare as both art and science. During the sixteenth and seventeenth centuries, in historian Michael Mallett's words, "Euro-pean warfare was passing through a transitional stage between the feudal hosts of the Middle Ages and the permanent professional armies of modern times."[2] A *condottiere* who fights by contract for the Venetian Republic, Othello reflects what European warfare would become. But his self-fashioned image of a romantic, chivalric hero who fights the infidel and wins fair damsel is a remnant of a medieval ideal. Confusion between the two constructs was inevitable. And

---

[1] Thomas Procter, *Of the Knowledge and Conduct of Warres* (London: Richard Tottell, 1578; repr. New York: Da Capo Press, 1970), p. iii of the Preface. I have removed the original italics for the reader's convenience.

[2] Michael Mallett, *Mercenaries and their Masters: Warfare in Renaissance Italy* (London: The Bodley Head, 1974), p. 4.

both images are defined to a certain extent by the military man's relationship to the female Other.

With the increasing frequency of military conflict in Renaissance Europe, war became more secular, more of an art to be mastered, a science to be studied. Soldiers were perceived as a different sort of men, separate from civilian society by training and by their legitimized resort to violent aggression. In the wars of the Middle Ages the peasant had temporarily exchanged his plow for his longbow; in the Renaissance, the soldier stayed armed and frequently joined the mercenary bands that moved around Europe.[3] Historian J. R. Hale notes that German and Swiss Renaissance artists realistically depicted soldiers with "the sexually aggressive strut, the bulging codpiece, the suggestive sword-hilt, the mixture of touseled peasant hairstyle with flamboyant costume that marked them as defying civilian morals."[4] Such dress signified that these men considered themselves – and were considered – a class apart from the normal confines of society; the bulging codpieces also suggest that they related masculine sexuality to fighting prowess.

If part of the lure of the soldier's life was its freedom from civilian restraint and its adventurous lifestyle, another attraction was a socially acceptable legitimation of masculine aggressiveness. Barnabe Rich, for example, who frequently wrote about his military experiences, voiced in *Opinion Diefied* (1613) the soldier's opinion of peacetime:

it infeebleth the mindes of young men, it maketh them become *Hermaphrodites*, halfe-men, halfe harlots, it effeminates their minds.[5]

Sir W. Segar directly linked a soldier's prowess to his sexuality, arguing that no eunuch or gelded man should bear arms, because "gelding did take from men the courage and viuacitie required in warre."[6]

To be most effective, a soldier must channel his sexual energies toward martial prowess. Hence the dire warnings about having women in camp.[7] Among Giles Clayton's rules to be observed in

[3] In addition to Mallett's study of Renaissance mercenaries in Italy, see J. R. Hale's *War and Society in Renaissance Europe, 1450–1620* (New York: St. Martins, 1985), esp. pp. 69–74; J. R. Hale, *The Art of War and Renaissance England* (Washington, DC: The Folger Shakespeare Library, 1961); and Henry J. Webb, *Elizabethan Military Science: The Books and the Practice* (Madison: University of Wisconsin Press, 1965).   [4] Hale, *War and Society*, p. 127.
[5] Barnabe Rich, *Opinion Diefied* (London: Printed for Thomas Adams, 1613), p. 27.
[6] Sir W. Segar, *Honor Military, and Ciuile, Contained in Foure Bookes* (London: Robert Barker, 1602), p. 9.   [7] See Hale, *War and Society*, p. 161.

military garrisons was: "that no man carry any woman to the Leaguor, or keepe her in the Towne, except she be his lawfull wife, upon paine to be punished as a vile person, or a vagabond, and neuer to be accounted a Souldier in any seruice."[8] Sometimes the rules were more stringent, prohibiting wives as well as prostitutes; in fact, most English regulations were firm against the presence of *any* women in camp. Yet, human nature was such that the rules were often more honored in the breach than the observance.[9]

A central change in the composition of armies during the sixteenth century was the increasing use of mercenary soldiers. Some theorists opposed the praçtice. Machiavelli, for example, argued in *The Arte of Warre* (translated into English as early as 1560) that "the straunge[r]s defence, shall hurt moche soner the common weale, then their owne: bicause thei be moche easier to be corrupted ... The same citee that useth straungers power, feareth at one instant the straunger, which it hireth."[10] Procter also contended that mercenaries were dangerous because, "being money men, by corruption or for a greater paye, they lightlie leaue their mayster in his greatest neade."[11] Lodowick Lloyd wrote in his 1602 historical survey of military practices that "seldome is found any constancie or soundnesse in mercenary souldiers, as by too many examples the Romanes and others found."[12] Despite these caveats, the practice of using mercenaries was nearly universal, and as I have indicated in chapter 1, Venetian state policy required the use of a foreign Captain General in times of national crisis.

Hale contends that what made a soldier a mercenary was "his dependence not on a political authority but on a contractor who had negotiated his own bargain with the government."[13] The English veteran Sir Roger Williams insisted that such duty was perfectly moral so long as one did not join the enemies of his native country. He wrote in 1590, "Thus did I enter into the *Spaniards* warres, and doo think it no disgrace for a poor Gentleman that liues by warres, to serue any estate that is in league with his owne."[14]

During the sixteenth century English writers began to translate

---

[8] Giles Clayton, *The Approoued Order of Martiall Discipline* (London: Printed by I. C. for Simon Watersonne, 1591), p. 35.   [9] See Mallett, *Mercenaries*, p. 189.
[10] Niccolò Machiavelli, *The Arte of Warre* (London: n.p., 1560), p. 14r.
[11] Procter, *Of the Knowledge*, fol. 35r.
[12] Lodowick Lloyd, *The Stratagems of Jerusalem* (London: Thomas Creede, 1602), p. 237.
[13] Hale, *War and Society*, p. 147.
[14] Sir Roger Williams, *A Briefe Discourse of Warre* (London: Thomas Orwin, 1590), p. 30.

Figure 2: The frontispiece to Machiavelli's *Arte of Warre*, translated into English in 1560.

Classical military texts into English and to codify for their readers "the ancient disciplines of the wars."[15] Implicit in their emphasis on codification is fear of the fluid and changing nature of military life. The commentaries bemoaned the lack of order in many military camps; to them, argues Paul Jorgensen, the authority on Shakespeare's use of the military, the violation of the "ideal orderliness" of war seemed potentially barbarous.[16] Such concern was understandable, for disciplined, scientific military practices were not fully established until well into the seventeenth century. Not only that, the "want of discipline and good guyde of warre" was, to use Procter's word, "effeminate."[17]

Hale notes that the "swift savagery of military justice" was both the cause and effect of numerous articulations of Ordinances and Articles of War.[18] Thomas Styward's *The Pathwaie to Martiall Discipline* (1581) lists more than sixty articles to be followed by army personnel. In 1591 William Garrard borrowed Styward's regulations in his treatise on *The Arte of Warre*, adding some extra regulations of his own. Both authors were particularly fearful of mutiny within the ranks. Styward's item 14 (Garrard's item 23) reads:

no souldier shall be suffered to be of a ruffianlike behauiour, either to prouoke or to giue any blow or thrust, or otherwise wilfully strike with his dagger, to iniurie any [of] his fellow souldiers with any weapon, wherby mutinies manie times ensue, vpon paine of the losse of his life.[19]

There were also rules against drunkenness on duty. Styward and Garrard proclaimed that "In Sobrietie consisteth great praise to the souldiers, who vsing the same are euer in state of preferment, such regard their dueties, and reproue the rash busibodies. Drunkerds, etc. are euer in danger of punishment."[20]

The reasons for such concern are obvious. Thomas Digges' *Stratioticos* makes it quite plain: "dronkennes doth turn men into beasts, and makes them many times vtter words tending to mutinies

---

[15] Webb, *Elizabethan Military Science*, provides a good summary of English treatises in pp. 3–50.

[16] Paul A. Jorgensen, *Shakespeare's Military World* (Berkeley and Los Angeles: University of California Press, 1956), p. 35. Jorgensen's study remains the most comprehensive analysis of the military material used by Shakespeare, and my discussion is greatly indebted to him.

[17] Procter, *Of the Knowledge*, fol. 2r.   [18] Hale, *War and Society*, p. 170.

[19] Thomas Styward, *The Pathwaie to Martiall Discipline* (London: Printed by T. E. for Myles Jenyngs, 1581), p. 51, and William Garrard, *The Arte of Warre* (London: Printed for Roger Warde, 1591), p. 39. Quoted from Garrard.

[20] Styward, *Pathwaie*, pp. 46–47; Garrard, *Arte*, pp. 30–31. Quoted from Garrard.

... If any man drink dronk, he shalbe chastised as an infamous person with a *Banne*, that shal publish his fault. "[21] Drunkenness was thus, as Cassio finds out, an enemy to reputation. Even more threatening to the fighting man was drink's power to rob him of his manhood. Sir John Smythe, a prominent but idiosyncratic sixteenth-century military strategist, viewed drunkenness as the "mother and nurse of effeminacy, of cowardice, of sensuality, of rebellion, of covetousness, and all other vices that can be imagined." Smythe decried the customary drinking of toasts: our men of war, he claimed, "drink to the health and prosperity of princes, to the health of counselors, and unto the health of their greatest friends both at home and abroad, in which exercise they neuer cease till they be dead drunk."[22] Such behavior was a disgrace to what Smythe believed was an honorable calling.

The sixteenth century was also a time of transition in the categorization of military rank. Definitions of the various offices were in flux,[23] and as Jorgensen concludes in his analysis of *Othello*, Shakespeare exploited this lack of clarity to heighten the tension between Cassio and Iago. Othello as general, Cassio as his lieutenant, and Iago as the ensign, are consistently represented as field-grade rather than company officers. But since Elizabethan officers often had a different company rank, it was perfectly consistent for Shakespeare to depict the appointment of Cassio and Iago on a company level. The field-grade level lends Othello his supreme authority over Cyprus; the company level makes his choice of his second in command legitimate. Like the double time-scheme, this military ambiguity looms much larger to armchair critics than to theatre audiences.[24]

As part of their efforts at codification, Elizabethan military writers carefully defined the duties of company officers, and despite the diversity of the treatises, they show remarkable agreement. The General (or Captain General in Venice) should be a patriarchal

[21] Thomas Digges, *An Arithmetical Warlike Treatise Named Stratioticos* (London: Richard Field, 1590), p. 288.

[22] Sir John Smythe, *Certain Discourses Military*, ed. J. R. Hale (Ithaca: Cornell University Press for the Folger Shakespeare Library, 1964), pp. 27–28.

[23] Procter, for example, uses the terms "general" and "captain" interchangeably. See *Of the Knowledge*, throughout.

[24] This is a summary of Jorgensen, *Shakespeare's Military*, pp. 100–18. See also Henry J. Webb, "The Military Background in *Othello*," *Philological Quarterly*, 30 (1951): 40–52, and John Robert Moore, "Othello, Iago, and Cassio as Soldiers," *Philological Quarterly*, 31 (1952): 189–94.

figure. In Sir W. Segar's words, "The office of a soueraigne Commander, may be compared vnto the skill of him that gouerneth well a priuate house: which is to command things fit, to make men obedient, to reward the good and punish the euill."[25] Sir John Smythe argued that a captain should lead by example, "not only by instruction but also by action in their own persons, accompting of their soldiers as of their own children."[26] Obedience was crucial to avoid barbarous disorder: "upon any transgression of orders it is lawful for the captains & higher officers to correct, reform, and punish according to the laws and ordinances military."[27]

To exact his soldiers' willing obedience, a General had to set an example. If they were to control their passions, he must control his. Claimed Styward, "A Generall ought to bee temperate, continent, and not excessiue in eating and drinking." If his men suffered hardship, he should share it with them; "in the time of turmoiles of the war," he should "bee the last that is wearie."[28] Garrard argued that the Captain (or General) "ought alwaies to lodge with his band, and remain with the same both in good and euill, and continually shewe himselfe louing and courteous, and take such as the souldiers do: for contrariwise, taking his ease, and suffering them to bee lodged or fed miserably breedeth his hatred or contempt."[29] Othello fits the ideal of a commanding officer when he finds "A natural and prompt alacrity ... in hardness" (1.3.229–30).

Iago's initial complaint against the General is his selection of officers. Elizabethan military treatises agree that the careful selection of subordinates is a General's most important duty. Garrard wrote that the General must "carry a speciall care to the choyse of his principall Officers, and that in the election, he haue more respect to the valour & vertue of the person, then to any particular fauour." He must take particular care in the selection of "a pollitike and practised Lieutenant, of a courageous *Alfierus* [Ensign], of a carefull Sergeant."[30] Digges maintained that a Captain "ought first to make choice of sufficient, expert, honest, paineful officers."[31] Giles Clayton echoed this theme in 1591; the commanding officer is "to haue an especiall and great care, in chusing of hys Lieutennant, for that he ought to be a man of great experience and knowledge in seruice."[32]

[25] Segar, *Honor Military*, p. 46.   [26] Smythe, *Certain Discourses*, p. 35.
[27] Ibid., p. 11.   [28] Styward, *Pathwaie*, pp. 2–3.   [29] Garrard, *Arte*, p. 144.
[30] Ibid., pp. 347, 139.   [31] Digges, *Stratioticos*, p. 95.
[32] Clayton, *Approoued Order*, p. 3.

A commanding officer should also have the gift of eloquence. Styward contended that "the Generall ought not to be chosen that knoweth not nor hath the grace in speaking, and that lacketh the facilitie and vtteraunce of speach." For nothing can so "inflame the mindes of men to take their weapons" than "the sugred talk of the Generall."[33] Garrard agreed, concluding that "I iudge it likewise verie necessarie for him to bee eloquent, since that qualitie hath great efficacie in perswading of mens minds."[34] Othello modestly disclaims such eloquence in Act 1, telling the Venetian Senate that he is rude in speech and "little shall I grace my cause / In speaking for myself" (1.3.81–88). Yet his "round unvarnished tale" easily persuades the Senate that he is innocent of the charge of witchcraft and moves the Duke to say, "I think this tale would win my daughter too" (1.3.170). Despite his insistence that he is the plain, blunt soldier,[35] Othello's grace in speaking indicates his stature as a military commander who can move men (and women) to feel and to act.

While the General (or Captain) took primary responsibility for the success or failure of his troops, his lieutenant played a strategic role. On the company level, the lieutenant was second in command, but as Henry Webb notes in his survey of military treatises, "his major tasks were to keep peace among the men, see that the noncommissioned officers performed their duties, post the guard, and, like the captain, make the round of the sentinels."[36] The Lieutenant was also the primary conduit of information between his superior and his soldiers. Garrard observed that the Lieutenant's part "is to giue willingly and readily counsell and advise to his captaine, as often as he is demanded." The Lieutenant was especially charged "to carie with him a diligent care of concord, for that particularly the pacification of discords & difference amongst ye souldiers of his company," which must be accomplished "without choler or passion."[37] The Lieutenant should also consult frequently with the Ensign. Garrard maintained that the Lieutenant must be careful "to avoide all stomaking and strife that might arise betwixt him and the *Alfierus*, for therby oftentimes great scandales haue falne out, and the diuision of the company, a thing aboue all other to be carefully forseene and shunned."[38] As Jorgensen indicates, Shakespeare's creation of tension

---

[33] Styward, *Pathwaie*, pp. 3–4.   [34] Garrard, *Arte*, p. 145.
[35] See Jorgensen's discussion of Shakespeare's use of the type in *Shakespeare's Military*, pp. 259–65.   [36] Webb, *Elizabethan Military Science*, p. 84.
[37] Garrard, *Arte*, pp. 68–69.   [38] Ibid., p. 71.

between the Lieutenant and the Ensign would not have surprised any Elizabethan soldier in his audience.[39]

Readers of *Othello* have long noted how the verbal irony in the phrase "honest Iago" reverberates throughout the play.[40] The phrase entails more than verbal irony, however. The Ensign, Elizabethan military treatises agree, must be selected for his honest, upright character. As the bearer of the company's standard, he must be a man the soldiers will trust and follow into battle. Barnabe Rich wrote in *A Path-Way to Military Practise* that "As the Ensigne in the fielde is the honour of the bande, so the Ensigne bearer in like use shoulde bee honoured by his company, and this reputation is best attained, by his owne curteous demeanour towards ye souldiours."[41] Garrard insisted that "The *Alfierus* must be a man of good account, of a good race, honest and vertuous, braue in apparell, thereby to honour his office."[42] Digges urged the Captain to bring all his company together and "deliuer the *Ensigne* to a chosen man for courage and honestie." The Ensign, he wrote, must be "a man of good account, honest and vertuous, that the Captaine may repose affiance in."[43] Clayton repeated this motif: "For that the Ensigne in the fielde is to be honoured of all men, so ye Bearer thereof ought to be a man of good courage, [and] knowledge, sufficient to discharge his duetie."[44] In sum, Renaissance military discourses reveal that the honor of the regiment was particularly dependent on the ensign who carried its flag.

Iago is hardly honest. When he professes his faith to the civilian Roderigo in the opening scene, he also proclaims his lack of loyalty to his superior officer: "not I for love and duty, / But seeming so for my peculiar end ... I am not what I am" (1.1.57–66). Iago is a self-seeker and profiteer. Roderigo's first speech, "I take it much unkindly / That thou, Iago, who hast had my purse" (1.1.1–2), tells the audience that Iago sells information about his commanding officer to interested civilians. Shakespeare represents Iago from the outset as duplicitous. As Hale puts it, Iago entered military life "on a strictly

---

[39] Jorgensen, *Shakespeare's Military*, p. 105.

[40] See Paul A. Jorgensen, "Honesty in *Othello*," *Studies in Philology*, 47 (1950): 557–67; Karina Williamson, "'Honest' and 'False' in *Othello*," *Studia Neophilologica*, 35 (1963): 211–20; and William Empson, "Honest in *Othello*," in *The Structure of Complex Words* (Ann Arbor: University of Michigan Press, 1967), pp. 218 49.

[41] Barnabe Rich, *A Path-Way to Military Practise* (London: Printed by John Charlewood for Robert Walley, 1587), sig. Giv.   [42] Garrard, *Arte*, p. 67.

[43] Digges, *Stratioticos*, pp. 94–95.   [44] Clayton, *Approoued Order*, p. 14.

business basis," in the hopes it would lead to "topsy-turvy fortune-making."[45]

Thus the question posed by analysts of the military in *Othello* (particularly Webb, Moore, and Jorgensen) – Would Shakespeare's audience believe Iago's complaints about his general's unwillingness to make him a lieutenant? – should be answered in the negative. Jorgensen argues that Iago has two genuine grievances against Cassio's appointment: It was attained by "letter and affection," and Cassio has no practical experience. As an experienced soldier who has fought beside Othello at Rhodes and Cyprus (if we believe him), Iago naturally resents the selection of a young theorist as lieutenant. But Jorgensen, like Webb and Moore, neglects the importance of the auditor of these opening speeches. Roderigo is a civilian, a "wealthy curled darling" of Venetian society who knows nothing about military affairs. To justify the money he has accepted from the young gull, Iago must explain why he hates Othello. His reasons satisfy Roderigo, but they do not bear scrutiny.

First, Iago himself has used influence to try to attain office. He admits that he persuaded "three great ones of the city" to make personal requests to Othello "to make me his lieutenant" but then found that Othello had already chosen his officer. Iago is just as guilty of trying to attain office by "letter and affection," as he claims Cassio to be. Roderigo believes Iago when he proclaims:

> 'Tis the curse of service;
> Preferment goes by letter and affection,
> Not by the old gradation, where each second
> Stood heir to the first.   (1.1.35–38)

Roderigo doesn't notice Iago's verbal legerdemain, but we should.

Second, while Cassio may have had less practical military experience than Iago, his "bookish theoric" was deemed crucial for a successful officer. The full title of Digges' military treatise makes the commander's need for mathematical expertise quite explicit: *An Arithmeticall Warlike Treatise names Stratioticos Compendiously Teaching the Science of Numbers ... as are requisite for the profession of a souldier.* Digges provided basic instruction in addition, subtraction, multiplication, fractions, equations, and more. Then he demonstrated how arithmetic could be used to resolve military questions. Sir W. Segar was equally adamant about the need for mathematics in his

---

[45] Hale, *War and Society*, p. 147.

1602 treatise: "For what man vnlearned can conceiue the ordering and disposing of men, in marching, in camping, and fighting without *Arithmetique*? Or who can comprehend the ingenious fortifications or instruments apt for Offence or Defence of Townes, or passing of waters unlesse he hath knowledge of *Geometrie*?"[46] No officer could be expected to manage fortifications and siege warfare, or even to arrange his squadrons in proper formation, if he did not have considerable training in arithmetic.

As a "gulled gentleman" and a "wealthy curled darling," Roderigo represents the effeminacy of peaceful, civilian life. Though the ostensible reason he puts on a false beard with his military garb is to disguise himself, the lack of hair implies a lack of virility. Certainly he is reluctant to fight. He only raises his sword when convinced that his prey will be easy and Iago will second him. Roderigo succumbs to Iago's murderous suggestions in a vain attempt to prove himself a man of "purpose, courage, and valour" (4.2.208). Even so, he readily admits

> I have no great devotion to the deed,
> And yet he hath given satisfying reasons.
> 'Tis but a man gone. Forth my sword. He dies! (5.1.8–10)

Of course, his feeble effort at valor fails; Cassio does not die, and Roderigo faints with the cry, "O damned Iago! O inhuman dog!" (5.1.67)

Cassio is the man Roderigo might like to be. He possesses the social skills of the courtier, and he is also a brave *condottiere*, with all the sexual attraction that implies. As a Florentine, he is a foreign mercenary fighting (as his general does) for Venetian pay. He knows Othello well enough to have served as a go-between during his courtship. The Senate also trusts and respects him or they would not have made him governor of Cyprus on Othello's recall. The text provides no evidence that he is, as Webb argues, "a perfect example of an inexperienced man who has obtained his rank by affection and favor."[47] He may have less experience than Iago, but he has the requisite moral qualities plus the proper training for a lieutenant.

Cassio's subsequent failure is not so much caused by drunkenness as by his inability to resist peer pressure. Though he knows he cannot handle liquor, he drinks because "the gallants desire it." Act 2, scene 3 demonstrates that Sir John Smythe was right to deprecate the

---

[46] Segar, *Honor Military*, pp. 200–01.   [47] Webb, "Military Background in *Othello*," 48.

drinking of toasts. Iago puts Cassio in a bind where he cannot refuse to drink without seeming discourteous. But Cassio is not the only one who drinks too much. By Iago's admission he has already caused Roderigo to carouse "Potations pottle deep" and "flustered" three men of Cyprus "with flowing cups." Though Cassio as a superior officer bears responsibility for the ensuing brawl, he is not the only drunk onstage.

The writers of Elizabethan military treatises would have shared Othello's outrage at the midnight disturbance on Cyprus. The general's reaction reflects any commander's fear of mutiny within an armed garrison:

> What, in a town of war,
> Yet wild, the peoples' hearts brimful of fear,
> To manage private and domestic quarrel,
> In night, and on the court and guard of safety?
> 'Tis monstrous.   (2.3.194–98)

If the military theorists were to fault Othello, it would probably be for leniency. Cashiering is mild compared to Styward's seventeenth article of war:

that no souldier or souldiers drawe his or their sword or swoords, or use anie other kinde of weapon with violence to do hurt within or without ye camp during the time of ye wars, upon paine of death.[48]

Cassio loses his lieutenancy and, for a time, his reputation. It is a mark of Othello's initial regard for him that he loses no more.

Cassio's concern for his damaged reputation is, of course, understandable. He errs gravely in going outside normal military channels by asking Desdemona to sue for him. In a chivalric context, the intercession of the knight's fair lady for a younger squire might be appropriate; in the milieu of military professionalism, the appeal must be rejected. Though she is Othello's "fair warrior," and Cassio's "great captain's captain," Desdemona's influence with Othello should have no sway on military matters which are defined by the treatises as entirely masculine.

Desdemona's and Emilia's very presence on Cyprus is laden with ambiguity. As mentioned earlier, wives were consistently discouraged from following their husbands on a military campaign. Respectable women would be content to stay at home, minding their domestic duties, in wartime as well as in peace, especially since military codes

---

[48] Styward, *Pathwaie*, p. 52.

seldom distinguished between wives and prostitutes.[49] Desdemona's request to follow Othello to enjoy her marriage "rites" might mistakenly imply lax morality. Like Emilia, who seems to accompany Iago wherever he goes, Desdemona subjects herself to misconstruction as a loose woman simply by being in the wrong place at the wrong time.

Othello's calling as a professional officer sets him apart from the society of women. Like other combat-oriented soldiers, Othello might claim:

> War is my country,
> My armour my home,
> And in every season
> Fighting is my life.[50]

And like the growing class of mercenaries who traveled across Europe, Othello enjoyed freedom from the restraints of civilian life. He puts this "unhoused free condition" "into circumscription and confine" by marriage to Desdemona. He is willing to relinquish much of his freedom, however, in pursuit of love.

Othello's description of his courtship characterizes the military adventures he has endured:

> most disastrous chances,
> Of moving accidents by flood and field,
> Of hair-breadth scapes i' th' imminent deadly breach,
> Of being taken by the insolent foe
> And sold to slavery. (1.3.133-37)

As many commentators have noted, this is the stuff of chivalric romance.[51] Othello's narrative of strange adventures beguiles the fair maiden's tears. Pity, as Chaucer was fond of saying, runneth soon in gentle heart. Desdemona loves Othello for his heroic narrative – for the dangers he had passed. He loves her because she pities him. Her pity, in turn, validates his existence as a romantic hero.

Aside from the enemies against which he opposes himself, the chivalric knight defines himself by the approval of a female of higher social station. If this woman loses her status, his self-fashioned identity is also in jeopardy. Thus when Edmund Spenser's Red Crosse Knight discovers the fair Fidelia is really the foul whore

---

[49] Hale, *War and Society*, p. 161.   [50] Quoted from ibid., p. 139.
[51] See, for example, Mark Rose, "Othello's Occupation: Shakespeare and the Romance of Chivalry," *English Literary Renaissance*, 15 (1985): 293–311 and Michael Louis Hays, "Shakespeare's Use of Medieval Romance Elements in His Major Tragedies," unpub. Ph.D. diss. University of Michigan, 1973.

Duessa, he is totally emasculated. When Othello becomes convinced that Desdemona is equally foul, his occupation is gone. The chivalric ideal upon which he has built his military vocation is destroyed.

Although he subscribes to a medieval ideal of selfless military service – the crusading spirit that pits him against the Turk – Othello is also a practical Renaissance military leader. He administers military justice swiftly and fairly; he sees to the fortifications at Cyprus; he consults with the captains of the citadel; he sends reports home to the Senate. In the second scene he is able to prevent a street brawl simply through his commanding presence. The Senate throws "a more safer voice" on Othello to lead its wars in Cyprus (1.3.223), and even Iago admits, "Another of his fathom they have none / To lead their business" (1.1.151–52). Thus everything we see of Othello in the first half of the play – what he does and what others say about him – makes him a truly professional military leader, a man who harmoniously combines heroic standards of virtue and valor with professional knowledge and experience. According to Jorgensen, Othello is "one of the most respected and capable military executives in Shakespeare."[52]

Even the temptation scene's passionate mood swings do not fully undercut Othello's status. His decision to proceed against Cassio and Desdemona is in many respects barbarous, but the swift justice he craves accords with military protocol. Styward's articles of war, for example, decree

that no man of what degree soeuer he be of, shal commit adulterie with maried wiues, nor inforce widdowes, maids or virgins & by violence defile them, [lest he] shall without mercie be punished with death.[53]

Othello's haste may seem to him justified, for as Procter proclaimed, "often times the greatnes of the mischiefe requireth sodaine iustice ... And therefore the Captaines dome, order, or sentence, in this case of spedie Iustice, standeth for law, and is called martial lawe."[54] On the other hand, Othello violates Styward's caution that the general meet with his warlike council to "deliberate upon euerie matter," for "if of others faithfull counsaile it be not holpen, easilie it [an individual judgment] maie beguile us, and manie times it is found full of errours."[55] Othello takes counsel with Iago whom he trusts completely. But because Cyprus is in a state of war, he treats Desdemona's

[52] Jorgensen, *Shakespeare's Military*, p. 117.
[54] Procter, *Of the Knowledge*, fol. 5v.
[53] Styward, *Pathwaie*, p. 55.
[55] Styward, *Pathwaie*, p. 5.

supposed adultery as a military matter subject to the hasty judgments of martial law. He does not consult those he might have – Montano, for example.

By Lodovico's appearance in Act 4, of course, Othello is too distracted to be reasonable. He construes Desdemona's every word and deed as proof of guilt. In the countless explanations of how Iago gets Othello to this state, one constant is Othello's inability to remain for long in a state of doubt. "No," he declares to Iago early in Act 3, scene 3, "to be once in doubt / Is once to be resolved" (181–82). He cannot believe two contradictory narratives at once; he must choose one version or another. This may serve him well in military decisions, though even there, taking counsel and sifting evidence were important. For example, further inquiry into Cassio's and Roderigo's drunken brawl might have led to recognition of Iago's duplicity, but Othello relies on one story only, Iago's. The compulsion to choose quickly serves even more poorly when he is faced with decisions about his wife's behavior.

Peter Stallybrass comments in his analysis of patriarchal territories that in *Othello* a "woman's body could be imagined as the passive terrain on which the inequalities of masculine power were fought out."[56] Nowhere were the inequalities of masculine power more apparent than in the struggle for military preferment. Iago's resentment over his rank coalesces with the desire to possess and then to destroy Desdemona's body. And rather tellingly, Othello cries in the midst of his jealous passion, "Cuckold me!... With mine officer!" (4.1.187–88). That Desdemona should be false is one sacrilege, but that she should be false with Othello's handpicked second-in-command is far more subversive.

A military ethos thus permeates Othello's thinking and his discourse even in the depths of his seemingly private, domestic crisis. If Desdemona is Othello's pronounced "fair warrior," her betrayal is not just a private affair but a public humiliation. No wonder that once he is convinced of her infidelity, he declares his military occupation gone.

When he first discovers the truth in Act 5, scene 2, Othello bemoans, "I am not valiant neither, / But every puny whipster gets

---

[56] Peter Stallybrass, "Patriarchal Territories: The Body Enclosed," in *Rewriting the Renaissance; The Discourses of Sexual Difference in Early Modern Europe*, ed. Margaret W. Ferguson, Maureen Quilligan, and Nancy J. Vickers (Chicago: University of Chicago Press, 1986), pp. 123–42, esp. p. 141.

my sword" (243–44). Without being overly Freudian, one can see
the swords and daggers in this bedroom scene as phallic imagery.
Othello reasserts his valor and his manhood by seizing a weapon from
the chamber: "A better never did sustain itself / Upon a soldier's
thigh" (258–59). With this sword he wounds Iago. Finally, Othello
finds a third weapon to use upon himself and, in so doing, to reassert
the military, masculine identity he had temporarily lost.

   Othello's final speech combines both images of military service
that inform the play. First, he asserts his status as a *condottiere*: "I have
done the state some service and they know't" (335). His mercenary's
contract is that he serve and they reward him fairly. But in the last
half of this speech, Othello reverts to the chivalric ideal of military
service he had asserted in the Senate scene. By stabbing the
"malignant and turbaned Turk," Othello destroys the crusader's
traditional enemy, the Infidel who violates the holy sepulcher. Then
in a passionate *Liebestod* the crusader affirms his union with the fair
and virtuous maiden of chivalric romance, dying upon a kiss.
Othello's tragedy is caused, in part, by his adherence to a romantic
ideal of military service. The chivalric story that he had fashioned, in
Stephen Greenblatt's terms, "the erotic as a supreme form of
romantic narrative, a tale of risk and violence issuing forth at last in
a happy and final tranquillity,"[57] can not withstand the deceptive
practices of a self-seeking cynic like Iago. The Ensign doesn't give a
"fig" for the old virtues and seeks only financial gain and power from
his service. Othello's lack of exposure to civilian life makes him
depend on this man, not his wife, for the truth. While the changing
categories embedded in sixteenth-century military discourse do not
directly cause the tragedy, they do provide Iago with linguistic tools
he can use with Roderigo, Cassio, and Othello. Despite Othello's
prowess and professionalism, his old-fashioned view of the world as a
battlefield between easily identified good and evil forces blinds him to
Iago's verbal legerdemain. Without the ability to penetrate the
deceptions of Iago, the true "super-subtle Venetian," Othello can
never be the complete model of a modern major general.

[57] Stephen Greenblatt, *Renaissance Self-Fashioning from More to Shakespeare* (Chicago: University
   of Chicago Press, 1980), p. 243.

CHAPTER 3

Racial discourse: black and white

If virtue no delighted beauty lack, / Your son-in-law is far more
fair than black.

Othello (1.3.285–86)

Black/white oppositions permeate *Othello*. Throughout the play,
Shakespeare exploits a discourse of racial difference that by 1604 had
become ingrained in the English psyche. From Iago's initial racial
epithets at Brabantio's window ("old black ram," "barbary horse")
to Emilia's cries of outrage in the final scene ("ignorant as dirt"),
Shakespeare shows that the union of a white Venetian maiden and a
black Moorish general is from at least one perspective emphatically
unnatural. The union is of course a central fact of the play, and to
some commentators, the spectacle of the pale-skinned woman caught
in Othello's black arms has indeed seemed monstrous.[1] Yet that
spectacle is a major source of *Othello*'s emotional power. From
Shakespeare's day to the present, the sight has titillated and terrified
predominantly white audiences.

The effect of *Othello* depends, in other words, on the essential fact
of the hero's darkness, the visual signifier of his Otherness. To
Shakespeare's original audience, this chromatic sign was probably
dark black, although there were other signifiers as well. Roderigo
describes the Moor as having "thick lips," a term many sixteenth-

---

[1] Marvin Rosenberg's *The Masks of Othello* (Berkeley: University of California Press, 1961)
documents the nineteenth-century penchant for light-skinned Othellos, as does Ruth
Cowhig's "Blacks in English Renaissance Drama and the Role of Shakespeare's *Othello*,"
The Black Presence in English Literature, ed. David Dabydeen (Manchester: Manchester
University Press, 1985), pp. 1–25. For a more recent and theoretical discussion of the impact
of Othello and Desdemona's union, see Karen Newman, "'And Wash the Ethiop White':
Femininity and the Monstrous in *Othello*," in *Shakespeare Reproduced: The Text in History and
Ideology*, ed. Jean E. Howard and Marion F. O'Connor (New York: Methuen, 1987), pp.
143–62.

century explorers employed in their descriptions of Africans.[2] But, as historian Winthrop Jordan notes, by the late sixteenth century, "Blackness became so generally associated with Africa that every African seemed a black man[,] ... the terms *Moor* and *Negro* used almost interchangeably."[3] "Moor" became, G. K. Hunter observes, "a word for 'people not like us,' so signalled by colour."[4] Richard Burbage's Othello was probably black. But in any production, whether he appears as a tawny Moor (as nineteenth-century actors preferred) or as a black man of African descent, Othello bears the visual signs of his Otherness, a difference that the play's language insists can never be eradicated.

Elizabethans were fascinated by travelers' accounts of foreign peoples, especially by tall tales of monstrous creatures, heathen customs, sexual orgies, and cannibalism. All were associated with blackness in the Elizabethan mind, a color that, in turn, suggested negation, dirt, sin and death.[5] From ancient and medieval lore, black meant the demonic. Thomas Wright's *The Passions of the Minde* also associates the color black (in any dark complexion) with sexuality;

> The redde is wise,
> The browne trustie,
> The pale peevish,
> The blacke lustie.[6]

And as the accounts of exploration spread, blackness joined additional signs of Otherness – nakedness, savagery, and general depravity.[7]

---

[2] See, for example, Leo Africanus' description of the kingdom of Casena, where "The inhabitants are extremely black, hauing great noses and blabber lips." Leo Africanus, *The History and Description of Africa*, ed. Robert Brown, trans. John Pory, 3 vols. (London: The Hakluyt Society, 1896), p. 830.

[3] Winthrop Jordan, *White Over Black: American Attitudes Toward the Negro, 1550–1812* (Chapel Hill: University of North Carolina Press for the Institute of Early American History and Culture, Williamsburg, VA, 1968), p. 5.

[4] G. K. Hunter, "*Othello* and Colour Prejudice," in his collection of essays, *Dramatic Identities and Cultural Tradition: Studies in Shakespeare and His Contemporaries* (Liverpool: Liverpool University Press, 1978), pp. 31–59; repr. from *Proceedings of the British Academy*, 53 (1967), 139–63. Quote from p. 41.

[5] See Jordan's discussion in *White Over Black*, p. 4. More recently John R. Aubrey argues that *Othello*'s references to monstrosity reflect the late-sixteenth-century popular association of blacks with monsters. See his "Race and the Spectacle of the Monstrous in *Othello*," *Clio*, 22 (1993): 221–38.

[6] Thomas Wright, *The Passions of the Minde* (London: Printed by Valentine Simmes for Walter Burre, 1604), p. 43.

[7] For detailed accounts of medieval and Renaissance discussions of blackness, see Eldred Jones, *Othello's Countrymen: The African in English Renaissance Drama* (London: Oxford University Press, 1965); Hunter, "*Othello* and Colour Prejudice"; Elliot H. Tokson, *The*

Renaissance commentators offered two possible explanations for the existence of skin color so different from their own. The quasi-scientific suggestion that blackness was nature's defense against intense tropical sun was quickly but not universally discredited when black men and women in northern climes produced equally black children. The second explanation relied on scriptural tradition and myth. Since George Best provides the most detailed account (and the one most frequently cited by modern commentators), I quote his Discourse from Hakluyt's *Voyages* at some length:

It manifestly and plainely appeareth by holy Scripture, that after the generall inundation and overflowing of the earth, there remained no moe men alive but Noe and his three sonnes, Sem, Cham, and Japhet, who onely were left to possesse and inhabite the whole face of the earth ... When Noe at the commandement of God had made the Arke and entred therein, and the floud-gates of heaven were opened, so that the whole face of the earth, every tree and mountaine was covered with abundance of water, hee straitely commaunded his sonnes and their wives, that they should with reverence and feare beholde the justice and mighty power of God, and that during the time of the floud while they remained in the Arke, they should use continencie, and abstaine from carnall copulation with their wives; and many other precepts hee gave unto them, and admonitions touching the justice of God, in revenging sinne, and his mercie in delivering them, who nothing deserved it. Which good instructions and exhortations notwith-standing his wicked sonne Cham disobeyed, and being perswaded that the first childe borne after the flood (by right and Lawe of nature) should inherite and possesse all the dominions of the earth, hee contrary to his fathers commandement while they were yet in the Arke, used company with his wife, and craftily went about thereby to dis-inherite the off-spring of his other two brethren: for the which wicked and detestable fact, as an example for contempt of Almightie God, and disobedience of parents, God would a sonne should bee borne whose name was Chus, who not onely it selfe, but all his posteritie after him should bee so blacke and lothsome, that it might remaine a spectacle of disobedience to all the worlde. And of this blacke and cursed Chus came all these blacke Moores which are in Africa.[8]

Chus and his descendants thus bear the double curse of blackness as the punishment for copulation against the patriarch's express

Popular Image of the Black Man in English Drama, 1550–1688 (Boston: G. K. Hall, 1982); and Anthony Gerard Barthelemy, *Black Face Maligned Race: The Representation of Blacks in English Drama from Shakespeare to Southerne* (Baton Rouge: Louisiana State University Press, 1987).
[8] From Richard Hakluyt, *The Principal Navigations Voyages Traffiques and Discoveries of the English Nation* (Glasgow: James MacLehose and Sons, 1904), vol. VII, pp. 263–64.

prohibition: Blackness signifies their unbridled lust and their inner spiritual state – a "naturall infection of the blood." To the Elizabethan mind, black skin thus denoted extreme Otherness, with overlays of satanic propensity and sexual perversion.[9]

Best's account mirrors but does not exactly parallel the version Shakespeare would have read in the Geneva Bible of 1560. In this narrative, Noah was found drunken one night,

> vncouered in ye middes of his tent. And when Ham the father of Canaan sawe the nakedness of his father, he tolde his two brethren without. Then toke Shem and Japheth a garme[n]t, and put it vpon bothe their shulders and we[n]t backward, and couered the nakednes of their father with their faces backwarde; so thei sawe not their fathers nakednes. Then Noah awoke from his wine, and knewe what his yonger sonne had done vnto him. And said, Cursed be Canaan: a seruant of seruants shall he be vnto his brethren. He said moreover, Blessed be the Lord God of Shem, and let Cannan be his seruant.[10]
>
> Genesis 9: 21–26

Here the punishment for violating a patriarchal taboo is not blackness but perpetual servitude; the damnable act is not copulation but viewing paternal privities, and the penalty is not in the skin but in slavery. In the Geneva version of Ham's fall, looking itself is perceived as voyeuristic and obscene. Like the sight of Othello's and Desdemona's bodies, it "poisons sight."

This account silently merged with Best's version of Ham's sin; blackness and perpetual servitude coalesced in the Elizabethan mind, a fusion justified by scriptural authority. And in either account, the original cause of the African's differentness was a sexual fall from grace. Blackness became a visual signifier of eternal sin. You could never, as the proverb reminds us, wash the Ethiopian white.[11] Nor could you change his scripturally ordained status of perpetual servitude. Thus blackness and forbidden sex, blackness and hea-

[9] As Kwame Anthony Appiah notes, during the Renaissance, both Moors and Jews were considered "unbelievers whose physical differences are signs (but not causes or effects) of their unbelief." Religious Otherness coalesces with physical differences in many contemporary texts, including *Othello*. See "Race," in *Critical Terms for Literary Study*, ed. Frank Lentricchia and Thomas McLaughlin (Chicago: University of Chicago Press, 1990), pp. 274–87; see p. 277. In an essay too recent to be incorporated fully into this chapter, Arthur L. Little, Jr. argues that accounts such as George Best's provided Shakespeare with a "pre-text, what the audience knows before it comes to experience the play," in particular, "the essence of blackness as the savage and libidinous Other." See "'An Essence That's Not Seen': The Primal Scene of Racism in *Othello*," *Shakespeare Quarterly*, 44 (1993): 304–24.

[10] *The Geneva Bible: A Facsimile of the 1560 Edition* (Madison: University of Wisconsin Press, 1969), pp. 4–5.

[11] Karen Newman rings the changes on this theme in "And Wash the Ethiop White."

thenism, blackness and slavery – all were linked in the English mind from the earliest descriptions of African people.

*   *   *   *

Stereotypes about blackness were reified in voyagers' accounts of what they saw in Africa. Nakedness bespoke depravity. *A Trve and Large Discovrse of the Voyage of the Whole Fleete of Ships* records for example that "The people are blacke and goe naked, saiuing that they weare short coates of Seales skinne, and a peece of the same skinne about their members, they are tall of stature, flat nosed, swift in running, they will pick & steale, although you looke on them."[12] *The Fardle of Facions* reported that "The moste part of them, for that they lye so under the Sonne, go naked: couering their privities with sheepes tayles." Along with nakedness went lechery, for "It is the maner emong theim, for euery man to haue many wiues: and the felowship of their wiues, that other use in secret: they use in open sighte."[13] To wit, Ham's voyeuristic sin was seen to be regularly reenacted among his descendants. The explorers who watched the natives watching nakedness apparently did not recognize their own prurient interests.

Ethnocentric travel accounts frequently stressed the bestiality and brutishness of African customs, especially in light of what they assumed was the "civilitie" of their own European customs. An English translation of Philippo Pigafetta's description of the Congo notes cannibalism among the Anzichi:

For their enemies whom they take in the warres, they eate, and also their slaues, if they can haue a good market for them, they sell: or, if they cannot, then they deliuer them to the butchers to be cut in peeces, and so sold to be rosted or boyled.[14]

Heathens by definition were lustful and brutish, Christians were not. Thus, Pigafetta reports, in the kingdom of Angola "euery man taketh as many wiues as hee listeth, and so they multiply infinitely: But they doe not vse to do in the kingdome of *Congo* which liueth after the manner of the *Christians*."[15]

[12] *A Trve and Large Discovrse of the Voyage of the Whole Fleete of Ships* (London: Printed by Thomas Thorpe for William Aspley, 1603), p. 3.

[13] *The Fardle of Facions Conteining the Auncient Maners, Customes, and Lawes, of the Peoples Enhabiting the Two Partes of the Earth Called Affrike and Asie* (London: Printed by John Kingstone and Henry Sutton, 1555), C3r and E8r.

[14] *A Report of the Kingdome of Congo, a Region of Africa.* trans. Abraham Hartwell (London: Printed by John Wolfe, 1597), p. 36.   [15] Ibid., p. 55.

Native customs were derided for their differentness and used as confirmation of the travelers' own prejudices. Pigafetta, for example, scorned the face markings common among the Agagi nation:

They doo vse to marke themselues aboue the lippe vpon their cheekes with certain lines which they make with *Iron* instruments and with fire ... [T]hose marks in their faces, it is a strange thing to behold them. For it is in deede a very dreadfull & deuillish sight. They are of bodie great, but deformed and liue like beastes in the fielde, and feede vpon mans flesh.[16]

John Leo, best known as Leo Africanus and a source for Shakespeare's *Othello*, was able to differentiate among the peoples he described. Within his *Geographical Historie of Africa*, translated into English by John Pory and published in London (1600), are accounts of treacherous tawny peoples and virtuous blacks. Leo's comparatively enlightened viewpoint reflects his own origins as an African Moor, albeit one converted to Christianity and living in Italy. His travels and adventures, including temporary slavery, have struck some modern commentators as similar to Othello's.[17] In any event, Leo could describe people "of a black colour" who were also "people of a courteous and liberall disposition, and most friendly and bountifull vnto strangers."[18] Aware that Muslims had a variety of different cultures, Leo classified Africans not only by color but according to town and tribe. Some struck him as civilized, some as savage. Still, Leo accepted and purveyed the biblical explanation of blackness, claiming that "For all the Negros or blacke Moores take their descent from *Chus*, the sonne of *Cham*, who was the sonne of *Noe*."[19] Leo's *Description* does not pursue the negative implications of this assertion, but to the informed Elizabethan reader they would have been clear. Thus, even in Leo's accounts of African people, signals were contradictory.

*   *   *   *

The texts described above were in print at the turn of the seventeenth century, available for the curious who could read. It is difficult to assess the attitudes of those who could not read, but we can examine the visual impressions that informed English Renaissance

[16] Ibid., pp. 204–05.
[17] See Lois Whitney's "Did Shakespeare Know *Leo Africanus*?" *Publications of the Modern Language Association*, 37 (1922): 470–83, and Rosalind Johnson's "African Presence in Shakespearean Drama: Parallels Between Othello and the Historical Leo Africanus," *African Presence in Early Europe* (*Journal of African Civilizations*, 7 [1985]): 276–87.
[18] Pory, trans., *History and Description of Africa*, p. 791.   [19] Ibid., p. 130.

MORO DI
CONDI-
TIONE.

Figure 3: The figure of "A Moor" from Cesare Vecellio's *Degli habiti* (Venice, 1590).

culture in general. There were blacks in England in the late sixteenth century. Their numbers were sufficiently substantial by 1601 for Elizabeth to license sea captain Caspar van Senden to transport all Negroes and blackamoors out of England. The royal proclamation seems to have followed up the Privy Council's attempt four years earlier to transport "such slaves" back to Spain and Portugal.[20] Presumably the earlier effort had failed; Elizabeth deemed it necessary to add her authority to her council's.

Who were these blackamoors and why did Elizabeth seek to oust them from England? Her proclamation declares that they had been carried into England since the late troubles with Spain – presumably as part of the booty brought home from Spanish ships by Drake, Essex, and other privateers. These Africans were almost certainly slaves, perhaps en route to Portuguese and Spanish colonies in the New World before they were seized by the British. In England they probably continued as slaves or very long-term servants. In either case, they took employment away from needy English subjects. In Elizabeth's words, they "are fostered and powered here, to the great annoyance of her own liege people that which co[vet?] the relief which these people consume, as also for that the most of them are infidels hauing no understanding of Christ or his Gospel." People "possessed of any such blackamoors" (i.e., slave owners) were directed to relinquish them under threat of Her Majesty's displeasure.[21]

Some members of Shakespeare's audience may have seen the emissaries from Barbary, led by the Moroccan Ambassador Abd el-Ouahed ben Messaoud, who visited London in late 1600. During their six-month stay, the Moroccans were regarded with mingled curiosity and contempt. Religious animosity spurred the disapproval of many English merchants and mariners, yet, observes Jack D'Amico, "Alongside mistrust and outright dislike of foreigners and infidels we find the grand, if somewhat fanciful, plans for a joint invasion of Spain."[22] Like Othello, the Moroccans were potential allies against a common enemy while remaining ineluctably different. Once the ambassadors departed, plans for a common military enterprise dissolved.

---

[20] Quoted from *Tudor Royal Proclamations*, ed. Paul L. Hughes and James F. Larkin (New Haven: Yale University Press, 1969), vol. III, p. 221n.   [21] Ibid., pp. 221–22.

[22] Jack D'Amico, *The Moor in English Renaissance Drama* (Tampa: University of Florida Press, 1991), p. 37.

By the time Shakespeare began writing *Othello*, the embassy was a distant memory. Any familiarity most Londoners had with "blackamoors" probably came from slaves and servants, not from "men of royal siege."

By 1603 Londoners had also been exposed to "blackamoors" in public pageants and the theatre. In his study of the popular image of blacks in English Renaissance drama, Elliot H. Tokson observes that "dramatists were more often drawn to the figure of the black man than other writers."[23] He suggests several reasons for this, including the visual impact of the actor's color. The audience, presumably composed of white English men and women and some foreigners, would necessarily view the black character to some extent as different, as Other, as object. And because their perceptions had been informed by negative associations with the color black and by lurid travellers' tales, their white gaze may have verged on voyeurism – a desire to see the black character in the context of illicit sex. Tokson contends that "there is hardly a black character created for the stage whose sexuality is not made an important aspect of his relationships with others."[24] The character's blackness was itself equated with paganism and an exotic but forbidden sexuality. Blackness had shock value. And if the black male character were linked with a white female, the prurient gaze would be even more excited.

Othello's dramatic forebears are well known and have been thoroughly analyzed elsewhere.[25] The three most notable figures, however – Muly Hamet, Aaron the Moor, and Eleazar – warrant attention here because they illustrate the kinds of choices Shakespeare had before him when he crafted Othello. Muly Hamet is a primitive ranter in the early revenge play, *The Battle of Alcazar*. The Chorus presents him in the play's opening lines:

> Blacke in his looke, ànd bloudie in his deeds,
> And in his shirt staind with a cloud of gore,
> Presents himselfe with naked sword in hand,
> Accompanied as now you may behold,
> With deuils coted in the shapes of men.[26]

---

[23] Tokson, *Black Man in English Drama*, p. 20.

[24] Ibid., p. 17. Little also describes the imagined scene of Othello and Desdemona coupling as the "sexual site and sight of the play's racial anxieties." See "An Essence That's Not Seen," 306.

[25] See Jones, *Othello's Countrymen*; Tokson, *Black Man in English Drama*; Barthelemy, *Black Face Maligned Race*; and D'Amico, *The Moor*, for full surveys of blacks on the Elizabethan stage.

[26] Cited from the Malone Society Edition, *The Battle of Alcazar*, ed. W. W. Greg (London: Chiswick Press, 1907). Quote from A2r.

Muly Hamet is frequently referred to as "the Negro Moor," his blackness associated with satanic evil. In a dumb show he murders his two younger brothers and his uncle. But despite frequent fits of braggadocio, Muly is a coward who can only succeed by stealth and deceit. As Eldred Jones notes, he "combines the grandiloquent extrovert and the subtle plotter."[27] Muly is a Marlovian overreacher who on his deathbed curses the fatal star that governs his fall. But he also curses his Negro mother: "Curst maist thou be for such a cursed sonne." The curse, of course, is blackness.

In *Titus Andronicus* Aaron continues Muly Hamet's bombastic villainy, but unlike his predecessor, he is no coward. Jones argues that Aaron is individualized and humanized by his passionate defense of his child and that, in his complex intriguing, he may be a forerunner of Iago.[28] Integral to Aaron's defiance of the white world around him is a sense of his own blackness. To Tamora's sons Chiron and Demetrius, Aaron exclaims:

> Ye white-lim'd walls! Ye alehouse painted signs!
> Coal-black is better than another hue,
> In that it scorns to bear another hue;
> For all the water in the ocean
> Can never turn the swan's black legs to white,
> Although she lave them hourly in the flood.   (4.2.98–103)

Aaron's paternal concern is also a form of black pride. "Aaron's only allegiance," contends D'Amico, "is to the image of himself seen in his son." Aaron is a father concerned for the future, his villainy mitigated by "the human capacity for survival and renewal."[29] Nevertheless, blackness remains the sign of Aaron's largely unmotivated, satanic villainy. While the play's white characters commit grossly despicable acts, they seek vengeance for injuries to themselves or their families. Aaron does evil for evil's sake. His final lines glorify his villainy:

> Even now I curse the day and yet I think,
> Few come within the compass of my curse –
> Wherein I did not some notorious ill ...
> But I have done a thousand dreadful things,
> As willingly as one would kill a fly,
> And nothing grieves me heartily indeed,
> But that I cannot do ten thousand more.   (5.1.125–44)

---

[27] Jones, *Othello's Countrymen*, p. 43.   [28] Ibid., pp. 52–60.
[29] D'Amico, *The Moor*, pp. 143 and 145.

Aaron's vaunts may be a last defiant gesture at the white world that surrounds him. Though his motives are never clarified, he remains one of – if not the most – interesting characters in Shakespeare's play. Perhaps as Emily C. Bartels notes, his purposelessness makes his villainy all the more insidious.[30] But to many in the white Elizabethan audience, Aaron's blackness would have seemed the immutable signifier of an inherited disposition to evil.

Like his predecessor Aaron, Eleazar of *Lust's Dominion* (*ca.* 1600) is a "striking combination of the Moor as man and as black devil,"[31] who has an illicit sexual relationship with a white woman of higher social status, in this case the Spanish Queen Mother. Like Aaron, Eleazar uses this relationship to gain power. And like Muly Hamet, he is an overreacher in the Marlovian vein. In his first-act soliloquy, Eleazar exclaims:

> Mischief erect thy throne and sit in state
> Here, here upon this head; let fools fear fate.
> Thus I defie my starrs, I care not I
> How low I tumble down, so I mount high.

When confronted with his relationship to the Queen Mother, Eleazar boasts:

> The Queen with me, with me, a *Moore*, a Devill,
> A slave of *Barbary*, a dog; for so
> Your silken Courtiers christen me, but father,
> Although my flesh be tawny, in my veines
> Runs blood as red, and royal as the best
> And proud'st in Spain.[32]

When he is finally ready to mount the Spanish throne, Eleazar emphasizes his military achievements:

> value me not by my sun-burnt
> Cheek, but by my birth; nor by
> My birth, but by my losse of blood
> Which I have sacrific'd in Spains defence.   (1794–97)

Later in the play, Eleazar tries to disassociate color and character:

---

[30] Emily C. Bartels, "Making More of the Moor: Aaron, Othello, and Renaissance Refashionings of Race," *Shakespeare Quarterly*, 41 (1990): 433–54.
[31] D'Amico, *The Moor*, p. 106.
[32] *Lust's Dominion: or The Lascivious Queen*, ed. J. Le Gay Brereton (Louvaine: Libraire Universitaire, 1931). Citations are from lines 260–63 and 227–34 respectively.

> Think you my conscience and my soul is so,
> Black faces may have hearts as white as snow
> And 'tis a generall rule in moral rowls,
> The whitest faces have the blackest souls.   (3607–10)

While the Duke of Venice's similar comments to Brabantio are true, here the white/black inversion is false. Eleazar *is* a self-proclaimed villain, his actions in accord with his audience's expectations.

In sum, black roles before *Othello*'s composition in 1603–04 tended to confirm the reports of travelers like George Best. Black skin signified, in addition to visual ugliness,[33] an ingrained moral infection, a taint in the blood often linked to sexual perversion and the desire to possess a white woman – her body, her status, her wealth, or her power. The subversive images of Muly Hamet, Aaron, and Eleazar must have fascinated yet frightened the Elizabethan audience. No wonder all three figures were killed or contained before the play's conclusion.

*   *   *   *

The threat of blackness outside the theatre was not so easily quelled. Elizabeth couldn't oust them; and as the seventeenth century progressed, the numbers grew. Increasingly containment came from the institutionalization of slavery. The English were well aware that the Portuguese had been bringing Africans to Europe since the late fifteenth century and to America since the early sixteenth. The English adventurer John Hawkins joined the slave trade himself during the 1560s. And as Winthrop Jordan observes, "By 1589 Negroes had become so preeminently 'slaves' that Richard Hakluyt gratuitously referred to five Africans brought temporarily to England as 'black slaves';... an equation had developed between African Negroes and slavery."[34]

When Europeans first encountered the West African slave trade, they found what was essentially a by-product of tribal warfare. Philippo Pigafetta remarked that the people of the Congo bring "thether with them slaues both of their own nation, & also out of *Nubia*."[35] Once Portuguese and Spanish traders began to collect slaves for shipment to America, the nature of slavery changed. The

---

[33] Later in the seventeenth century, Bishop Joseph Hall was to describe the sight of a blackamoor as a man "whose hew showes him to bee farre from home, his very skin bewrayes his Climate; it is night in his face, whiles it is day in ours." See *Occasional Meditations* (London: Set by R. H., 1630), p. 93.

[34] Jordan, *White Over Black*, p. 60.   [35] Hartwell, trans., *Report on the Congo*, p. 35.

sporadic result of war was transformed into a giant economic enterprise. Pigafetta noted that in Angola

> there is also a greater trafficke and Market for slaues ... then in any place els. For there are yearely bought by the Portingalles aboue fiue thousand head of *Negroes*, which afterwardes they conveigh away with them, and so sell them into diuers parts of the worlde.[36]

In Africa, the slave's status had been more neutral, his possibilities more fluid. Leo Africanus narrates the example of a Negro slave in the kingdom of Gaoga:

> This slaue lying vpon a certaine night with his master that was a wealthie merchant, & considering that he was not far from his natiue countrey, slue his saide master, possessed his goods, and returned home: where haiuing bought a certaine number of horses, he began to inuade the people next adioning, and obtained for the most part the victorie: ... And by this means he tooke great numbers of captiues, whom he exchanged for horses that were brought out of Egypt: insomuch that at length (the number of his souldiers increasing) he was accounted by all men as soueraigne K. of Gaoga.[37]

This Negro warrior's captives were probably sold into slavery, but, as this narrative demonstrates, status within Africa was comparatively liminal. A courageous man like Othello could be captured in battle, sold into slavery, escape, and fight in triumph over his former owners. And as later chapters will indicate, this historical shift to a more rigid, exploitative system influenced future representations of Othello, most dramatically during the nineteenth century.

*   *   *   *

The Renaissance texts surveyed here have often been searched for clues to Shakespeare's conception of *Othello*. They yield no certain conclusions, of course, for the texts themselves are contradictory, combining savage images along with the exotic. Moreover, we can never be certain what Shakespeare retained, let alone read. And even if Shakespeare had only encountered Leo Africanus's book, for example, he might have created different representations from different portions of the text.

It is not surprising, then, that scholars have drawn conflicting conclusions from these materials. For the most part, they agree that the dominant discourse of Shakespeare's culture was ethnocentric in its assumptions about color and foreign customs. They disagree, however, as to what degree Shakespeare shared those assumptions

---

[36] Ibid., p. 62.   [37] Pory, trans., *History and Description of Africa*, p. 835.

and to what extent they informed his tragedy. In 1965 Eldred Jones concluded that "in the end Othello emerges, not as another manifestation of a type, but as a distinct individual who typified by his fall, not the weaknesses of Moors, but the weaknesses of human nature."[38] Two years later G. K. Hunter advanced a similar theme in his seminal lecture on "*Othello* and colour prejudice." The characterization of Othello initially contradicts the stereotype of the black man, Hunter argued, but as the play progresses, Iago succeeds in "making the deeds of Othello at last fit in with the prejudice that his face at first excited."[39] Winthrop Jordan wrote in the following year that Shakespeare did not necessarily accept his society's fears about miscegenation, but that he exploited the theme of black/white sexuality to explode his society's beliefs, particularly "the notion that Negroes were peculiarly sexual men."[40]

Symptomatic of the 1960s new awareness of race, K. W. Evans contended that no analysis of *Othello* "can be adequate if it ignores the factor of race." Iago, he argued, "comes to personify the more virulent aspects of Venetian prejudice against Moors," while Othello reifies the legend of Moorish credulity with "his own superstitious fatalism." Evans concluded that Othello's blackness "is correlated with a character which spans the range from the primitive to the civilised, and in falling partially under Iago's spell Othello yields to those elements in man that oppose civilised order."[41]

Tokson's 1982 survey of black men on the English Renaissance stage does not address *Othello per se*, but his conclusions are equally negative. "A black man," Tokson admitted, "could on rare occasions turn out to be a decent human being, but only if he reached a consciousness and an acceptance of Christian ethics and white manners."[42] The framework in which he appeared remained unabashedly ethnocentric. Anthony Barthelemy's 1987 survey, *Black Face Maligned Race*, argued that the dramatist toyed with his culture's racial stereotypes, but "[h]owever successful Shakespeare's manipulation of the stereotype may be, Othello remains identifiable as a version of that type." As the play ends, Venetian hegemony continues, for "Shakespeare's black Moor never possesses the power or desire to subvert civic and natural order."[43]

[38] Jones, *Othello's Countrymen*, p. 87.
[39] Hunter, "*Othello* and Colour Prejudice," p. 55.   [40] Jordan, *White Over Black*, p. 38.
[41] K. W. Evans, "The Racial Factor in *Othello*," *Shakespeare Studies*, 5 (1969): 124–40; quotes from 125, 127, 135, and 139.   [42] Tokson, *Black Man in English Drama*, p. 135.
[43] Barthelemy, *Black Face Maligned Race*, p. 161.

Karen Newman was less harsh on Shakespeare in 1987. She contended that

Shakespeare was certainly subject to the racist, sexist, and colonialist discourses of his time, but by making the black Othello a hero, and by making Desdemona's love for Othello, and her transgression of her society's norms for women in choosing him, sympathetic, Shakespeare's play stands in a contestatory relation to the hegemonic ideologies of race and gender in early modern England.[44]

Michael Neill agreed in 1989, stating that though *Othello* does not directly oppose racism, the play nevertheless "illuminates the process by which such visceral superstitions were implanted in the very body of the culture that formed us."[45] And as recently as 1990 Emily C. Bartels concluded that in *Othello* Shakespeare "invokes the stereotype of the Moor as a means of subverting it, of exposing its terms as strategic constructions of the self and not empirical depictions of the Other."[46]

D'Amico's 1991 analysis of the Moor in English Renaissance drama takes a similar stance. "In *Othello*," he asserts,

Shakespeare explored the tragic consequences of a cultural frame of reference that made the alien Moor something other than human. Working with the dual image of the noble, tawny Moor and the dark-complexioned devil, Shakespeare revealed how a man could be destroyed when he accepts a perspective that deprives him of his humanity ... Othello is debased by a role that he adopts.[47]

Note that this assortment of critics from varied backgrounds and perspectives agrees on one thing – the stereotype is there, deeply embedded in the text of Shakespeare's play. Their disagreement lies in the analysis of how Shakespeare's text exploits that stereotype. Obviously there is no single answer to this debate, but perhaps a close examination of Shakespeare's lines can illuminate how these contradictory conclusions came into being.

Despite Venice's need for Othello's military acumen, the Venetian outlook in Shakespeare's play is predominantly racist.[48] Roderigo,

[44] Newman, "And Wash the Ethiop White," p. 157.

[45] Michael Neill, "Unproper Beds: Race, Adultery, and the Hideous in *Othello*," *Shakespeare Quarterly*, 40 (1989): 383–412; quote from 412.

[46] Bartels, "Making More of the Moor," 447.   [47] D'Amico, *The Moor*, p. 177.

[48] I recognize that some would disagree with me. Edward Washington argues, for example, in an unpublished paper, "'At the Door of Truth': The Hollowness of Signs in Shakespeare's *Othello*," that Venice is more tolerant of others than Othello thinks it is. Martin Orkin also contends that the play's racist sentiment is "to an important degree confined to Iago,

the wealthy curled darling, refers to Othello as "the thick-lips" (1.1.65), and Iago's shouts below Brabantio's window stress the association between blackness and bestial sexuality:

> an old black ram
> Is tupping your white ewe ...
> you'll have your daughter covered with a Barbary
> horse, you'll have your nephews neigh to you, you'll
> have coursers for cousins, and jennets for germans.
>
> (1.1.89–90, 111–13)

Roderigo describes the Moor as "lascivious," while Iago cries, "the devil will make a grandsire of you" (1.1.92). Iago's purpose, to arouse Brabantio's wrath, is achieved with verbal images of his daughter copulating unnaturally with a bestial creature, a satanic figure of vice and depravity.

Iago also perpetuates the myth of Moors having promiscuous sexual appetites: "These Moors are changeable in their wills" (1.3.336). Clearly Iago thinks of Othello as "an old black ram," who has probably seduced Emilia, which suggests (among other things) envy of powers he imagines to be greater than his own. At this point in the play, suggests G. K. Hunter, "[t]he sexual fear and disgust that lie behind so much racial prejudice are exposed for our derisive expectations to fasten upon them. And we are at this point bound to agree with these valuations, for no alternative view is revealed."[49]

Roderigo and Iago have reason to hate the Moor; the former is a rival for Desdemona's love, the latter believes he has been passed over for promotion. But until Act 1, scene 1, line 82 Brabantio has had no such motive, and his entertainment of Othello in his home might bespeak his openmindedness. Yet he too is prejudiced. Why else would he jump to the conclusion that Othello used witchcraft on his daughter? Only enchantment, he claims, could have made her

> Run from her guardage to the sooty bosom
> Of such a thing as thou – to fear, not to delight.   (1.2.70–71)

Though Othello argues eloquently that this is not so, by the middle of the temptation scene he seems to believe it himself. When Iago suggests that Desdemona's decision to shun "many proposed matches

Roderigo, and Brabantio." See "Othello and the 'Plain Face' of Racism," *Shakespeare Quarterly*, 38 (1987): 166–88; quote from 168. But Brabantio is a respected Senator and part of the power structure. I might add that Emilia also shows signs of color prejudice.
[49] Hunter, "*Othello* and Colour Prejudice," p. 45.

of her own clime, complexion, and degree" indicated "a will most rank, / Foul disproportion, thoughts unnatural" (3.3.231–35), Othello remains quiet.

At the play's finale, Emilia's outrage may – as Kent Cartwright has shown – vent the audience's own anger and, perhaps, its racism.[50] When Othello reports that Desdemona's last words are a lie, Emilia cries

> O, the more angel she
> And you the blacker devil!...
> She was too fond of her most filthy bargain!...
> O gull! O dolt!
> As ignorant as dirt! (5.2.131–32, 156, 162–63)

Dirt, filth, blackness, and the devil – all are intertwined.

But while racism's voice is heard intermittently throughout the play, Othello denies the stereotype. Unlike Muly Hamet, Aaron, and Eleazar, he is not a manipulative scheming villain. Those characteristics appear instead in the white Venetian ensign, Iago. And other characters in the play speak well of the Moor. Desdemona praises Othello's virtue:

> I saw Othello's visage in his mind
> And to his honours and his valiant parts
> Did I my soul and fortunes consecrate. (1.3.248–50)

On Cyprus Montano reports that "I have served him, and the man commands / Like a full soldier" (2.1.35–36). Iago admits in the midst of his hate

> The Moor, howbeit that I endure him not,
> Is of a constant, loving, noble nature;
> And I dare think he'll prove to Desdemona
> A most dear husband. (2.1.269–72)

Lodovico also expresses the high regard Venice once had for its Moorish general:

> Is this the noble Moor whom our full senate
> Call all-in-all sufficient? Is this the nature
> Whom passion could not shake? Whose solid virtue
> The shot of accident nor dart of chance
> Could neither graze nor pierce? (4.1.255–59)

[50] See Kent Cartwright, "Audience Response and the Denouement of *Othello*," in *Othello: New Perspectives*, ed. Virginia Mason Vaughan and Kent Cartwright (Newark: Fairleigh Dickinson University Press, 1991), pp. 161–76.

As Cassio later remarks, the Othello rewarded by the Venetian Senate was "great of heart," a man respected for military prowess, courage, and steady character. And Othello's initial appearance in Act 1, scene 2 – "Keep up your bright swords or the dew will rust them" – confirmed that judgment.

On the other hand, the Senate is proved wrong. Iago's and Roderigo's prejudices do become reified by the end of the play. Desdemona thinks that Othello "[i]s true of mind and made of no such baseness / As jealous creatures are." He could not be jealous because "the sun where he was born / Drew all such humours from him" (3.4.26–27). But we know that Othello is jealous, a fact that confirms Renaissance stereotypes about Moorish behavior – the sun was believed to create passionate furies, not dry them up. Moors, in fact, were stereotyped as unusually jealous, as in Leo Africanus' oft-cited comment:

> For by reason of iealousie you may see them daily one to be the death and destruction of another, and that in such sauage and brutish manner, that on this case they will show no compassion at all.[51]

When Othello claims that he wants to chop Desdemona into messes and tear her to pieces, he confirms his audience's expectations.

Leo Africanus also reports that Moors' "wits are but meane, and they are so credulous, that they will beleeve matters impossible, which are told them."[52] Iago reiterates this theme in his opening soliloquy:

> The Moor is of a free and open nature,
> That thinks men honest that but seem to be so,
> And will as tenderly be led by the nose
> As asses are. (1.3.381–84)

To a certain extent, the temptation proves Africanus correct, for as many commentators have noted, Desdemona and Cassio could not have committed adultery in the brief time since Othello's marriage.

Othello's epileptic fit demonstrates his passionate nature but it also marks him as the member of an alien race. According to Leo Africanus, "This falling sicknes likewise possesseth the women of Barbarie, and of the land of Negros, who, to excuse it say that they are taken with a spirite."[53]

---

[51] Pory, *A Geographical Historie of Africa*, p. 154.   [52] Ibid., p. 185.
[53] Ibid., p. 182.

Another source of ambiguity in the play is the connection between blackness and slavery. Othello's narrative of his life to Desdemona includes stories

> Of being taken by the insolent foe
> And sold to slavery; of my redemption thence,
> And with it all my travels' history. (1.3.136–38)

These lines rush by in performance, but set against the context of the nascent English slave trade, they resonate with meaning. And even though Othello is ostensibly a "free" man in Venice, by terms of his mercenary contract, he remains the "servant" of the Venetian state, subject to its commands. His status, in short, is liminal. Yet the final irony of the play is that the white Iago is the one led in chains, the one called "damned slave," the one about to be tortured. Just as Iago turns out to be the white villain with the black heart, he also becomes the true slave while Othello asserts his freedom to choose his own death.

Shakespeare plays with us throughout *Othello*, exploiting stereotypes, arousing expectations, alternately fulfilling and frustrating our preconceptions. Othello's rhetoric, for example, is inherently ambiguous. On the one hand, the "Othello music" is a mark of the hero's greatness,[54] but boastful language is also the mark of Othello's villainous predecessors Muly Hamet, Aaron, and Eleazar. Compare, for example, Othello's

> I fetch my life and being
> From men of royal siege, and my demerits
> May speak unbonneted to as proud a fortune
> As this that I have reached. (1.2.21–24)

to Eleazar's

> Although my flesh be tawny, in my veines
> Runs blood as red, and royal as the best
> And proud'st in Spain. (231–33)

Is this boasting? Or is it an exercise in black pride, an attempt at what Stephen Greenblatt calls "self-fashioning" that empowers the black caught in the grips of a white political system?[55]

---

[54] G. Wilson Knight coined the term "Othello music" in *The Wheel of Fire: Essays in Interpretation of Shakespeare's Sombre Tragedies* (London: Humphrey Milford [Oxford University Press], 1930), pp. 107–31.

[55] See Stephen Greenblatt, "The Improvisation of Power," *Renaissance Self-Fashioning from More to Shakespeare* (Chicago: University of Chicago Press, 1980), pp. 222–54.

The threads of this argument may recall Othello's own confusion in the temptation scene:

> I think my wife be honest, and think she is not;
> I think that thou art just, and think thou art not. (3.3.385–86)

I think this play is racist, and I think it is not. But Othello's example shows me that if I insist on resolving the contradiction, I will forge only lies and distortion. As this exploration of texts has shown, the discourse of racial difference is inescapably embedded in the play just as it was embedded in Shakespeare's culture and our own. To be totally free of racism, one would have to invent a new language with no loaded words, no color discriminations, and no associations of blackness with evil, whiteness with good. White and black are opposed in the play's language – in what we hear – and in what we see during performance. When Shakespeare tackled Cinthio's tale of a Moor and his ancient, he had no choice but to use this discourse. Shakespeare, and we, are necessarily implicated in its tangled web.

The wonder of *Othello* is that Shakespeare was able to exploit the full complexity of that discourse, showing expectations gone topsy-turvy with a white villain opposed to a black man of heroic proportion. Even though the predominant typology of white over black is only temporarily subverted in fits and starts within the play, that subversion is itself an incredible artistic triumph.

As the performance history of *Othello* shows, Shakespeare's manipulation of white and black has never lost box-office appeal. The play has admittedly enjoyed varied interpretations and emphases through the centuries, with its racial themes muted in the Restoration and eighteenth century, accentuated in the twentieth. The confrontation it portrays between black and white continues to touch our deepest prejudices, fears, and hopes.

CHAPTER 4

Marital discourse: husbands and wives

[W]hat should such a fool / Do with so good a wife?

(5.2.231–32)

The progression of chapters in Part I, beginning with global contexts and ending with the marriage bed, would have struck an Elizabethan reader as entirely appropriate. It was a commonplace of Renaissance sermons, pamphlets, and treatises that the family was the state in microcosm. The husband was its governor, the wife and children his loyal and obedient subjects. Just as civilized societies like England and Venice must use vigilance and force to preserve their integrity against barbarous enemies, the watchful husband must repel the forces – particularly erotic impulses – that disrupt marital harmony.[1]

Robert Cleaver's popular marriage treatise, *A Godly Forme of Hovsehold Government* exemplifies this patriarchal power structure; the wife must obey, for "if she be not subiect to her husband, to let him rule all household, especially outward affaires: if she will make head against him, and seeke to haue her owne waies, there will be doing and vndoing. Things will goe backwarde, the house will come to ruine."[2] Edmund Tilney's *The Flower of Friendship* admonishes, "let hir indevor to increase a perfection of love, and above all imbrace chastitie. For the happinesse of matrimonie, doth consist in a chaste matrone."[3] Moral treatises like Cleaver's and Tilney's consistently

---

[1] For a valuable overview of English Renaissance marriage tracts, see Valerie Wayne's introduction to Edmund Tilney's *The Flower of Friendship: A Renaissance Dialogue Contesting Marriage* (Ithaca: Cornell University Press, 1992), pp. 1–93.

[2] R. Cleaver, *A Godly Forme of Hovsehold Government for the Ordering of Priuate Families, According to the Direction of Gods Word* (London: Printed by Thomas Creede for Thomas Man, 1603), p. 88. Cleaver's treatise was extremely popular. The *Short-Title Catalogue* lists nine editions, beginning in 1598 and running to 1624; I quote from the 1603 edition as the closest to the time of *Othello*'s composition.   [3] Tilney, *Flower of Friendship*, p. 128.

argue that by her speech, the wife disrupts household harmony, by her unchastity she subverts patrilineal inheritance, and by her disobedience she destroys right rule and order in her little state. In these admonitions the treatises reveal the contradictions inherent in Renaissance marriage ideology, for the ability to disrupt, subvert, and destroy provides, in a sense, the ability to control.

Fear of the "feminine" – passion, sexual appetite, unruliness – underlies Cleaver's and Tilney's construction of gender roles. And these are the fears that Iago uses so successfully to turn Othello from Desdemona. Critics of the Renaissance construction of gender have, accordingly, found the patriarchal structure of *Othello* ripe territory for investigation. They have reexamined Othello's psychology and have often found in masculine codes of behavior the root of his tragedy and in Desdemona's submission to patriarchal ideology a cause of her victimization. While these views are well known, a brief survey of interpretations from the 1980s will set Othello and Desdemona's marriage within this modernist context.

Irene Dash was a pioneer in the decade's reassessment of Othello and Desdemona in *Wooing, Wedding, and Power: Women in Shakespeare* (1981). Dash argued that while Desdemona is initially portrayed as a spirited and independent woman, marriage to a soldier subjects her to conventions that regulate her behavior. Gradually she loses her self-confidence. Like Emilia, a precursor of modern "battered wives," Desdemona abandons her ability to think for herself. Both women are portrayed as victims of patriarchal marriage conventions.[4]

Carol Thomas Neely also sought to reevaluate male and female characters in *Broken Nuptials in Shakespeare's Plays* (1985). For Neely, the play's central conflict is between men and women. Cassio, Iago, and Othello, she contended, do not measure up to Renaissance ideals of courage and manliness; their competition leads to aggression that ultimately destroys the women they fight over. Desdemona, Emilia, and Bianca, "in contrast, are indifferent to reputation and partially free of vanity, jealousy, and competitiveness." The play's tragic ending does not reconcile the men and women; if anything, "the separation between them widens."[5]

[4] Irene Dash, "A Woman Tamed: *Othello*," *Wooing, Wedding, and Power: Women in Shakespeare's Plays* (New York: Columbia University Press, 1981), pp. 103–30.
[5] Carol Thomas Neely, "Women and Men in *Othello*," *Broken Nuptials in Shakespeare's Plays* (New Haven: Yale University Press, 1985), pp. 105–35; quotes from pp. 122 and 134.

Neely disagreed with Dash's view that there is a radical shift in Desdemona from the play's initial scenes to the willow song scene; "Desdemona's spirit, clarity, and realism do not desert her entirely in the latter half of the play."[6] Even so, many have wondered why the young woman who stood against her father before the Venetian Senate goes so submissively to her death. Peter Stallybrass maintained in 1986 that in the first half of the play, Desdemona is an active agent. When she becomes "the object of surveillance," however, she must be purified. The play thereby "constructs two different Desdemonas: the first, a woman capable of 'downright violence' (1.3.249): the second 'a maiden never bold' (1.3.94)."[7] Instead of looking for psychological consistency in her characterization (and needing, in consequence, plausible explanations for any changes in behavior), we must see her refracted through patriarchy's bifurcated lens.

Critics of the 1980s have also seen Othello as patriarchy's victim. Stephen Greenblatt began the exploration of the hero's sexual anxiety in 1980 with his analysis of Othello's longing "for a final *release* from desire, from the dangerous violence, the sense of extremes, the laborious climbing and falling out of control that is experienced in the tempest." Greenblatt noted that the early Church fathers and Renaissance marriage manuals counselled "that the active *pursuit* of pleasure in sexuality is damnable."[8] Desdemona's frank, erotic submission troubles Othello and renders him credulous. In the same year Edward A. Snow took a more openly psychoanalytic position: Othello demonstrates repressed guilt and disgust with coition itself. According to Snow, Othello sees Desdemona's sexuality as sinful and himself as both cuckold and adulterer. The superego within him tries to destroy his own erotic impulses by destroying Desdemona.[9]

Equally psychoanalytic is Marianne Novy's analysis of gender relations in *Othello*. Novy contended that Othello's compulsion to subdue womanish passion and his desire to assert his manliness are

[6] Neely, *Broken Nuptials*, p. 116.
[7] Peter Stallybrass, "Patriarchal Territories: The Body Enclosed," in *Rewriting the Renaissance: the Discourses of Sexual Difference in Early Modern Europe*, ed. Margaret W. Ferguson, Maureen Quilligan, and Nancy Vickers (Chicago: University of Chicago Press, 1986), pp. 123–42, esp. p. 141.
[8] Stephen Greenblatt, "The Improvisation of Power," *Renaissance Self-fashioning from More to Shakespeare* (Chicago: University of Chicago Press, 1980), pp. 222–54; quotes from pp. 243 and 249.
[9] Edward A. Snow, "Sexual Anxiety and the Male Order of Things," *English Literary Renaissance*, 10 (1980): 384–412.

symptoms of a "fantasy of love as fusion with a woman both maternal and virginal." Othello is fixated, in other words, on "a symbiosis possible only for the mother and infant before the infant's discovery of sex." After the temptation scene, Othello reasserts the masculine code of revenge in a final effort to dominate and control Desdemona.[10] Patriarchal psychology is also the key to Coppelia Kahn's gloss on cuckoldry in *Othello*. The Elizabethan and Jacobean preoccupation with cuckoldry stemmed, according to Kahn, from (1) misogyny (the belief that women are inherently lustful), (2) the double standard, and (3) patriarchal marriage's belief that a husband's honor is dependent on his wife's chastity. *Othello* embodies all three causes. It shows a husband becoming convinced of the veracity of fears he already harbors about women.[11]

This brief survey demonstrates that recent discussions of Desdemona and Othello use modern psychological and psychoanalytic theories to assess and understand their relationship. Such treatments imply what C. S. Lewis called the doctrine of the unchanging human heart – the assumption that human nature now is much the same as it was in the Renaissance and that modern concepts and Freudian terminology can accurately describe Shakespeare's characters.[12] But these paradigms were not Shakespeare's. His age was interested in human psychology and marital relationships, but its rhetoric and categories were quite different from those of the late twentieth century. My purpose is to examine the sources and contexts available to Shakespeare as he composed *Othello* and to analyze how Renaissance marital discourse affected the construction of Othello and Desdemona.

Two such attempts have already been made for Desdemona. In *Shakespeare and His Social Context* Margaret Loftus Ranald urged a reevaluation of Desdemona's behavior in light of Renaissance homilies, ballads, canon laws, and marriage treatises. These sources unfailingly preach the importance of wifely submission. They emphasize female chastity, the need for parental permission before marriage, and the importance of tact, discretion, and circumspection in any wife. Desdemona violates this code repeatedly – in her

[10] Marianne L. Novy, "Marriage and Mutuality in *Othello*," *Love's Argument: Gender Relations in Shakespeare* (Chapel Hill: University of North Carolina Press, 1984), pp. 125–49; quotes from pp. 133 and 132.

[11] Coppelia Kahn, "'The Savage Yoke': Cuckoldry and Marriage," *Man's Estate: Masculine Identity in Shakespeare* (Berkeley: University of California Press, 1981), pp. 119–50.

[12] See C. S. Lewis, *The Allegory of Love* (Oxford: Oxford University Press, 1956), pp. 3–4.

clandestine marriage, in entertaining Cassio without Othello's permission, in speaking for Cassio despite Othello's evident displeasure, and in concerning herself with affairs outside the household. In short, "if one keeps in mind the precepts of the courtesy books, Desdemona is at fault in her wifely conduct and innocently supplies the evidence that leads to her own death through her assertion of her own independence."[13]

Mary Beth Rose also situated Desdemona within the context of Elizabethan and Jacobean marital discourse, but her approach is more positive. Rose argued that Desdemona "presents herself to the Senate as a hero of marriage." In accord with Puritan marital tracts, Desdemona "analogizes public and private life, drawing them together and granting them equal distinction." Othello, however, falls short of the Puritan heroic ideal of marriage by insisting on a hierarchy that subordinates the private to the public. He is unable to embrace the patience and humility required by a heroic marriage. Eventually Desdemona retreats into passive victimization.[14]

As Rose indicates, Desdemona's initial independence, however transgressive of dominant ideologies, is a major aspect of her appeal. And she was not alone. Other Jacobean tragedies – *The White Devil*, *The Duchess of Malfi*, and *Antony and Cleopatra* come readily to mind – highlighted women who violated patriarchy's codes. Though their voices were stopped by tragic conclusions, Vittoria, the Duchess, and Cleopatra asserted their independence and spoke their mind, giving voice to feelings transgressive of patriarchal constructions.

If Desdemona's outspokenness violates Renaissance marriage ideology, so does Othello's behavior. By marrying a younger woman of a different social station, he ignores Cleaver's warning that there should be "a wise and holy regard had of equalitie in yeeres, of an agreement in religion, of similitude in nature, in manners, in outward estate, condition and qualitie of person, and such like necessarie circumstances. For what is more vnmeet, then for an olde person to promise to bee contracted to a young one?"[15] Ideally, concludes Tilney's Master Pedro, husbands should be no more than four or five years older than their wives.[16]

[13] Margaret Loftus Ranald, "The Indiscretions of Desdemona," *Shakespeare and His Social Context: Essays in Osmotic Knowledge and Literary Interpretation* (New York: AMS Press, 1987), pp. 135–52, esp. p. 151.

[14] Mary Beth Rose, *The Expense of Spirit: Love and Sexuality in English Renaissance Drama* (Ithaca: Cornell University Press, 1988), pp. 131–55; quotations from p. 138.

[15] Cleaver, *Household Government*, p. 131.   [16] Tilney, *Flower of Friendship*, p. 110.

Marriage to a younger woman makes Othello particularly susceptible to concerns about the control of her sexual appetite.[17] Possession is the issue. Tilney defines jealousy as "a certaine care of mans minde, least another shoulde possesse the thing, which he alone would enjoye. There is no greater torment, than the vexation of a jeolous minde."[18] Cleaver warns that when a husband or wife becomes jealous, "they beleeue euery word that they heare spoken touching theyr passion, albeit it beare no apparance of truth."[19]

Othello errs in believing Iago in the first place. In *Tell-Trothes New Yeares Gift* Robin Goodfellow exposes "ill counsel" as a primary cause of jealousy. Often the wicked

(whose immaginations are only to soe discentions by bruting euil supposes, bred of a suspitious braine & vttered with colored hipocrisie) labour to sette debate betweene true hartes, and to shuffle in suspition amongst those that are free from thought thereof. They will striue to perswade by liklyhoods & confirme ascertions with false oathes[,] ... their heads studying how to bring them to like of the practise of their premeditated mischiefe ... They will tatle tales as if fraught with truth: and vtter slanders, with protestations. They will inuent to perswade, and sweare to confirme.[20]

As Valerie Wayne persuasively argues, Othello soon becomes entwined in Iago's discourse of misogyny, a discourse that defined woman as whore and was directed against marriage itself. Iago's misogyny is but one of several ideologies about women and marriage that interact within the play.[21] Moreover, Iago's speech acts – protesting, inventing, and swearing – were well-known slanderous devices. Othello's readiness to believe them violates the pamphlets' and treatises' everyday wisdom far more than Desdemona's behavior violates the marriage manuals.

*   *   *   *

These treatises concern a husband and wife's daily behavior, outlining what men and women should and shouldn't do. On the whole they do not address the question of why men and women act as they do. Yet texts concerned with human psychology were available to Shakespeare when he was writing *Othello*. The terms used

---

[17] Cf. January in Chaucer's *The Merchant's Tale*.
[18] Tilney, *Flower of Friendship*, p. 122.   [19] Cleaver, *Household Government*, p. 186.
[20] Anon., *Tell-Trothes New Yeares Gift Being Robin Good-fellowes Newes ... With his Owne Invective Against Ielosy* (London: Imprinted by Robert Bourne, 1593), sig. B2r.
[21] Valerie Wayne, "Historical Differences: Misogyny and *Othello*," in *The Matter of Difference: Materialist Feminist Criticism of Shakespeare*, ed. Valerie Wayne (Ithaca: Cornell University Press, 1991), pp. 153–79.

to describe the human mind were obviously not Freudian, but there was nonetheless a significant attempt to understand human passions, where they come from, and how they manifest themselves in a marital relationship.

One of the primary passions in Jacobean texts is jealousy. Shakespeare's fascination with the workings of the jealous mind is evident not just in *Othello* but also in *Much Ado About Nothing*, *The Merry Wives of Windsor*, and *The Winter's Tale*. In all but *The Merry Wives* (where jealousy is more of a Jonsonian humor), the sudden pathological transformation of a man's love into hate results in violence against a woman. To understand this passion in the context of Shakespeare's time, it will be helpful to examine Thomas Wright's lengthy and influential study, *The Passions of the Minde in Generale*.

Shakespeare probably knew Wright's work. A truncated version appeared in 1601, and the corrected and expanded edition of 1604, dedicated to the Earl of Southampton, might have been available in manuscript before publication. If the dramatist did study Wright, he found not just theoretical discussion of human emotions but a detailed outline of how passions are revealed through speech and gesture. In other words, Wright's analysis would have provided abundant verbal and visual material for someone interested in representations of human conflict on the stage.

Wright defined a passion as "a sensual motion of our appetitive facultie, through imagination of some good or ill thing." Such "affections" influence, in turn, the bodily humors, causing perturbations that corrupt the judgment and seduce the will.[22] If such passions are not "moderated according to reason ... immediatly the soule is molested with some maladie." At the same time, passions should not be completely extinguished, "but sometimes to be moved, and stirred vp for the service of vertue." Passions can stir up "sluggish and idle soules,"[23] and if they are moderated with "right reason," they can lead to good effects. If left unchecked, however, they inevitably result in destruction. Wright uses the same political analogy Cleaver employed to describe the family; inordinate affections, he wrote, in "many waies disquiet the Minde, and trouble the peaceable state of this pettie commonweale of our soule."[24] The

---

[22] Thomas Wright, *The Passions of the Minde in Generale* (London: Printed by Valentine Simmes for Walter Burre, 1604), p. 8. I was first directed to Wright's analysis of human behavior by Professor Keir Elam at a workshop sponsored by the Folger Institute's Center for Shakespeare Studies. [23] Ibid., pp. 17–18. [24] Ibid., p. 68.

central issue for both marital relations and the individual mind is control; in each case, feminine or womanish emotions are feared as destabilizing forces.[25]

Wright cautioned that the heart of a passionate man becomes "tossed like the Sea with contrary windes." And like a storm at sea, passion can suddenly appear from nowhere: "some times a man will bee in the prime of his ioy, and presently a sea of griefe overwhelmeth him."[26] When passion does strike, claimed Wright, it demands immediate satisfaction:

Inordinate Passions...neither observe time nor place: but vpon every occasion would be leaping into action, importuning execution. Let a man fall a praying or studying, or be busie in any negotation [of] importance, and very often he shal feele a headlesse Passion to rush in vpon him, importuning him even then to leave all, and prosecute revenge...or some other vnbridled desire."[27]

Motivation is not an issue for Wright. Passion is a given of human nature, like the need to eat and sleep. Thus to Wright it is not necessary to explain sudden changes in behavior. The problem is to resist sudden changes, to bridle desire, put a head on passion, and maintain a calm and tranquil mind.

Even if Shakespeare did not know Wright *per se*, he would have found in the texts he did use abundant descriptions of sudden, seemingly inexplicable changes in a husband's personality. These "perturbations of the mind" center on the husband's desire for his wife, his ensuing jealousy, and his subsequent murder of the woman who aroused such passions in the first place.

Richard Knolles' *Generall Historie of the Turkes* offers a rich example. Scholars have longed recognized this text as a source for details of the Venetian-Turkish wars,[28] but they have not considered Knolles' account of Bassa Ionuses and his wife Manto as a precursor of Othello and Desdemona. Because this section of Knolles is so little known, I quote at length:

---

[25] The repetition of the "kingdom" analogy from the family to the microcosmic individual may seem like a recycled version of Tillyard's "doctrine of correspondences," and in some sense, it is. The analogy does exist in Elizabethan and Jacobean texts, especially homiletic texts that exhort control of possible threats to order and stability. While Tillyard assumed that everyone in the English Renaissance subscribed to this ideology, I see it as a furious effort to contain that which could not be contained. Although it is currently fashionable to discard Tillyard altogether, I suggest we leave his dogmatism behind but continue to use his concepts where they are relevant. See E. M. W. Tillyard, *The Elizabethan World Picture* (New York: Vintage Books, 1959).   [26] Wright, *Passions*, p. 71.   [27] Ibid., pp. 72–73.
[28] See chapter 1 above, pp. 24–25.

This great Bassa, whilest he yet liued and flourished in the court, in nothing
so much offended the minds of the people (who generally both loued and
honoured him) as by the crueltie by him shewed vpon the person of the faire
ladie *Manto* his best beloued wife ... [T]his great Bassa *Ionuses*[,] ... finding
her outward perfections graced with no lesse inward vertues, and her
honourable mind answerable vnto her rare feature, tooke her vnto his wife;
honouring her farre aboue all the rest of his wiues and concubines: and she
againe in all dutifull loyaltie seeking to please him, for a space liued in all
worldly felicitie and blisse, not much inferiour vnto one of the great
Sultanesses ... For in short time, the Bassa more amorous of her person than
secured in her vertues, and after the manner of sensuall men still fearing least
that which so much pleased himselfe, ... began to haue her in distrust,
although he saw no great cause why, more than his owne conceit, not
grounded vpon any her euill demeanor, but vpon the excesse of his owne
liking. Which mad humour (hardly to be euer purged) of it selfe still more
and more in him encreasing, he became so froward and imperious, that
nothing she could say or doe could now so please or content him, but that
he still thought some one or other, although he wist not who, to be therein
partakers with him. So fearfull was the jealous man of his owne conceits.

Exhausted by his jealous tirades, Manto made plans to escape which
were treacherously disclosed to her husband, "Who therewith
enraged, and calling her vnto him, forthwith in his furie, with a
dagger stabd her to the heart and slew her: so togither with the death
of his loue, hauing cured his tormenting jealousie."[29] Notice that by
this account Manto does nothing until the end to provoke the Bassa's
jealousy. The root cause is what Wright calls an "inordinate
affection," leading to perturbation of the mind. Or, in Emilia's
words, jealous souls "are not ever jealous for the cause, / But jealous
for they're jealous. 'Tis a monster / Begot upon itself, born on itself"
(3.4.154–56). The Bassa succumbs because he is "more amorous of
her person than secured in her vertues;" he is a sensual man who
feared "least that which so much pleased himselfe, gaue no lesse
contentment to others."[30] Once his passion is aroused, Ionuses will
believe anything of his wife. The only way to still his beating mind is
to destroy her.

   While I cannot prove that Shakespeare had this passage in mind as
he composed *Othello*, he must at least have noted the engravings of

---

[29] Richard Knolles, *The Generall Historie of the Turkes* (London: Printed by Adam Islip, 1603),
p. 557.
[30] Manto's desire to destroy his wife, caused by his erotic feelings toward her, perhaps indicates
what Snow describes as a "pathological male animus toward sexuality." See Snow, "Sexual
Anxiety," 388.

Figure 4. (See facing page.)

Ionuses and Manto on folios 558 and 559 of Knolles' text. Manto is
the only woman portrayed in this richly illustrated volume. Under
her portrait Knolles printed a commemorative poem:

> If feature braue thou doest respect, thou canst none
>   fairer see,
>   Nor in whose chast and constant brest could greater
>   graces lie.
> But whilst mismatcht she liu'd to mourne, enthrald to
>   jealous braine,
>   Vnhappie she, with cruell hand was by her husband
>   slaine.[31]

[31] Knolles, *Generall Historie*, p. 559.

Figure 4 and 5: Sultan Ionuses and his wife Manto from Richard Knolles' *Generall Historie of the Turkes* (1603).

While skimming Knolles for background, Shakespeare may have noticed Manto's picture and Knolles' poem. Curiosity whetted, he could easily have turned to page 557 to read of her life and death.

The dramatist would also have encountered a more detailed account of perturbed masculine affection if, as Paul Siegel argues, he used Geoffrey Fenton's *Tragical Discourses* as a source for *Othello*.[32] Fenton began his translation of Bandello's Discourse IV with a theatrical metaphor: "I have here to expose unto you a myserable accident, happening in our tyme, whiche shall serve as a bloddy skaffolde, or theaterye, wherin are presented such as play no partes

[32] See Paul N. Siegel, "A New Source for *Othello*," *Publications of the Modern Language Association*, 75 (1960): 480.

but in mortal and furious tragideies."[33] This scaffold will demonstrate that "jelosye is an evill excedinge all the tormentes of the
world, supplantinge oftentymes bothe wytt and reason."[34] Fenton
then narrated the story of an "Albanoyse captain" who marries a
woman "constant wythout cause or argument of dishonesty, and that
(whiche is the chiefest ornement and decoracion of the beautie of a
woman) to bee of disposition readye to obeye her husbande, yeldinge
hym suffraintye with a deutifull obedience."[35] Like Knolles' Bassa,
this Albanoyse captain, "doating without discrecion uppon the
desyer of his newe lady, and rather drowned beastely in the
superfluitie of her love than waighing rightly the meryte and vertue
of true affection, entred into such tearmes of fervent jelowsie, that
every fle that wafteth afore her made hym sweate at the browes with
the suspicion he had of her bewty."[36] Once again, the husband's
excessive and sensual desire for his wife leads to obsessive jealousy.
The wife's virtuous behavior only confirms the husband's suspicions:
"the more she sought to prefer a show of sinceritie and honestie of life,
the more grew the furye and rage of his perverse fancie, thinking the
compaignye and fellowship of his wife to be as indifferente to others
as peculiar to himselfe."[37] Despite his savage fury, the wife continues
to show her love and duty. Finally, to relieve his "hagarde mynde"
and his unnatural fury "(far excedinge the savage and brutishe
maner of the tiger, lyon, or libarde, bredd in the desertes of Affrike,
the common norsse of monsters and creatures civil without reason),"
he embraced and kissed her, then killed her by slashing her ten or
twelve times. His knife penetrated her head, her arms, and even her
legs in a violent orgasm, so that "no parte shoulde escape free from
the stroke of his malice."[38] For the Turkish Bassa and the Albanoyse
captain, violence against the wife is not an attempt to restore lost
honor so much as a desperate effort to relieve the pressure of pent-up
passions. With the wife's death, the object of the husband's inordinate
affection is removed; the violence provides, in Wright's words, "a
firme rest" and satisfaction of the "streame of his Passions."[39]

According to Fenton, the Albanoyse captain's jealous rage comes
from excess passion, not from outside provocation. Othello's passionate love, expressed on the Cyprus quay, is initially kept in check by

[33] Geffraie (Geoffrey) Fenton, *Certaine Tragical Discourses of Bandello* (London: David Nutt,
   1898), vol. I, p. 165.   [34] Ibid., p. 164.   [35] Ibid., p. 167.
[36] Ibid., p. 176.   [37] Ibid., p. 178.   [38] Ibid., pp. 188–89.
[39] Wright, *Passions*, p. 74.

Desdemona's matter-of-fact response and by the military business at hand. But the strength of his passion makes him vulnerable to Iago's insinuations; having invested so much of himself in this woman – "My life upon her faith" – he is unraveled by the mere possibility of adultery. While Iago's machinations make Othello a more plausible character than the Captain, Shakespeare's Moor neverthless shares the same pathology. Once jealous, he exclaims, "I will chop her into messes" (4.1.188). Only by destroying Desdemona can he quell the emotions that tear him apart.

Shakespeare's immediate source for *Othello* was Giraldi Cinthio who, unlike Knolles and Fenton, provided an outside instigator in the husband's jealousy. The first transformation from love to hate in Cinthio is his, for according to Bullough's translation, the Ensign began by falling "ardently in love with Disdemona." He then "bent all his thoughts to see if he could manage to enjoy her." When she did not respond to his overtures, "the love which he had felt for the Lady now changed to the bitterest hate." Like the two texts described above, excess of desire engenders the will to destroy. His anger flails outward; first it is directed at Disdemona, then at the Corporal (the Cassio figure), and finally at the Moor. Iago, in contrast, begins with hatred of the Moor, using Desdemona as a pawn. Thus in Shakespeare's text, Desdemona's death is a necessary by-product of Iago's hatred.

Cinthio also differs from Knolles and Fenton by characterizing the wife more fully than simply as the object of her husband's passions. When his Disdemona brings up the Corporal's reinstatement, she comments impetuously, "But you Moors are so hot by nature that any little thing moves you to anger and revenge." But as soon as these words are spoken, she backs off, terrified at her husband's reaction. She then humbly promises, "Only a very good purpose made me speak to you about this, but rather than have you angry with me I shall never say another word on the subject."[40] It is too late. Her husband asks the Ensign for ocular proof, sees the stolen handkerchief, and together they beat Disdemona to death with a sandfilled stocking.

Cinthio offered Shakespeare ample material for the temptation scene: the Ensign's insinuations about the Corporal, his manipulation of evidence, and his suggestion that Disdemona dislikes the Moor's

[40] Geoffrey Bullough, ed., *Narrative and Dramatic Sources of Shakespeare* (London: Routledge and Kegan Paul, 1973), vol. VII, pp. 241–52.

blackness. What he did not provide is a deep portrait of the husband's pathology, the perturbations of the mind that lead him to believe such insinuations in the first place. So while Shakespeare relied on Cinthio for plot, he got the nuances of his characters elsewhere.

Another fascinating account of marital jealousy may have been available to Shakespeare during 1603 in manuscript form. Lady Elizabeth Cary's closet drama, *Mariam*, was written between 1602 and 1604 though it remained unpublished until 1613. George W. Williams suggested that this play's portrayal of a "Judean queen" may have been the source of the Quarto's hotly-debated reference to a "base Judean."[41] More important to my purposes than direct verbal parallels are the structural parallels to many of the situations and several speeches. In probing the pathology of male jealousy, Shakespeare may have turned not to Cinthio but to a play written by a woman.

Lady Cary's tragedy begins with Mariam alone, torn between sorrow that her husband has died and relief that she will no longer suffer from his tyranny. She blames "*Herods* Iealousie" which "Had power euen constancie it selfe to change." Yet, she says, "too chast a Scholler was my hart, / To learn to loue another then my Lord."[42] Every character in the play, except perhaps Herod's manipulative sister Salome, fears his excessive rages. He had killed Mariam's father and brother, and for love of her had divorced his wife Doris. He is perceived, in other words, as a man given to inexplicable perturbations of the mind. As his speeches in Act 4 demonstrate, when he thinks positively of Mariam, he idealizes her into a creature more than human. When he suspects her, he sees her as the blackest devil imaginable. His mood swings are thereby symptomatic of his traditionally bifurcated view of the female Other as goddess or whore.

This double view is reinforced in *Mariam* by the opposition between Mariam and her sister-in-law Salome. While Mariam's

41 George W. Williams, "Yet Another Early Use of Iudean," *Shakespeare Quarterly*, 34 (1983): 72. Barry Weller and Margaret W. Ferguson also discuss this verbal parallel in *The Tragedy of Mariam, the Fair Queen of Jewry* (Berkeley: University of California Press, 1994), pp. 42–43; unfortunately, this critical edition of Elizabeth Cary's play was published too recently to be cited here.

42 E[lizabeth] C[ary], *The Tragedie of Mariam, the Faire Queene of Iewry* (London: Printed by Thomas Creede for Richard Hawkins, 1613; repr. for the Malone Society, ed. A. C. Dunstan [Oxford: Oxford University Press, 1914]). Quotations are from the Malone Society reprint and will be cited by line numbers within the text. The lines quoted here are 25–30.

chastity is never in doubt, Salome has had one husband killed before
the play begins. During the play she divorces her second husband to
marry a third. Constabarus, the second husband, warns his successor
Silleus that "She meerly is a painted sepulcher, / That is both faire,
and vilely foule at once." Though fair in outer graces,

> Her mind is fild with worse then rotten bones
>
> ...
>
> Her mouth though serpent-like it neuer hisses,
> Yet like a Serpent, poysons where it kisses.   (880–89)

Mariam, in contrast, is the "chast Queene." There is

> neuer woman with so pure a heart.
> Thine eyes graue maiestie keepes all in awe,
> And cuts the winges of euery loose desire:
> Thy brow is table to the modest lawe.   (1211–14)

Instead of providing a spectrum of female sexual mores, as Shakespeare does with Bianca the prostitute, Emilia the earthy matron,
and Desdemona the chaste bride, Cary presents her major female
characters as polar opposites.[43]

Evil though she may be, Salome is compelling. She argues
passionately in the first act that the Hebrew law that allows men to
divorce wives they're tired of, but which denies this privilege to
women, is unfair. In what may be an inspiration for Emilia's
reflections on the double standard, Salome questions:

> Why should such priviledge to man be giuen?
> Or giuen to them, why bard from women then?
> Are men then we in grater grace with Heauen?
> Or cannot women hate as well as men?   (315–18)

But Salome, unlike Emilia, is a villain. Mariam claims in the previous
scene that her sister-in-law had "vsde the art, / To slander haplesse
Mariam for vnchast" (265–66), and as the play unfolds, it becomes
clear that Salome will commit any evil to get what she wants. Finally
she succeeds in provoking Herod to kill his wife.

Salome's wickedness ought to highlight chaste Mariam's virtue.
Strangely enough, in this play written by a well-educated woman,
the heroine's tragic flaw is her penchant for expressing her in-

---

[43] Graphina combines chastity with silence, but as a result, she speaks so few lines that she can
hardly be called a major character.

dependent thoughts. In Act 3, when Herod unexpectedly returns
alive from Egypt, Mariam forswears his bed. She knows that she
could win him back with smiles and gentle words, but she opts instead
for integrity, refusing to do what she does not feel. Salome predicts
that "Vnbridled speech is *Mariams* worst disgrace, / And will
indanger her without desart" (1186–87). Like Iago, Salome resolves
to turn Mariam's "virtue into pitch, / And out of her own goodness
make the net / That shall enmesh them all" (*Othello*, 2.3.327–29).
The Chorus agrees with Salome, pronouncing Mariam's doom in a
strange conjunction of admiration and condemnation:

> Tis not enough for one that is a wife
>   To keepe her spotles from an act of ill:
>   But from suspition she should free her life,
> And bare her selfe of power as well as will.
>   Tis not so glorious for her to be free,
>   As by her proper selfe restrain'd to bee.
>   ...
> That wife her hand against her fame doth reare,
> That more then to her Lord alone will giue
> A priuate word to any second eare,
> And though she may with reputation liue.
>   Yet though most chast, she doth her glory blot,
>   And wounds her honour, though she killes it not.
>   ...
> Then she vsurpes vpon anothers right,
> That seekes to be by publike language grac't:
> And though her thoughts reflect with purest light,
> Her mind if not peculiar is not chast.
>   For in a wife it is no worse to finde,
>   A common body, then a common minde.   (1219–48)

The Chorus, no doubt, would exalt the Stepford Wives as the ideal of
womanhood. By its judgment, Mariam's determination to speak her
thoughts condemns her. Or, as Herod puts it later in the play, "Her
mouth will ope to eu'ry strangers eare" (1706). Mariam is thus a
stronger version of Desdemona, whose outspoken pleas for Cassio are
so easily misconstrued.

The similarities between Herod and Othello are also clear. Under
Salome's insistence, the tyrant, like Othello, ponders the means to kill
his wife. Whenever he thinks of her beauty, his heart softens. Like
Othello, he sees "the pity of it" and dwells on his wife's virtues. When
Salome suggests her treachery, Herod can only think of her death.

Finally, Herod resolves, "She shall not liue, nor will I see her face."
Then he turns on Salome as Othello turns on Iago, "Hence from my
sight" (1776–90).

After Mariam's death, Herod turns again. When he discovers that
Mariam was innocent of Salome's accusations, he exclaims

> I had but one inestimable Iewell,
> Yet one I had no monarch had the like,
>
> ...
>
> Twas broken by a blow my selfe did strike.
> A pretious Mirror made by wonderous art,
> I prizd it ten times dearer then my Crowne,
> And laide it vp fast foulded in my heart:
> Yet I in suddaine choler cast it downe.
> And pasht it all to peeces.
>
> ...
>
> She was my gracefull moytie, me accurst,
> To slay my better halfe and saue my worst.   (2061–76)

The parallels to Othello's final words are obvious. The Moor, like
Herod, cast away a pearl richer than all his tribe, then his better half
destroys his worser side by killing the Turk within. *Mariam* closes with
Herod still alive, raving against Mariam's heavenly beauty that
made him think "That it with chastitie could neuer dwell" (2186).

Cary exposes in *Mariam* the contradictions in patriarchal conceptions of the female Other, but she does not condemn them. Mariam's
beauty arouses Herod's passion, yet the excess of feeling he has for her
is easily transformed to jealous rage. She could win his favor,
temporarily at least, by being submissive. She chooses instead to be
independent, and that decision guarantees her destruction.

In *Othello* Shakespeare manipulates the same contradictions; the
more Desdemona pleads for Cassio, the more she insures her own
death. Like Herod, Othello does not understand how his assumptions
about women contribute to his tragedy, but unlike the Judean, he
takes responsibility for his decision and executes the Turk within
himself. And Emilia expresses what one wishes a character would say
to Herod, "O gull! O dolt! / As ignorant as dirt!" (5.2.162–63)

Mariam allows no voice for such feelings. The result is a
disconcerting disjunction between Mariam's role as virtuous heroine
and the Chorus' condemnation of her.

As these texts demonstrate, narratives about the sudden onset of
jealousy that results in violence against women appealed to Elizabe-

than and Jacobean authors and readers. Such stories might have had even greater appeal to dramatists, for scenes of jealous passion could titillate with fantasies of sexual activity without compromising the chaste heroine. Moreover, the enactment of the passions of the mind fully challenged a tragedian like Richard Burbage. Wright outlined how passions like jealousy could be represented. First, they appear in a man's speech. Too much or too little talk, slowness in speech, or rash, disconnected speech would reveal a perturbation of the mind. Thus it is a truism of *Othello* criticism that after the temptation scene arouses Othello's jealousy, his speech radically changes. He begins to speak in Iago's accents, using grotesque animal images. His speeches are no longer stately, but explosive and disjointed.

External actions could also reveal the workings of the inner soul. Wright cautioned his readers to examine "motions of the eyes, pronuntiation, managing of the hands and bodie, [the] manner of going." Desdemona fears Othello, for example, when his eyes "roll so" (5.2.38). Wright would also have approved of the use of the handkerchief, for he claimed, "it ought seriously to be considered, that the presence of any visible obiect, moueth much more vehemently the passion, than the imagination or conceit thereof."[44]

Othello's responses to Desdemona and to Iago can be seen as physical manifestations of a troubled mind. When he compares Desdemona to "The fountain from the which my current runs / Or else dries up" (4.2.58–59), he echoes Wright: "the passion which is in our brest must be the fountaine and origen of all external actions."[45] That such passion leads to sudden changes in mood and turns his love to hate would not have surprised a Jacobean audience accustomed to such stories. Nor would it have been surprised that such passion was rooted in erotic desire and sexual jealousy, for in the narratives of Fenton and Cinthio, women were catalysts for male frenzy.

Note, too, that with the exception of the Albanoyse captain, the husbands described here are situated outside Christian culture: Ionuses is a Turkish sultan, Herod a Judean king. These husbands confirm Christian stereotypes about Turkish cruelty and Jewish tyranny. Like them, Othello is constructed in opposition to European culture, fulfilling the audience's expectations that a Moor will be violently jealous. In other words, while his behavior suits con-

---

[44] Wright, *Passions*, p. 158.　　　　　　[45] Ibid., p. 174.

temporary conceptions of male desire and susceptibility to passion, it is also imbricated in the discursive fields outlined in chapters 1 and 3.

The contradictions in Othello's construction were inherent in contemporary debates about love, marriage, and the role of women.[46] As the "weaker vessel," Renaissance women were believed to be more passionate then men. If a husband could not control his wife, his other self, how could he control his own passions in the patriarchy of his own psyche? Or, to reverse the relationship between women and passion, where else should he vent his own uncontrollable erotic impulses if not on the woman, the representative of his weaker nature? The need to keep women silent, chaste, and obedient was thus the drive for order both without and within. Simply by serving as the object of a husband's desire, a woman could become the locus of disorder, of perturbations, of violence. The more she disturbed him, the more she had to be controlled. For Knolles' Bassa, Fenton's Captain, and Lady Cary's Herod, excess of love brings not just the desire to possess but the desire to destroy. Only with the woman's death do the disturbing passions cease.

The feminist critics discussed in the first section of this chapter have taught us to see Othello and Desdemona as constructed characters who are imbricated in contemporary conceptions of gender. Their analysis of *Othello* has provided valuable correctives to the male-dominated criticism of the mid-twentieth century and accorded Desdemona, Emilia, and Bianca the attention they deserve. My discussion of narratives contemporary to *Othello* should be seen as a complement to their analyses and an antidote for the presentist impulse to see the play solely in post-Freudian terms.

Within that historical context, a Jacobean audience would have been less puzzled by Othello's transformation from doting husband to jealous murderer than we are. They would have expected Desdemona's love to be expressed in obedience and forgiveness. If the play surprised them at all, I suspect, it was by Emilia, a woman neither saint nor whore, who speaks against her husband's command to silence what might have been said of Knolles' Bassa, Fenton's Captain, and Cary's Herod: "O murderous coxcomb, what should such a fool / Do with so good a wife?" (5.2.231–32)[47]

---

[46] Cf. Valerie Wayne's Introduction to Tilney, *Flower of Friendship*, pp. 52–64.

[47] Here I admit to being among what Carol Thomas Neely describes as "the Emilia critics," for I see her as one of Shakespeare's most remarkable creations. See Neely, *Broken Nuptials*, p. 108.

PART II

Representations

CHAPTER 5

Othello *in Restoration England*

> the neighing steed and the shrill trump,
> The spirit-stirring drum, th'ear-piercing fife,
> The royal banner, and all quality,
> Pride, pomp, and circumstance of glorious war!
>
> *(Othello,* 3.3.352–55)

When the Restoration[1] adapters began "improving" Shakespeare, they left *Othello* relatively unscathed.[2] Two explanations for this uncharacteristic reverence may be the play's acting history and its subject matter. Until the acting companies united in 1682, *Othello* was performed by the King's Company.[3] Theatre historian Gunnar Sorelius demonstrates that "at an early stage the King's Men established themselves as custodians of the dramatic heritage," whereas Davenant's Duke's Company "felt a need to 'reform' and 'make fit' Shakespeare's dramas."[4] As a King's Company play, *Othello* was less likely to be tampered with.

Unlike many Restoration tragedies, *Othello* was never censored for political reasons. A critic like Thomas Rymer might find its violation of the classical unities culpable.[5] But of all Shakespeare's tragedies, it appealed most to Neo-Classical tastes: it had one unified plot, and

---

[1] I use the term "Restoration" for convenience's sake, realizing that, as Robert D. Hume demonstrates, it does not do justice to the multiplicity of dramatic texts produced between 1660 and 1710. See Robert D. Hume, *The Development of Drama in the Late Seventeenth Century* (Oxford: Clarendon Press, 1976).

[2] See George C. D. Odell, *Shakespeare from Betterton to Irving* (New York: Charles Scribner's Sons, 1920), vol. I, p. 26.

[3] For analysis of the repertories of the Duke's and King's Companies, see Robert D. Hume, "Securing a Repertory: Plays on the London Stage 1660–5," in *Poetry and Drama, 1570–1700,* ed. Antony Coleman and Antony Hammond (London: Methuen, 1981), pp. 156–71, and Gunnar Sorelius, "The Rights of the Restoration Theatrical Companies in the Older Drama," *Studia Neophilologica,* 37 (1965): 174–89.

[4] Gunnar Sorelius, *"The Giant Race Before the Flood": Pre-Restoration Drama on the Stage and in the Criticism of the Restoration* (Uppsala: Studia Anglistica Upsaliensis, 1966), pp. 40 and 201.

[5] Rymer particularly criticized the movement from Venice to Cyprus between Acts 1 and 2. See Thomas Rymer, *A Short View of Tragedie* (London: Richard Baldwin, 1693), p. 106.

once the clown was eliminated, it was no mongrel mixture of comedy and tragic action.

At the same time, *Othello*'s popularity was partly due to its striking use of a black man as romantic warrior and hero. Rymer ranted about this unusual feature in palpably racist exclamations:

shall a Poet thence fancy that [the Venetians] will set a Negro to be their General, or trust a *Moor* to defend them against the *Turk*? With us a Black-a-moor might rise to be a Trumpeter, but *Shakespear* would not have him less than a Lieutenant-General. With us a *Moor* might marry some little drab, or Small-coal Wench: *Shake-spear*, would provide him the Daughter and kin of some great Lord, or Privy-Councellor.[6]

Charles Gildon, who later countered Rymer's quarrels with Shakespeare, agreed on the shock value of a black hero: that a woman such as Desdemona should admit " a *Negro* to a Commerce with her, " why "every one almost starts at the Choice. "[7] Shocking as it was, or *because* it was, the dramatic representation of the union of a white woman and a black man was popular throughout the Restoration and the manner of its performance reinforced Restoration concerns and values. The decision to perform *Othello* without major alteration – but to highlight particular aspects of the play as opposed to others – was *inherently* ideological.

While it is admittedly difficult to identify Restoration concerns and values through twentieth-century lenses, *Othello*'s acting history and its acting context – in particular, the texts offered by the Duke's Company in imitation of Shakespeare's original – provide valuable clues to what audiences looked for in Shakespeare's tragedy.

*　　*　　*　　*

A brief review of what we know about *Othello* from its earliest performances, familiar ground though that may be, sets the stage. From its initial performance, sometime around 1604, until the closing of the theatres in 1642, *Othello* was a popular commercial play and was also staged at Court well into the reign of Charles I. It was performed at the Banquetting House at Whitehall in 1604, for the Princess Elizabeth's wedding in 1612–13, and at Hampton Court in 1636.[8] Early on the lead was acted by the King's Company's major

[6] Ibid., pp. 91–92.
[7] Charles Gildon, *Remarks on the Plays of Shakespeare* (London: Printed with the Seventh Volume of the Works of Shakespeare, 1710), p. 410.
[8] E. K. Chambers, *William Shakespeare* (2 vols., Oxford: Oxford University Press, 1930), vol. I, p. 462; vol. II, pp. 331–53.

tragedian, Richard Burbage, who (according to an elegy published at his death) excelled in the role.[9] After 1618, the Moor was played by Eyllaerdt Swanston; Joseph Taylor was recognized for his rendition of Iago.

In 1648 members of the King's Company (Lowin, Taylor, and Pollard who had known Shakespeare) tried to start acting again, but the government suppressed their efforts. Associated with these old-timers were some younger actors, men who had begun their careers in the 1630s playing women's roles. During the Civil War the younger actors were allied with the Royalists; several fought with Prince Rupert's forces. And when the theatres reopened in 1660, these actors – not so young anymore – formed the new King's Company, managed by Thomas Killegrew, a Royalist who had also participated in Charles II's exile. *Othello* became part of its repertory.

The first Restoration Othello was Nicholas Burt, succeeded by Charles Hart in the 1670s. The first Iago was Walter Clun. James Wright records in his *Historia Histrionica* (1699) that Clun and Hart "were bred up Boys at the *Blackfriers*; and Acted Women's Parts."[10] If Wright was correct, they must have seen *Othello* in the 1630s, even if they were too young to perform in it, and therefore *they* represent an unbroken line of tradition reaching back to Shakespeare's own acting company. At the same time, much had changed since the closing of the theatres. Burt and Hart's Othello may have echoed the resonant tones of Burbage, but as produced by Killegrew, the play was probably stamped by Interregnum experiences as well.

The illustration for Nicholas Rowe's edition (1709), which may reflect actual performances, depicts Othello as a black man dressed in the uniform of a British army officer,[11] a tradition that continued throughout much of the eighteenth century. Francis Gentleman writes in *The Dramatic Censor* (1770) that while actor James Quin's "magpye" appearance – with black face under powdered wig – was absurd, it was nonetheless striking to see the contrast between Othello's gloved white hand and the blackness of his skin when he removed his gloves.[12] Gentleman refers here to performances in the

---

[9] See Horace Howard Furness, ed., *Othello: A New Variorum Edition* (New York: J. P. Lippincott and Co., 1886), p. 396.

[10] James Wright, *Historia Histrionica* (London: n.p., 1699 [Facs. ed. New York: Johnson Reprint Corporation, 1972]), p. 3.

[11] Nicholas Rowe, ed., *The Works of Mr. William Shakespeare* (London: Jacob Tonson, 1709–1710), vol. V.

[12] Francis Gentleman, *The Dramatic Censor* (London: J. Bell, 1770), vol. I, pp. 151–52.

first half of the century; Quin last appeared as Othello at Covent Garden in 1751 and retired altogether in 1754.[13] Given the continuous chain of *Othello* tradition, it is reasonable to assume that Shakespeare's Moor was meant to be black and that he was played black throughout the Restoration.

Even though England was heavily involved in the slave trade by the last half of the seventeenth century, such economic activity did not preclude the stage presence of a noble black African hero. Othello's ebony skin could even have been interpreted as a sign of his nobility, for dramas like Dryden's *The Conquest of Granada* were extremely popular during this period and Aphra Behn's novel of an African prince sold into slavery, *Oroonoko*, was published in 1688. Othello easily fit familiar Restoration stereotypes of the exotic, blameless hero, and, despite Rymer's reaction to his color, his blackness was not necessarily a stumbling block to audience sympathy. His color may have contributed an aura of forbidden sexuality that heightened the play's appeal. Not until the nineteenth century did actors and audiences insist he be a white man, admittedly dark but certainly not black.[14]

It is difficult to know how Restoration actors interpreted the play's major roles. We do know that as former Cavaliers, most actors were associated with the Court. Robert D. Hume concludes in his study of late seventeenth-century drama: "Carolean drama derives conspicuous and trend-setting support from the Court circle, and ... many of the plays very naturally express the tastes, values, and prejudices of this group."[15] Carolean actors may also have been affected by their experience as Royalist officers during the Civil War. The cast list from the 1681 Quarto, a text reprinted with little alteration from Q2 (1630) perhaps sheds some light. The Moor, played by Hart (probably from Burt's retirement until Betterton took over the role in 1682) is described as "Othello, the Moor, General of the army in Cyprus."[16] During the early eighteenth century, Othello appeared in the uniform of a British general; audiences were startled in 1744 when he was clothed for the first time after the "Custom of his

---

[13] See *The London Stage, 1660–1800*, ed. George Winchester Stone (Carbondale: Southern Illinois University Press, 1962), part 4, vol. I, p. 236.

[14] For more information see Ruth Cowhig, "Blacks in English Renaissance Drama and the Role of Shakespeare's Othello," in *The Black Presence in English Literature*, ed. David Dabydeen (Manchester: Manchester University Press, 1985), pp. 1–25.

[15] Hume, *Development*, p. 487.

[16] *Othello, the Moor of Venice* (London: R. Bentley and M. Magnes, 1681).

native Country."[17] We can't know when this tradition began, but we can assume that at least by Betterton's time, Othello and his officers were dressed in military garb.[18] The General's uniform would have made his military status preeminent to the audience, mitigating any negative effects of his skin color. Moreover, Hart's experience as Lieutenant of Horse in Prince Rupert's regiment may have helped him convey Othello's military bearing. John Downes praised Hart's performance and reported the comment "That *Hart* might Teach any King on Earth how to Comport himself."[19]

That actors stressed Othello's basic nobility is strongly supported by the evidence of the Smock Alley Promptbook. Its editor, G. Blakemore Evans, concludes that "many of the cuts and other changes, which now appear for the first time in the Smock Alley PB, were in fact importations from London.... [T]he Smock Alley PB preserves for us in its essentials *Othello* as it was performed in Restoration London."[20] Evans notes that the cuts could not have been inspired by Rymer, who did not write specifically on *Othello* until 1693 in *A Short View of Tragedie*, whereas the Smock Alley Promptbook dates from sometime between 1675 and 1685.[21] The Smock Alley deletions may be attempts to make the play more decorous, as Marvin Rosenberg contends;[22] by eliminating difficult or obsolete words, they reflect Restoration tastes in language.[23] The cuts also emphasize the Moor's nobility; passages that stress Othello's age, his unattractiveness, or his ferocious passion have been deleted. Othello's "For since these arms of mine had seven years' pith... " (1.3.83) is gone. So is "Nor to comply with heat the young affects / In my distinct and proper satisfaction" (1.3.258–59), though this may have been cut for its obscurity rather than its suggestion of Othello's age. In Act 3, scene 3, references to Othello's appearance

[17] See *The London Stage, 1660–1800*, ed. Arthur H. Scouten (Carbondale: Southern Illinois University Press, 1961), part 3, vol. II, p. 1088.

[18] Rymer remarked in *Short View*, "*Jago*, I hope, is not brought on the Stage, in a Red-Coat" (p. 94).

[19] John Downes, *Roscius Anglicanus* (London: H. Playford, 1708), p. 16. See also the most recent edition, ed. Judith Milhous and Robert D. Hume (London: Society for Theatre Research, 1987).

[20] G. Blakemore Evans, *Shakespearean Promptbooks in the Seventeenth Century* (Charlottesville: University of Virginia, 1980), vol. VI, p. 10.   [21] Ibid., p. 3.

[22] See Marvin Rosenberg's analysis of the Smock Alley Promptbook in *The Masks of Othello* (Berkeley: University of California Press, 1961), pp. 20–24.

[23] See Gino J. Matteo, *Shakespeare's Othello: The Study and the Stage, 1604–1904* (Salzburg: Institut für Englische Sprache und Literatur, 1974), pp. 65–75 for analysis of the Smock Alley Promptbook in regard to Restoration canons of taste.

– but not to his blackness – are omitted. His claim, "For she had eyes, and chose me" (193) disappears, as does "for I am declin'd into the vale of years" (269–70). Othello's "Farewell the neighing steed" and "Arise, black Vengeance!" are cut. The trance remains, but the passionate stuttering before it, "we say, lie on her when they belie her" (4.1.36) is eliminated. Gone too in the final scene, is Othello's "O cursed slave! Whip me, ye devils!" (5.2.275) In sum, Othello's extremes of passion are carefully modulated to comply with the late-seventeenth-century conception of how the noble hero should comport himself – with decorum.

The 1681 cast list includes Michael Mohun as Iago, who played the role as early as 1669, and was for Pepys a disappointing successor to Walter Clun, who was killed in 1664. Like Hart's, Mohun's acting training began before 1642. He had worked with Christopher Beeston at the Cockpit; during the Civil War he had been a Captain with the Royalist army and "served in Flanders at the pay of a major."[24] His other roles included Face in *The Alchemist*, Volpone, True Wit, and Cassius. Iago is described in the cast list as "standard-bearer to the Moor, a Villain." Iago's villainy must be stressed, of course, in any production that emphasizes Othello's basic nobility. In the Restoration, accordingly, Iago seems to have been played as a one-dimensional stage villain.

The rest of the cast list is fairly straightforward. Cassio, played by Edward Kynaston (a pre-Restoration actor who was also noted for playing the woman's part), is simply, "the Moor's Lieutenant General." Roderigo is "a foolish Gentleman that follows the Moor in hopes to Cuckold him"; Desdemona is "Daughter to Brabantio, and Wife to the Moor"; and Bianca is "Cassio's wench."

Performance records indicate *Othello*'s popularity. At least three performances took place in 1660; the play was revived in 1669, though Pepys was disappointed: "ill acted in most parts, Mo[h]one (which did a little surprize me) not acting Iago's part by much so well as Clun used to do: nor another Hart's, which was Cassio's; nor indeed Burt doing the Moor's so well as I once thought he did."[25] Hart took over the lead in 1675 and 1676. Performances are also recorded in 1683, twice in 1685, and twice in 1686.

[24] Philip Highfill et al., *Biographical Dictionary of Actors and Actresses, Etc.* (Carbondale: Southern Illinois University Press, 1984), vol. X, p. 272.

[25] Samuel Pepys, *Memoirs of Samuel Pepys, Esq.* (London: Henry Colburn, 1828), vol. IV, p. 243.

By this time Betterton must have acceded to the title role, in which he was said to excel, although, as Marvin Rosenberg justly observes, we have little besides impressionistic accounts of his interpretation.[26] According to Charles Gildon, Betterton believed that at the height of the temptation scene Othello must speak "with an elevated Tone and enraged Voice, and the accents of a Man all on Fire, and in a Fury next to Madness."[27] Colley Cibber thought Betterton played Othello better than he did Castalio:

For though in Castalio he only excell'd others, in Othello he excell'd himself; which you will easily believe, when you consider, that in spite of his Complexion, Othello has more natural Beauties than the best Actor can find in all the Magazine of Poetry, to animate his Power, and delight his Judgment with.[28]

Steele's *Tatler* recalls Betterton in the handkerchief scene:

The wonderful Agony which he appeared in, when he examined the Circumstances of the Handkerchief of *Othello*; the Mixture of Love that intruded upon his Mind upon the innocent Answers *Desdemona* makes, betrayed in his Gesture such a Variety and Vicissitude of Passions, as would admonish a Man to be afraid of his own Heart, and perfectly convince him, that it is to stab it, to admit the worst of Daggers, Jealousy.[29]

If Betterton's Othello was admirable, his control destroyed only by the vicissitudes of jealous passion, the Iago played opposite him by Samuel Sandford, Mohun's successor, was thoroughly evil. Robert H. Ross, Jr., notes that Sandford became typed in the Villain's role because his "personal appearance and histrionic techniques suited his audience's preconceptions of stage villainy."[30] Colley Cibber's description of Mr. Sandford in the role is emphatic on this point:

Mr. Sandford, upon the Stage, was generally as flagitious as a Creon, a Maligni, an Iago, or a Machiavel, could make him ... [P]oor Mr. Sandford was not the Stage-Villain by choice, but from Necessity; for having a low and crooked Person, such Bodily Defects were too strong to be admitted into great, or amiable Characters; so that whenever, in any new or revived Play,

---

[26] See Rosenberg, *Masks*, pp. 19–20 for a discussion of Betterton.
[27] Charles Gildon, *The Life of Mr. Thomas Betterton* (London, 1710), pp. 115–16.
[28] Colley Cibber, *The History of the Stage* (London: J. Miller, 1742), p. 20.
[29] Richard Steele, *The Tatler*, no. 167, 2–4 May 1710.
[30] Robert H. Ross, Jr., "Samuel Sandford: Villain from Necessity," *PMLA*, 76 (1961): 367–72; quote from 367.

there was a hateful or mischievous Person, Mr. Sandford was sure to have no competitor for it.[31]

This assessment is echoed by Anthony Aston, who remarks that

Mr. SANDFORD, although not usually deem'd an Actor of the first Rank, yet the Characters allotted him were such, that none besides, then, or since, ever topp'd; for his Figure, which was diminutive and mean, (being Round-shoulder'd, Meagre-fac'd, Spindle-shank'd, Splay-footed, with a sour Countenance, and long lean Arms) render'd him a proper Person to discharge *Iago Foresight*, and *Malignii*, in the VILLAIN ... This Person acted strongly with his Face, – and (as King *Charles* said) was the best Villain in the World.[32]

Iago's obvious villainy was another source of aggravation to Rymer. He wrote that

what is most intolerable is *Jago*. He is no Black-amoor Souldier, so we may be sure he should be like other Souldiers of our acquaintance; yet never in a Tragedy, nor in comedy, nor in Nature was a Souldier with his Character.

If Othello's jealous passions "are no part of a Souldiers Character," to Rymer Iago's diabolic plotting was even less appropriate.[33]

The noble Moor was the victim of Sandford's crookback villain. So too was Desdemona. After 1660, the role was acted by women.[34] When played by Anne Bracegirdle, whose "style in tragedy was pathetic,"[35] Desdemona became the passive victim she was to remain well into the nineteenth century. Her passivity was reinforced by cuts in the text.[36] The Smock Alley Promptbook eliminates Desdemona's account of her Mother's maid Barbara and her willow song. It also cuts Emilia's ruminations on the double standard, further reinforcing women's subordinate role.

These cuts aside, the text of *Othello* stayed in the Restoration much as Shakespeare had written it. The result was a play that, as Marvin Rosenberg argues, satisfied Restoration appetites for amorous

---

[31] Cibber, *History of the Stage*, p. 35.

[32] Anthony Aston, *A Brief Supplement to Colley Cibber, Esq; His Lives of the Late Famous Actors and Actresses* (London: Printed for the Author, ?1748), p. 11.

[33] Rymer, *Short View*, p. 93.

[34] See John Harold Wilson, *All the King's Ladies: Actresses Of the Restoration* (Chicago: University of Chicago Press, 1959) for discussion of how actresses affected Restoration drama. [35] Highfill, *Biographical Dictionary*, vol. II, p. 279.

[36] For a perceptive discussion of how cuts in Desdemona's lines can affect interpretations of her character, see Irene G. Dash, *Wooing, Wedding, and Power: Women in Shakespeare's Plays* (New York: Columbia University Press, 1981), pp. 103–30. See also James R. Siemon, "'Nay, that's not next': *Othello*, V. ii in Performance, 1760–1900," *Shakespeare Quarterly*, 37 (1986): 38–51.

intrigue and exotic language.[37] But there was more to the Restoration
Othello than eroticism; as performed, the play reflected social concerns
peculiar to the post-1660 period.

*   *   *   *

It is usually difficult to determine what audiences thought several
centuries ago. We have evidence of *Othello*'s popularity, but other
than the scanty comments in Pepys' diaries, no critical accounts of it
from the Restoration. We do, however, have an "intertextual"
framework that indicates what audiences were looking for. Hume
contends that the Duke's and King's Companies "competed hotly,
vying to outdo each other in whatever had caught the audience's
fancy," and the playwrights, in turn "imitated each other, plagi-
arized, adapted, and burlesqued each other's works."[38] We know
from contemporary mass culture that imitation is not only a form of
flattery: when a rival company seeks to capitalize on its competitor's
success by imitating a product, it often exaggerates the characteristics
of the product it believes are most popular. By examining the
imitation, we may learn what was so appealing about the original.

When *Othello* proved to be popular with Restoration audiences,
The Duke's Company, composed of younger actors, chose to imitate
the original with its own play, Thomas Porter's *The Villain*.[39] Later,
The Villain became part of the repertoire of the united companies, so
that (as indicated earlier) Colley Cibber could admire Samuel
Sandford as Iago and as his counterpart, Maligni, in *The Villain*.
Written in 1662 and published the next year, *The Villain* is a strange
hodgepodge, perhaps best described as a grafting of *Othello* and *The
Rover*. Like other plays written in the early 1660s, *The Villain*
resembles common Caroline types, particularly what Hume describes
as the *précieuse* court drama fostered by Queen Henrietta Maria.[40]
Not surprisingly, Hume classifies it as a "villain play" and describes
it as a "rousing and popular exercise in Jacobean blood-and-
thunder."[41] It also shares Cavalier and "heroic" drama's "preoccupation with human emotions strained to their utmost capacity,
and, in addition, an increased interest in the conflict between
contending passions."[42]

---

[37] See Rosenberg, *Masks*, pp. 18–20.   [38] Hume, *Development*, p. 17.
[39] I was first directed to *The Villain* by Nancy Klein Maguire. See her "Origins and
Development of Serious Drama in the 1660s," *DAI*, 44 (1984): 3696–97A.
[40] Hume, *Development*, p. 237.   [41] Ibid., pp. 168 and 245.
[42] Sorelius, "*The Giant Race*," p. 119.

Porter's plagiarism is obvious. In scenes borrowed step by step from Shakespeare's original, the villain Maligni tempts the officers of his regiment to deadly jealousy. Theatre historian J. P. Vander Motten argues that "Porter appears to have viewed him as the play's protagonist, a figure of cunning endowed with extraordinary oratorical powers and motivated by malice and sexual jealousy."[43] For example, "honest Maligni" convinces Beaupres that his wife has been unfaithful, using Iago's techniques of reticence and innuendo:

> MALIG: Heaven guard your brest from evil thoughts,
>   You will not, sure, conclude that there is harm in this.
> BEAU: No, no, meet a man privately,
>   Disguis'd as you do tell me,
>   One that durst wrong me too, her husband,
>   Most excellent Meaning sure there is in this,
>   O, I could tear her from my memory,
>   Nay, tear the heart that ever did contain
>   So base a Guest, as her base Whorish Love.
> MALIG: Fye, Sir, 'tis not so bad yet.
> BEAU: 'Tis not the body, but the mind
>   Can ever make it bad,
>   I'de rather have my wife 'twice ravish'd,
>   Then once dare think the means how she may act it,
>   But thou art honest *Maligni*
>   And know'st not half the cunning of these Women.[44]

Beaupres shares the honors for hero with a fellow officer, Brisac, a role played by the young Betterton. With the war over, these two gentlemen use their leisure to court two young ladies: Beaupres woos and weds Bellmont, Brisac's sister, while Brisac pursues Charlotte, daughter to the town Governor. The plot is too complex to summarize – Pepys needed several performances before he could follow it. Suffice it to say that all four young people die, as does General Clairmont (who though a general is portrayed as a young man also in love with Charlotte), as well as Boutefeu, an officer of the regiment who becomes embroiled in Maligni's intrigues. At the finale Maligni – described as a "horrid Monster" – is hauled offstage with an Iago-like note of defiance: "I will not answer thee, do what thou wilt." But unlike Iago, we have evidence of his torture; from within he first

[43] J. P. Vander Motten, "Iago at Lincoln's Inn Fields: Thomas Porter's *The Villain* on the Early Restoration Stage," *Studies in English Literature, 1500–1800,* 24 (1984): 415–28; quote from 423–24.

[44] Thomas Porter, *The Villain: A Tragedy* (London, 1663), p. 88. Further passages from *The Villain* will be cited by page number within the text.

cries, "O, O! ye Cruel Dogs!" then "O, O, O!," and finally we have the intriguing stage direction, "Malig. *discover'd peirc'd with a stake*"(pp. 93–94). That the audience enjoyed this is attested by Tatler no. 134's recollection:

When poor *Sandford* was upon the Stage, I have seen him groaning upon a Wheel, stuck with Daggers, impaled alive, calling his Executioners, with a dying Voice, Cruel Dogs, and Villains! And all this to please his judicious Spectators, who were wonderfully delighted with seeing a Man in Torment so well acted.[45]

If Sandford played his Iago in the same way he acted Maligni – and contemporary accounts indicate he did – he must have been a flamboyant villain indeed.

It seems probable that the Duke's Company, with the help of that young rake and infamous duellist, Thomas Porter, deliberately imitated *Othello*, appropriating much of its plot and its villain. At the same time, partly because their actors were younger, they made Shakespeare's tragedy into a soap opera of the regiment. Alfred Harbage concludes that *The Villain* "would be uninteresting were it not for several scenes of realism which take us directly into the military barracks of the seventeenth century."[46] While stealing *Othello*, Porter emphasized the military aspects of the play, adding typical Restoration plotting about comrades in arms who woo the same lady, who must choose between love and honor, and who honorably kill each other while duelling over a lady. Or, as Dorvile announces in the opening scene

> For Friendship in Young-men breeds a delight
> In doing great and worthy things, whereby
> They may tie fast the bond of Friendship sworn.   (p. 2)

Gone is Othello's blackness, his exotic "Otherness." Instead we have two barely distinguishable gentlemen who are deceived by a crafty villain.

The Villain depicts military officers at leisure, billeted in civilian homes, prone to duelling and general mayhem – symptomatic of the problems England faced after 1660, when for the first time a standing army was maintained in peacetime.[47] But for Porter, the problems of

[45] *Tatler*, no. 134 (14–16 February 1709).

[46] Alfred Harbage, *Cavalier Drama: An Historical and Critical Supplement to the Study of the Elizabethan and Restoration Stage* (New York: Modern Language Association, 1936), p. 250.

[47] I am grateful to John G. A. Pocock for pointing out the military implications of *The Villain*'s regimental setting.

the standing army were not caused by the young officers and their elaborate honor system, but rather by the junior officer who envied his superiors.[48]

The Villain was extremely popular. First performed in 1662, according to Downes, it ran ten successive nights. Like most of Davenant's plays, it was larded with song and dance, especially in a comic subplot. More important, its depiction of young army officers upheld Cavalier values espoused by Charles' followers while simultaneously scapegoating forces opposed to those values in a recognizable villain who is contained and destroyed.

What does this have to do with *Othello*? This appropriation of a text by a rival acting company indicates in exaggerated form, I believe, what audiences saw in *Othello*. Set in Venice, a city ruled by Duke and Senate, *Othello* seemed eminently safe. It did not address issues of governance or royal prerogative. Its hero, a gentleman and a general (who happened to be black) was noble to the core. Its subject matter – the marriage of a black man to a white woman coupled with the suggestion, but not the fact, of adultery – could arouse sexual titillation yet remain satisfyingly moral.

Performed by ex-army officers who had fought in Charles II's cause, *Othello* privileged their values: virtue, as Harbage contends, consisted of "Physical courage, prowess in arms, magnanimity, and fidelity to a code of personal honor." This ideal produced heroes who are "heroical in speech and action because of their obligations under a code of gallantry."[49] As they projected this code, their antagonist (Iago) countered with what Susan Staves describes as "the mob's morality of self-preservation."[50]

The Cyprus scenes, moreover, depict a situation of some concern to Restoration audiences – the difficulties of manning a peacetime garrison. This scene, unfortunately, is not available in the extant Smock Alley Promptbook because the relevant pages have been lost. We do have, however, a 1755 acting edition which shows that although part of the scene on the Cyprus quay was cut, probably for

[48] See John Childs, *The Army of Charles II* (London: Routledge and Kegan Paul, 1976) for discussion of the discipline problems encountered in Restoration military barracks. For a thorough analysis of the forces opposed to the creation of a standing army, see Lois G. Schwoerer, *"No Standing Armies!" The Anti-Army Ideology in Seventeenth-century England* (Baltimore: The Johns Hopkins University Press, 1974).

[49] Harbage, *Cavalier Drama*, pp. 55–56.

[50] Susan Staves, *Players' Scepters: Fictions of Authority in the Restoration* (Lincoln: University of Nebraska Press, 1979), p.55. See also Laura Brown, *English Dramatic Form, 1660–1760* (New Haven: Yale University Press, 1974).

propriety's sake, Cassio's cashiering is kept in its entirety. If this edition reflects continuing tradition, the scene may have appeared on the Restoration stage as well.

Act 2, scene 3 (in modern editions) depicts the realities of barracks life more than any scene in *Othello*. Throughout, rank and its prerogatives are stressed. Iago insistently addresses Cassio as "lieutenant," whereas superior rank permits Cassio to use the familiar "Iago" to his subordinate. The scene begins with Othello's charge to Cassio to supervise the guard. Pressured by Iago to be a "good fellow" and join the carousing, Cassio quickly gets drunk. His words – "the lieutenant is to be saved before the ancient" – must rankle Iago, whose first stated motive is his envy of Cassio's promotion. At the same time, he takes pleasure in the success of his plan to have Cassio cashiered.

This scene must have struck home to Restoration audiences. From 1662 to 1674 they had heard reports from Tangier, a British military outpost designed to guard trade routes in the Levant – much like Cyprus to the Venetians. Pepys' "Notes on Tangier" record popular opinion that the Tangier garrison was a nest of "swearing, cursing, and whoring." The worst vice of all was widespread drunkenness that interfered with discipline. Such behavior violated the 1642 "Lawes and Ordinances of Warre" which state:

Whatever officer soever shall come drunk to his guard, or shall quarrel in the quarter, or commit any disorder, shall be cashiered without mercy, and the next officer under him shall have his place, which he may pretend to be his right, and it shall not be refused to him.[51]

Othello's anger and sudden dismissal of Cassio would not have surprised a Restoration audience. His strict adherence to a military code would have seemed another indicator of his nobility and his skill as a professional military officer. And this same code determines his decision to mete justice to his "fair warrior," Desdemona.

As described in contemporary accounts, Hart's and Betterton's noble Othello affirmed not only the worth of military service and the male right of property in women but also the need for a personal honor code. When Charles II's courtiers, who had resided with him

---

[51] "The Lawes and Ordinances of Warre" were issued by Essex in 1642 and imitated by the Royalist army. Actors who had served with Prince Rupert, who was a strict disciplinarian, would have been familiar with such codes of behavior. See Peter Young and Wilfred Emberton, *The Cavalier Army: Its Organisation and Everyday Life* (London: George Allen and Unwin, 1974), pp. 62–71 and 172–86. The quotation above is from p. 181.

in France, returned with him to England, they brought with them a complicated code of "civility." Outlined by Antoine de Courtin, *The Rules of Civility* create an elaborate protocol for behavior between equals, inferiors and superiors, and vice versa. More important here, they culminate in an image of the perfect courtier, an image that coincides amazingly with the qualities Othello prides himself on. According to Courtin, a wise man

hears rather than talks, believes not easily, judges seldom, and then upon examination, deliberates before he resolves; is constant in his resolutions, fears not to repent; he speaks well of all, defendeth the fame of the absent; is courteous, nor [sic] flattering, readier to give than to receive; loves his friends, but doth nothing unworthy for their sakes; is ready to assist and pleasure all men, many times unknown; he considers events before they happen, and then is neither exalted nor dejected, he will avoid anxiety and moroseness, is even in his carriage, true in his words; the same in reality as he is in shew; admires few, derides none, envies none, despiseth none, no not the most miserable; he delights in the company of wise and vertuous persons; profereth not his counsel when he understands not well; is content with his condition; he doth not any thing through contention, emulation, or revenge, but endeavours to do good for evil.[52]

This standard of behavior resembles Othello's desire to be known as a man of honor, who was "not easily jealous, but being wrought, / Perplex'd in the extreme; ... threw a pearl away, / Richer than all his tribe." This noble hero is tricked by a diabolic villain away from his better nature and his code of honor into the passionate throes of jealousy.

*   *   *   *

The Villain's emphasis on the conflicts between love and friendship, passion and honor, reflect continuities from Cavalier drama. A decade later, however, tastes had changed. The 1670s saw the rise of the rhymed heroic play with its extravagant exaltation of the hero.[53] In the early 1670s Dryden established the paradigm of heroic tragedy with a plot and characters that resemble those of Shakespeare's *Othello – The Conquest of Granada* began a new wave of Restoration tragedies that exalted the exotic hero torn between friendship and love.

---

[52] Antoine de Courtin, *The Rules of Civility; or, Certain Ways of Deportment Observed in France Amongst All Persons of Quality, Upon Several Occasions* (London: Printed for J. Martyn, 1675), pp. 171–72.   [53] See Hume, *Development*, p. 269.

With heroic drama came an emphasis on the exemplary. John M. Wallace contends that Dryden justified the exaggerations of heroic drama by "an appeal to his belief in the power of the dramatic illusion; given the harness of the rules to keep the action believable, no images of virtue could be too high. But the exaggerations also helped to pose the topical questions in the most exalted and conceptual terms." Heroic drama, in other words, reflected the "exemplary" rather than the metaphorical nature of experience.[54]

The rise of the exemplary hero coincided in the 1670s with renewed interest in the villain-oriented play, as in Henry Nevil Payne's *The Fatal Jealousie* (1673). This time the villain (once again acted by Samuel Sandford) has a plausible motive: Jasper seeks revenge against the hero, Don Antonio, because:

> *Don Sancho De Monsalvo* [Jasper's] Grandsire
> Was for a while Vice Admiral of Spain,
> But then disgrac'd turn'd Pyrate and Reveng'd
> With Fire and Sword on all Mankind, the wrongs
> He thought the Court had basely plac'd on him;
> At last he was betray'd and lost his head,
> [Jasper's] Thy Father turn'd Bandetto,
>
> ...
>
> his Fate
> Betray'd him too to Death by Execution:
>
> ...
>
> And thou [Jasper] art forc'd to serve –
> That very Lord, who does those Lands
> Possess should have been thine.[55]

Jasper is distinguished from nobility by his behavior (he sleeps with the heroine's nurse), his language (he speaks much of the time in earthy prose), and by his appearance. Despite – or perhaps because of – his marginality and his motivation, he remains a professed villain. He stabs himself at the end and declaims in Aaron-like rhetoric of the many evils he has committed.

Jasper's greatest strength is deceitfulness. Everyone believes him except Caelia, the Desdemona figure, Don Antonio's wife. His intrigue to promote jealousy in Don Antonio, motivated by revenge and greed, is an easier task than Iago's or even Maligni's. Don

[54] John M. Wallace, "Dryden and History: A Problem in Allegorical Reading," *ELH*, 36 (1969): 269–90; quote from 286.

[55] Henry Nevil Payne, *The Fatal Jealousie*, repr. with an introduction by Willard Thorpe (Ann Arbor: The Augustan Reprint Society, 1948), p. 24. Quotations from *The Fatal Jealousie* will be cited by page number within the text.

Antonio is beset by jealousy from the play's opening lines. Stage directions read, " *The Curtain drawn Discovers* Don Antonio *and* Caelia *in Morning-Gowns, Chamber and Bed*" (p. 1). This is their wedding day, but already Antonio, racked with jealousy, has killed a man he believed (having been told so by Jasper) was Caelia's lover. Antonio's language echoes Othello's, except that the Moor's lines occur midplay, Antonio's at the very beginning:

> Can you believe me stupid, or an Ass?
> To think my Wife should meet a Man i' th' Night;
> Nay, more; a Man that was my seeming Friend:
> Yet taken in at Window privately!
> Nay, which was most, stay with him two full hours,
> And in a Room made proper by a Bed,
> And yet not Cuckold me; the thing's too plain,
> I do not doubt the deed, which Iv'e [*sic*] Reveng'd
> In part, by killing him. (p. 1)

Jealousy is Antonio's humor. Jasper does not create it; he merely plays upon it.

Still, plagiarism from *Othello* abounds. The following passage, for example, mirrors the temptation scene:

> JASP: Nay, nothing it may be, my Lady is my Lady, and
> You are a kind Lord, that's all I know; so begging
> Your Lordships Discharge, I'm gone, and then your
> Fears are over.
> ANTO: Villain, thou'st given me poyson; my veins swell
> With it, produce the Antidote, or I'le dissect thy Soul
> To find it out; what is't you know that can disquiet me?
> JASP: I know little, my Lord, to th' purpose, besides, it will
> But vex you, since there may be no harm in it.
> ANTO: Come, come, no going back, tell quickly what you know.
> JASP: I know, why, I know that my Lady hates me
> Because I told your Lordship the time she was to
> Deliver the Jewels and Money to *Don Lewis*, and
> Still she calls me false in being true to you – but-
> ANTO: But what?
> JASP: But if I should say all I know – well, but let
> That alone, good, my Lord, your Discharge.
> ANTO: Vile Dog, dost raise my Anger for to play with it?
> I'le vent it upon thee then.
> [*Draws, and cuts at him.*] (pp. 17–18)

Antonio, unlike Othello, is convinced from the play's beginning, and his credulity results in the deaths of all the major characters.

Antonio, I suspect, is meant to be an exemplary hero, noble except for his predisposition to jealousy. Why else would his friend and admirer Gerardo frequently deliver presentational sententiae on the evils of jealousy? Take this example:

> Doubt is th'effect of fear or Jealousie,
> Two Passions which to Reason give the Lye
> For fear torments, but never does assist,
> And Jealousie is love lost in a Mist.
> Both Hood-wink truth, then go to blind-man's buff,
> Cry here, then there, seem to direct enought:
> But all the while shift place making the mind
> As it goes out of breath despair to find.
> And if at last something it stumbles on,
> Perhaps it calls it false and then 'tis gone.
> If true, what's gained only just time to see
> A breachless Play a Game at Liberty:
> That has no other end then this, that men
> Run to be tyr'd just to set down agen.   (p. 25)

Amidst this domestic plot, Payne supplies spectacular effects characteristic of the Duke's Company. Witches and devils ascend, gypsies dance and sing, and spirits chant prophecies reminiscent of *Macbeth* – all calculated to horrify the audience.

Unlike *The Villain*, *The Fatal Jealousie* is not concerned with the military. It reflects, instead, what Hume describes as "pathetic tragedy." "In its bloodbath manifestations the pathetic play can encroach on villain-horror drama."[56] Caelia, innocent and virtuous, suffers from the play's beginning to her death. In a "willow song scene" she bids her maid Flora sing the dying lyrics of Cloris, a maid who perishes from grief over her jealous lover Chloridon. Caelia's suffering is paralleled in that of her less innocent sister who also perishes through Jasper's machinations.

Like Desdemona, Caelia dies in her bed. When Antonio finds his servant Pedro in the chamber, he runs him through. Caelia's outburst of grief for the slain innocent, like Desdemona's cry for Cassio, proves her undoing:

ANTO: Now Monster of thy Sex, see this, and tell me
    What are the effects you do expect from it?
CAEL: Death, that's less terrible than is your Anger,
    Which I perceive by it's effects already,
    Upon that Innocent Man cannot stay there.

---

[56] Hume, *Development*, p. 218.

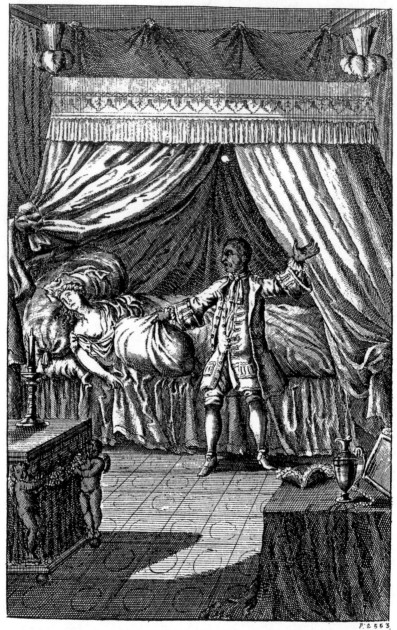

P. 2 553

Figure 6: The frontispiece to Nicholas Rowe's edition of *Othello* (1709).

ANTO: Are your concerns for him, when they should be
    Employ'd to Heav'n for mercy to your Soul?
    Nay, then Hell take it's Quarry; this for *Don Lewis*,
    This for *Don Francisco*; and take this last
    For thy insatiate Lust with that damn'd Hind.
  CAEL: Thus killing me, my Lord, is very cruel;
    Since I ne're sinn'd in thought against your Honour.
    This, as I do expect Eternall Rest,
    Is such a Truth, that I can dye in it.   (p. 69)

She perishes, the pathetic victim of jealousy and deception. Antonio, wounded by Jasper, dies pronouncing her innocence.

What does Payne's domestic bloodbath tell us about *Othello*? First, the link between Iago, Maligni, and Jasper (all performed by Samuel Sandford until the end of his career in 1700) indicates that *Othello* was perceived as a villain play.

The picture of Sandford as archetypal Restoration villain emerges with some clarity: "a small man of mean figure, hunched, spindly-legged, with a meager and sour countenance, a strident voice; an actor who frequently resorted to the leer or grimace and, probably, broad gesticulation."[57] Such an obvious villain should stretch our credulity and lessen our opinion of Othello. To the Restoration, however, a noble hero like Othello, Beaupres, or Antonio would be admired for his heroic traits but pitied for his victimization by a fiendish enemy.

The Fatal Jealousie also demonstrates, especially in Caelia's death, audience preoccupation with feminized pathos. Desdemona's final words must have aroused similar feelings. This taste for the innocent female, lying helpless in her bed (the object of the audience's voyeuristic gaze), overcome by a knife-bearing Moor, may explain the popularity of illustrations from Act 5, scene 2 of Desdemona in her bedchamber.[58] While Rymer ranted against Shakespeare's lack of poetic justice, the sight of a bare-breasted, helpless, prone, yet innocent Desdemona, murdered violently in her bed, probably aroused primal emotions that insured the drama's continuing popularity.

Finally, we may infer from Payne's exemplary drama that *Othello* was also believed to be a play primarily about jealousy. It

---

[57] Ross, "Samuel Sandford," 370.
[58] See, for example, the frontispiece to Rowe's 1709 edition, the engraving from Jennen's 1773 edition, and two illustrations from Boydell's Gallery, one by Josiah Boydell (1803) and another by George Romney (1799).

demonstrated the evils inherent in succumbing to passion, in believing too easily what others say, in taking revenge. The heroic Moor is noble, yet jealousy proves his fatal flaw. The result is a drama that could arouse pity and fear but would not disturb the audience's basic preconceptions and values.

Whether Porter and Payne realized it or not, they had borrowed from *Othello* elements calculated to appeal to Restoration audiences. Unadapted as it was, the Restoration's *Othello* represented aspects of the era's dominant ideologies. Shockingly black, Othello, as acted by Hart and Betterton, was nevertheless a noble hero of military experience and aristocratic bearing. Iago – and Maligni and Jasper – represented, by contrast, the forces of anarchy that seek to destroy the social order. Iago hates Cassio's daily beauty, Maligni is aware of his lower social rank, and Jasper seeks revenge against the Court and the aristocrat who has stolen his land. All three try to subvert the Cavalier code. No wonder audiences of the early Restoration loved to see Maligni not only contained, as Iago is, but violently destroyed. The stake through his heart visually fulfilled the audience's wishes: with Maligni's destruction, the code of civility is preserved.

The slim but suggestive evidence about Restoration performance indicates, in sum, that Hart's and Betterton's portrayal privileged the noble Moor and repressed his savagery. Despite his blackness, he was part of the aristocracy, not marginalized from it. His nobility in the face of Iago's villainous challenge reinforced the actors' most cherished ideals. This explains, I contend, why the play could be performed with so little alteration and why it was so popular. Whether audiences realized it or not, the Restoration's *Othello* was a mirror of its time.

CHAPTER 6

Amateur versus professional: the Delaval Othello

Pleasure and action make the hours seem short.

(*Othello*, 2.3.344)

7 March 1751: Sir Francis Blake Delaval, heir to Northumberland's Seaton Hall and the vast Delaval estate, enacted *Othello, the Moor of Venice*, in an amateur performance at the Theatre Royal, Drury Lane. Normally relegated to footnotes in histories of the eighteenth-century stage,[1] this production warrants the cultural historian's attention because Delaval's rental of a professional theatre, his distribution of tickets to the royal family, and his performance in the title role constituted not simply an elaborate and expensive public assertion of his wealth, class, and breeding, but also a complex statement about the role of Shakespeare in eighteenth-century self-fashioning. As amateur performers – lovers of theatrics and admirers of Shakespeare – Delaval's family and friends invited public comparison with the professional actors of Covent Garden and Drury Lane. The entire production – costumes, music, blocking – reveals shared assumptions about what a performance should be, particularly a performance of a major Shakespearean tragedy. The details of this production illustrate some cultural assumptions about the roles of Othello and Iago and how they should be represented on stage.[2]

---

[1] Cf. John Genest, *Some Account of the English Stage from the Restoration in 1660 to 1830* (Bath: H. E. Carrington, 1832), vol. IV, p. 325; George Winchester Stone, Jr. *The London Stage, 1660–1800* (Carbondale: Southern Illinois University Press, 1962), part 4, vol. I, p. 240; and William W. Appleton, *Charles Macklin: An Actor's Life* (Cambridge: Harvard University Press, 1960), pp. 93–94. Sybil Rosenfeld discusses the Delaval *Othello* at greater length in her study of eighteenth-century amateur theatricals. See *Temples of Thespis: Some Private Theatres and Theatricals in England and Wales, 1700–1820* (London: Society for Theatre Research, 1978), pp. 96–100.

[2] See Erika Fischer-Lichte, "Theatre and the Civilizing Process: An Approach to the History of Acting," in *Interpreting The Theatrical Past: Essays in the Historiography of Performance*, ed.

Eighteenth-century productions of *Othello* expanded on the foundation laid during the Restoration; they maintained Othello's basic nobility and military heroism, but placed greater emphasis on his role as a romantic lover. By the middle of the century, acting styles had changed from the static, oratorical style of the Restoration to more fluid, energetic modes of representing the passions. Othello's rapid shift from doting husband to jealous murderer provided a wonderful opportunity for actors to demonstrate their prowess at making such a change. In accord with the new emphasis on "natural" representation, Othello began to appear in Moorish garb; by the end of the century, he had abandoned for all time the regalia of a British military officer.

*   *   *   *

According to accounts in the *London Advertiser* and Literary Gazette (3 March 1751) and the *London Evening Post* (5 March 1751), the Delavals had originally planned to stage their play at Samuel Foote's Little Theatre in the Haymarket. But, as the *Post* reports, "having been much importuned by their Friends and Acquaintances for Tickets, they found a larger House would be necessary." They applied to David Garrick, manager of Drury Lane, and he agreed "without Hesitation" that "the Run of *Alfred* should be interrupted for one night to oblige them." Such complaisance was not merely a sign of Garrick's good nature, for by some accounts Delaval paid £1,500 for use of the theatre.[3] In 1751 the Drury Lane Theatre held approximately 1,200 spectators; a full house would gross £190, whereas the average daily receipts were £134. The audience normally consisted of footmen and workmen in the upper galleries, people of the "middling sort" (small businessmen and professionals) in the pit, and aristocrats in the boxes.[4] This heterogeneous audience

Thomas Postlewait and Bruce A. McConachie (Iowa City: University of Iowa Press, 1989), pp. 19–36 for a theoretical discussion of the social implications of various acting styles.

[3] See Robert A. Smith, "The Delavals of Seaton," *The Lady* (16 March 1978): 476. Garrick could have expected approximately £150 for a successful performance of *Alfred*. The £1,500 figure mentioned in most newspaper accounts may include, however, the cost of lavish costumes, new scenes painted just for this performance, and a special orchestra. Still, the figure, if accurate and not the result of Delaval self-promotion, does seem extravagant. Sibyl Rosenfeld suggests that total expenses were £1,000–1,500, with £150 the fee for the rental of the theatre (Rosenfeld, *Temples*, p. 97).

[4] For background on the mid-eighteenth-century theatre, see Harry William Pedicord, *The Theatrical Public in the Time of Garrick* (New York: King's Crown Press, 1954), pp. 15–43; Allardyce Nicoll, *The Garrick Stage: Theatres and Audience in the Eighteenth Century*, ed. Sybil Rosenfeld (Manchester: Manchester University Press, 1980), pp. 36–44; and James J.

included people who attended the theatre regularly, who knew the actors and their roles, and who argued fiercely for and against their favorites.[5] Among them on a random evening – either in the boxes or sitting prominently on the stage where he could be seen by all – was the stage-struck rake, Sir Francis Delaval.

Although Garrick was later to improve lighting in the Drury Lane Theatre Royal, in 1751 the stage was lit by masses of candles, ranged in hoops over the platform, in sconces at the side of the boxes, along the scenic devices, and in footlights. The actors, knowing they would not be seen if they strayed back into the scenery, played toward the front of the platform. Even so, as Allardyce Nicoll observes, "if we were suddenly enabled to be present at a performance in Garrick's Drury Lane, our eyes would certainly be continually conscious of and oppressed by its dim outlines."[6] The scenic designs for *Othello* normally came from those in stock: "Temples, Tombs, City Walls and Gates, Outsides and Insides of Palaces, Streets, Chambers, Prisons and 'Rural prospects.'"[7] Venice could easily be represented by the outside of a palace, Cyprus by a city gate, and any chamber could be turned to a bedchamber with the addition of a bed.

By the mid-eighteenth century, theatre had become essential to London's cultural life. In his *Memoirs of Samuel Foote*, William Cooke recalled that "The Bedford [coffee house] principally laid claim to dramatic criticism:... the wits generally supped after the play, and passed judgment freely on the several authors, actors, and managers." But such discussion was not confined to the wits alone. "The stage at that time formed a general topic of conversation among all ranks of people": Drury Lane partisans versus Covent Garden devotees, Garrick fans versus Barry fans – none hesitated to join the fray.[8] The *Theatrical Review* bemoaned in 1758 that "almost every coffee-house, and every news-paper, prove the truth of the observation; no body can talk or write about our theatres, but he is immediately possessed with this demon of party, and praises or condemns, not from his feelings, but his prejudices."[9] By attending performances and then debating them, Londoners expressed, cri-

---

Lynch, *Box, Pit, and Gallery: Stage and Society in Johnson's London* (Berkeley: University of California Press, 1953), pp. 199–207.   [5] Lynch, *Box, Pit, and Gallery*, p. 297.

[6] Nicoll, *Garrick Stage*, p. 116.   [7] Ibid., p. 131.

[8] William Cooke, *Memoirs of Samuel Foote* (London: Printed for Richard Phillips, 1805), vol. I, pp. 32–33.

[9] *The Theatrical Review for the Year 1757 and Beginning 1758* (London: Printed for J. Coote, 1758), Preface, p. i.

tiqued, and affirmed a shared body of cultural, social, and political assumptions. Among these assumptions were standards for the proper behavior for ladies and gentlemen, the civilizing of disruptive physical forces through polite discourse and manners.[10]

Acting itself was also a subject of debate. According to mid-eighteenth-century treatises and pamphlets, the first requisite of a good actor was the ability to express the passions. Francis Delaval's companion, Samuel Foote, defined "passion" in his 1747 *Treatise*: "The word Passion is applied to the different Motions and Agitations of the Soul, according to the different Objects, that present themselves to the Senses; how or by what means this mutual Action, or Communication between Soul and Body is effected, remains a secret to us." Foote divided the passions into "Passions of Desire, such as Pleasure, Pain, Love, Hatred, &c and the irascible ones, namely, Courage, Anger, Despair, &c., but the most natural Division of them in my Judgment, is into painful and pleasureable, and in this Sense, all the Passions may be reduced to Love and Hatred, nay perhaps to one, Love."[11] Both – Hatred and Love – were crucial to contemporary representations of Shakespeare's Othello.

While the wits were discussing acting, David Garrick introduced a new acting style to London's theatres, a style that theatre historian James R. Roach describes as a "revolutionary paradigm shift." The seventeenth-century view of acting as a combination of oratorical style and rhetorical gesture was replaced by "a more streamlined model of the human body and its passions: the machine."[12] Like a moving statue, the body could be trained to express particular emotions and attitudes and to make swift, fluid changes from one to another. When an actor prepared a new role, he would try to recreate its passions rationally in his mind by observing and defining the body language and tones of voice that should accompany it. He would then work out the transitions from passion to passion. The role became a sequence of such passions, later known as "points," not a conceptualized rendition of the entire character.[13]

---

[10] See, for example, Norbert Elias, *The History of Manners*, trans. Edmund Jephcott (New York: Pantheon Books, 1978), esp. pp. 51–204.

[11] Samuel Foote, *A Treatise on the Passions, So Far As They Regard the Stage* (London: Printed for C. Corbet, 1747), pp. 10–11.

[12] James R. Roach, *The Player's Passion: Studies in the Science of Acting* (Newark: University of Delaware, 1985), pp. 56–57.

[13] See George Taylor, "'The Just Delineation of the Passions': Theories of Acting in the Age of Garrick," in *The Eighteenth-Century Stage*, ed. Kenneth Richards and Peter Thomson (London: Methuen, 1972), pp. 51–72, esp. pp. 60–65.

Roach contends that eighteenth-century attempts to externalize the Passions were also an attempt to open "them to the domain of public surveillance where their activity may be regulated by the meticulous enumeration of their expressive signs. They promulgate the circumscriptions of style by subjecting the body to ordered sequences of behavior. They transform Passions into manners, for if Passions may not be controlled, style can."[14] Acting became a set series of gestures and movements that expressed in public the unruly human emotions that would normally be hidden.

Many eighteenth-century acting theorists agreed with Descartes that each passion could "be identified by its effects, a set of bodily postures and physiognomical manifestations."[15] Particular moments in *Othello* could thus be translated into a physical semiotic code. For example, Garrick described in a letter to painter Francis Hayman the proper body language for Othello at the moment he learns the truth (in Act 5, scene 2): "Othello (ye Principal) upon ye right hand (I believe) must be thunderstruck with Horror, his Whole figure extended, w'th his Eyes turn'd up to Heav'n & his Frame sinking."[16]

While Garrick portrayed this new conception of acting on stage, Charles Macklin stressed it in the lessons he gave to amateurs such as Sir Francis Delaval and Samuel Foote. John Genest's *Some Account of the English Stage* outlines his technique:

the principal part of his method seemed to be, in breaking his pupils from those artificial habits of speaking, which for some time past had been conceived to belong to the stage; it was his manner to check all the cant and cadence of Tragedy; he would bid his pupils first speak the passage as they would in common life, if they had occasion to pronounce the same words; and then giving them more force, but preserving the same accent, to deliver them on the stage.[17]

According to biographer William Cooke, Macklin restrained his pupils

from those *artificial* habits of speaking which are too generally pre-conceived to belong to the stage. Putting them thus in a course of Nature, they felt the effects of her powers; and, instead of that *titum tum* manner of speaking which

---

[14] Joseph R. Roach, "Power's Body: The Inscription of Morality as Style," in Postlewait and McConachie, *Interpreting*, pp. 99–118. For discussion of acting theory, particularly in regard to the passions, see Taylor, "The Just Delineation of the Passions."

[15] Roach, *Player's Passion*, p. 64.   [16] Ibid., p. 74.

[17] Genest, *Some Account*, vol. IV, p. 76.

Representations

Figure 7: Francis Hayman's engraving of Othello and Desdemona from Thomas
Hanmer's 1743–44 edition of Shakespeare.

was the predominant mistake of the old school, those who were capable of attending to his advice, spoke the language of the character they represented, as little mixed with *art* as stage performances will admit of.[18]

This, presumably, is the way Sir Francis Delaval was taught to play Othello.

When a mid-eighteenth-century audience came to see *Othello*, it expected a noble hero, a gentleman who displayed good manners and civility. As Julie Hankey concludes in her analysis, during the eighteenth century, "the noble rank of the Moor was a presumption in favor of his noble heart."[19] What made the role of Othello so exciting, however, was the shattering of this facade. Francis Gentleman summarized the popular conception of the role in 1777:

There is not, in the whole scope of the drama, a character which demands greater requisites, than *Othello*; nor is there one which gives more support to, or calls for more from, the actor. His appearance should be amiably elegant, and above the middle stature; his expression full and sententious, for the declamatory part; flowing and harmonious, for the love-scenes; rapid and powerful, for each violent climax of jealous rage.[20]

The interaction of order and disorder, control and lack of control, was the key to the part. Thomas Wilkes argued, for example, that in Othello we find a full range of emotions: "Love was his prevailing passion, jealousy his prevailing foible; and the former takes all its tincture and hue from the latter, even when his passion is wrought up to the most interesting pitch."[21]

Spranger Barry succeeded in conveying both Othello's innate nobility and his jealous rage. Cooke praised "the harmony of his voice, and the manly beauty of his person" that "spoke him alike the hero and the lover." In Barry's Moor, spectators could see Shakespeare's grand design "in forming a mutual passion between ... the *black* Othello, and the *fair* Desdemona." They saw in Barry "that mere colour could not be a barrier to affection."[22] Garrick believed that the Moor's customary blackface hindered the actor's ex-

[18] William Cooke, *Memoirs of Charles Macklin, Comedian* (London: Printed for James Asperne, 1804), p. 149.

[19] Julie Hankey, ed., *Othello* (Bristol: Bristol Classical Press, 1987), p. 40.

[20] Francis Gentleman, ed., *Othello: A Tragedy by Shakespeare* (London: J. Bell, 1777), p. 10n.

[21] Wilkes, *A General View of the Stage*, (London: J. Coote, 1759), p. 120.

[22] Cooke, *Memoirs of Macklin*, p. 155.

pression,[23] while Samuel Foote claimed that Othello's "black Covering...hinders our discerning the Action of the Muscles."[24] Whatever effect burnt cork had on Garrick, it did not inhibit Spranger Barry. The *Theatrical Review* argued that Barry's critics, "if they are not absolutely blinded by their prejudice, they may experience the dumb eloquence of his eyes, when their colour, set off by the hue of the Moorish complexion, and rendered thereby more striking, becomes capable of conveying his soul's meaning to the most distant spectator."[25]

Besides, nature had crafted Barry for the role. "[F]irst, the graces of manly beauty are so favourably blended in his person, with majesty and softness, as equally to make him look the warrior, command the respect due to a general, and make the greatest excess of love appear natural, both in him who loves, and in the person who loves him."[26] Excess is made to appear natural, expressed through carefully coded body language. John Bernard, who saw Barry play Othello later in the century, recalled that "His gradual preparation for the volcanic burst of – 'I'll tear her all to pieces,' and the burst itself, in its exquisite agony, as well as power, surpassed the grandest" of stage effects. "You could observe the muscles stiffening, the veins distending, and the red blood boiling through his dark skin – a mighty flood of passion accumulating for several minutes – and at length bearing down its barriers, and sweeping onward in thunder, love, reason, mercy, all before it." Note Bernard's metaphor here; like Othello's Propontic Sea, Barry's passion flowed relentlessly onward, seeming to break the barriers of control as it went. Females in the audience shrieked, and Bernard confessed that "the thrill it gave me took away my sleep the entire night."[27] Francis Gentleman's *Dramatic Censor* lauded Barry's success in the role: "he happily exhibited the hero, the lover, and the distracted husband, he rose through all the passions to the utmost extent of critical imagination, yet still appeared to leave an unexhausted fund of expression behind."[28]

Remarkably, in none of these discussions is Othello's race a major factor. At the height of the slave trade Londoners conceived

---

[23] See Hankey, *Othello*, p. 38.   [24] Foote, *Treatise*, p. 25.

[25] *Theatrical Review*, p. 25.   [26] Ibid., p. 23.

[27] John Bernard, *Retrospections on the Stage* (London: Henry Colburn and Richard Bentley, 1830), vol. I, p. 28.

[28] Francis Gentleman, *The Dramatic Censor; or Critical Companion* (London: J. Bell, 1770), vol. I, p. 151.

Shakespeare's Moor as a high ranking, noble, courageous general, an English gentleman, represented by a white actor in blackface. Any anxiety over miscegenation was repressed; any taint of barbarism in Shakespeare's hero was civilized out of existence. The very incongruity of James Quin's famous quip comparing Garrick's Moor to Pompey with his tea kettle suggests that though there were black servants in London, audiences did not normally relate them to Shakespeare's Othello. Historian Anthony J. Barker claims this dissociation of attitudes was not uncommon in eighteenth-century London. Individual negroes in London might be termed "African princes" because such overcompensation enabled Englishmen to "differentiate individual Negroes from the predominant stereotypes."[29] Portrayed by Barry, Othello was not a former slave; the actor's dark complexion indicated instead an exotic nobility.

Opposite Barry's Othello was Macklin's Iago. In the Restoration, as indicated in chapter 5, Iago had been represented as a villain: Samuel Sandford and later Colley Cibber mugged their maliciousness to the audience. They embodied the character's essential evil by a distorted countenance and figure, and by wearing a black costume.[30] The effect clearly signified the popular view of Shakespeare's Ensign. In Kirkman's words, Iago is "full of subtilty, irascibility, and villainy – devoid of every good and tender feeling – mean, hypocritical, and vindictive – base enough to do any bad action underhand, but without resolution to avow or vindicate his wickedness."[31] Like Samuel Sandford before him, Macklin seemed framed by nature for the villain's part. John Bernard remembered him as a "broad-breasted, bald-headed, shaggy-browed, hooked-nosed individual, as rough and husky as a cocoa-nut, with a barking or grunting delivery more peculiar than pleasing."[32] This view was seconded by a treatise written in opposition to Foote which charged that Macklin "has such a strong Stamp of the Villian [*sic*] imprinted in his Countenance, even when he endeavors to appear most honest; that we can't help thinking it a Weakness in *Othello* to have any Concerns with him at all."[33] Whatever his physiognomy, Macklin

[29] Anthony J. Barker, *The African Link: British Attitudes to the Negro in the Era of the Atlantic Slave Trade, 1550–1805* (London: Frank Cass, 1978), pp. 25–26.

[30] See Nicoll, *Garrick Stage*, p. 164.

[31] James Thomas Kirkman, *Memoirs of the Life of Charles Macklin, Esq.* (London: Lackington, Allen, and Co., 1799), vol. I, p. 300.   [32] Bernard, *Retrospections*, vol. II, p. 119.

[33] Anon., *A Letter of Compliment to the Ingenious Author of a Treatise on the Passions* (London: Printed for C. Corbett, ?1747), p. 27.

applied his own teachings about natural acting to Iago's role. First, he changed the Ensign's traditional black garb. Wilkes observed that "formerly he [Iago] was dressed in such a manner, as to be known at first sight; but it is unnatural to suppose, that an artful villain, like him, would chuse a dress which would stigmatize him to everyone: I think, as Cassio and he belong to one regiment, they should both retain the same regimentals."[34]

Foote, Macklin's former pupil, wrote that his mentor's Iago displayed just the right amount of obsequiousness toward Othello, his superior officer. To Foote, class and rank were important distinctions and should be represented as such onstage. Especially during the temptation scene, "from his modest and decent Deportment, you are always taught that he has a Superior, both in Quality and Character, on the Stage."[35] According to Cooke, Macklin's "gradual disclosure of the character; his seeming openness, and concealed revenge; and, above all, his soliloquies, were so much the natural workings of real character, as to demand the profoundest attention."[36] John Hill agreed, noting Macklin's delivery of the aside, "If I can fasten but one cup upon him [Cassio]," in Act 2: "Mr. *Macklin* first set an example which has been followed by Mr. *Garrick*, of delivering plainly and without ornament, a speech in which we have been us'd to see a world of unnatural contortion of face and absurd bye-play."[37] Once again, in the name of natural acting, the body was subjected to greater control.

Macklin's obsequious yet subtly villainous Ensign highlighted Othello's (Barry's) nobility, heroism, and good manners. When these two professional actors performed the roles together, the London audiences readily responded to Shakespeare's piteous spectacle with shrieks, sighs, and tears.

*　　*　　*　　*

Such was the professional actor's *Othello* in 1751. What about the amateurs? Why did they select *Othello* in the first place? How did the Delaval clan's production compare to the professional performances of *Othello* described above?

First, some context on the instigator, Sir Francis Blake Delaval. Born in 1727, Sir Francis was twenty-four in 1751. Heir to a

[34] Wilkes, *General View*, p. 159.　　　　[35] Foote, *Treatise*, p. 39.

[36] Cooke, *Memoirs of Macklin*, p. 407.

[37] John Hill, *The Actor: A Treatise on the Art of Playing* (London: R. Griffiths, 1750), p. 282.

considerable estate in Northumberland, the young noble had been educated at Eton and Oxford. He enjoyed all the wealth and privilege that mid-eighteenth-century England could afford. By 1751 he was a Member of Parliament for Hinden. In 1752 his father died and he became, in consequence, a baronet. He had run through one fortune (£9,000 a year) and tried to recoup it by marriage in 1750 to Samuel Foote's cast-off mistress, a wealthy widow, Lady Isabella Paulet. Her fortune, to both Foote's and Delaval's surprise, was rigidly entailed.[38] Still, by means of this sordid and unhappy marriage, Sir Francis had money to spend. And in March of 1751 spend he did – £1,500 for one night's entertainment.

Delaval's London extravaganza was not unusual for him. Robert A. Smith records in "The Delavals of Seaton" that

> when Francis, or Frank as he was known to his friends, was at Seaton, banquets for anything up to four thousand guests were a regular occurrence. Overnight guests were likely to be pitched into a bath of water as their bed collapsed, and partitions between rooms were slid along to reveal the occupants in various stages of undress, to hoots of laughter from the onlookers.[39]

It is not surprising that the Delavals should have continued their recreations in London. That they would perform in public at the Theatre Royal – to be judged by professional actors and their fellow nobles – shows remarkable nerve, however, even for them.

Apparently Frank had always been stage-struck. Biographer Francis Askham marvels that at Drury Lane, Covent Garden, and the Haymarket, Sir Francis knew not only "the players, but the property-men, the candle-snuffers, the prompters and the authors, and took in all the players' cant, together with their diet of pint pots of porter and mutton-pies in the greenroom."[40] In the process he became friends with both Macklin and Foote.

One day, as they were conversing in the coffee house, Foote apparently suggested to Sir Francis that he should "get up some creditable play, in which himself and friends might fill up the characters."[41] The play was to be *Othello*, a longtime favorite of Frank's.

[38] See Smith, "The Delavals of Seaton," for background on Sir Francis and his family. See also Francis Askham, *The Gay Delavals* (London: Jonathan Cape, 1955), and John Robinson, *The Delaval Papers* (Newcastle: Browne and Browne, *ca.* 1890).

[39] Smith, "The Delavals of Seaton," 476.   [40] Askham, *The Gay Delavals*, p. 33.

[41] Cooke, *Memoirs of Foote*, vol. II, p. 71.

Several reasons for the choice of *Othello* are likely. First, the title role as it was then portrayed by Barry – hero and lover – must have appealed to Frank's vanity. In London he was known as a lover. Later in the century, Miss Ambross recollected that Sir Francis' "person was elegant, his face handsome, his manner polished, his education liberal, his conversation sprightly and pleasing. Few men possessed so many of those qualities which fascinate the ladies, and few ever succeeded better in obtaining their favours by humbling their proud hearts."[42] By 1751 he was openly living with Elizabeth Roach, a girl he had seduced soon after her arrival at Seaton Hall from a French convent. When he took her to London, her sister Deodata Quane accompanied her. Mrs. Quane seems an unlikely Desdemona, but perform Shakespeare's chaste heroine she did.[43]

The role of Othello also fit Frank's self-image. Tate Wilkinson recalled that "Sir Francis' person was noble, handsome, and commanding, and very proper to give a striking resemblance of the Moorish general."[44] Archivist John Robinson noted that Sir Francis seems from all descriptions to have been tall and well made: "His figure being remarkably attractive, and having an uncommon taste in dress, he was soon distinguished by society as a fine fellow."[45] *Othello* would enable him to display his face and figure before the best of London society. The hero's blackface does not seem to have been a deterrent either; Othello's darkened hue apparently added an exotic flavor to the role.

In addition to the play's suitability to Delaval's personality, it was, especially as cut in mid-eighteenth-century versions,[46] more suitable for amateur theatrics than Shakespeare's other popular tragedies, *Hamlet* and *Macbeth*, which required large casts. *Othello*, by contrast, could be performed with a minimum cast of five men and two women. If Othello, Iago, and Desdemona were credible in their

---

[42] Miss Ambross, *The Life and Memoirs of the Late Miss Ann Catley, the Celebrated Actress* (London: J. Bird, ?1789), p. 13. During the 1760s Sir Francis seduced the aspiring actress Ann Catley, and kept her as his mistress for several years. His reputation as a womanizer was extreme, even for the eighteenth century.

[43] See George Winchester Stone, ed., *The London Stage, 1660–1800* (Carbondale: Southern Illinois University Press, 1962), part 4, vol. I, pp. 240–41 for a record of that performance.

[44] Tate Wilkinson, *Memoirs of His Owne Life* (York: Printed for the Author, 1790), vol. II, p. 221.   [45] Robinson, *Delaval Papers*, p. 7.

[46] See Marvin Rosenberg, *The Masks of Othello* (Berkeley: University of California, 1961), pp. 34–38; Gino M. Matteo, *Shakespeare's "Othello": The Study and the Stage, 1604–1904* (Salzburg: Institüt für Englische Sprache und Literatür, 1974), pp. 108–17; and Hankey, *Othello*, pp. 44–48.

performances, the play could survive a mediocre Cassio, Roderigo, Brabantio (doubled with Lodovico), and Emilia. The Delaval *Othello* could succeed if the three principals were well drilled.

If Frank intended to become the talk of the town, he certainly succeeded. Cooke observed that

Private theatricals were at this period very rare; – so that the report of this intended *fete*, as a novelty, drew much of the attention of the town. The scenery was for some months in preparation, the dresses were magnificent, and tickets of admission were distributed to only the first people of quality.[47]

Four days before the scheduled performance, the *London Advertiser and Literary Gazette* (3 March 1751) proclaimed, "The Dresses provided for this Occasion, are the richest and most elegant that could be devised." John Hill later reported that the costumes were not only magnificent, "but well fancied, and much better adapted to the characters than any we have seen before."[48] The amateurs, notes Rosenfeld, could afford new costumes that were "vastly superior to the stock costumes of the patent theatres."[49] In accord with Macklin's teachings, "Othello's was a robe in the fashion of his country; Roderigo's an elegantly tawdry modern suit, and Cassio's and Iago's very rich uniforms."[50]

While these elaborate costumes and new scenes were being prepared, Sir Francis selected his cast. He assigned Iago to his brother John, Cassio to brother Edward, Roderigo to Captain Stevens, Brabantio/Lodovico to Sim Pine, Desdemona to Mrs. Quane, and Emilia to his mistress, Betty Roach. The *London Evening Post* (7–9 March 1751) reported that the Delavals' Preceptor "was Mr. *Macklin*; who has often Shewn Abilities in these Matters; and heretofore, as well as on this Occasion, has *deservedly got great Honour* by his Pupils." Presumably Macklin coached the Delavals according to his principles of natural acting.

When 7 March finally arrived, the Delavals were prepared. In addition to providing extravagant costumes and new scenes, they hired a first-rate orchestra and added extra wax lights to illuminate the house. They had distributed tickets to the royal family and packed the rest of the Drury Lane Theatre with their friends. They

---

[47] Cooke, *Memoirs of Foote*, p. 271.
[48] John Hill, *The Inspector* (London: R. Griffiths, 1753), vol. I, p. 11. *The Gentleman's Magazine* and Kirkman, among others, report Hill's account verbatim. His review may, in fact, have been authorized and distributed by the Delaval family.
[49] Rosenfeld, *Temples*, p. 168.   [50] Hill, *The Inspector*, vol. I, p. 11.

had also commissioned a special prologue and epilogue for the
occasion by Christopher Smart. John Delaval delivered the Prologue
to a packed house. It began

> WHILE mercenary Actors tread the Stage,
> And hireling Scribblers lash or lull the Age,
> Ours be the Talk t'instruct, and entertain,
> Without one thought of Glory or of Gain.

The gauntlet was thus thrown before the professional actors –
Garrick among them – in the audience. Smart's poem continued
with predictable homage to the Bard:

> The shade of *Shakespear*, in yon azure sky,
> On yon high cloud behold the Bard advance,
> Grasping all Nature with a single Glance:
> In various Attitudes around him stand
> The Passions, waiting for his dread Command.

These passions were expressed in particular "attitudes," agreed-
upon poses, and by a conventional code of gesture – love as sighs,
hope as upward glances, and terror as trembling:

> First kneeling Love before his Feet appears,
> And musically sighing melts in Tears.
> Near him fell Jealousy with Fury burns,
> And into Storms, the amorous Breathings turns;
> Then Hope with Heaven-ward Look, and Joy draws near,
> While palsied Terror trembles in the Rear.

Presumably if one knew this semiotic code, he or she could convey the
proper feeling. Delaval concluded the Prologue with the conventional
apology; if we fail, he said, "your Censure still defer, / When Truth's
in View 'tis glorious e'en to err."[51]

The Epilogue was left to Desdemona. Her speech parodies – and
thereby seeks to divert – possible criticism from this most aristocratic
audience:

> *Prudella* first in Parody begins,
> (For Nonsense and Buffoonery are Twins),
> "Can Beaux the Court for Theatres exchange?
> "*I swear by Heaven, 'tis strange, 'tis passing strange*
> "And very whimsical, and mighty dull,
> "*And Pitiful, and wond'rous pitiful*:

---

[51] Christopher Smart, *An Occasional Prologue and Epilogue to Othello* (London: Printed for the
Author, ?1751), pp. 5–6.

"*I wish I had not heard it* – Blessed Dame!
Whene'er she speaks the Audience wish the same.
Next *Neddy Nicely* – "Fye, oh fye, good lack,
"A Nasty Man to make his Face all black."
The Lady *Stiffneck* shews her pious Rage,
And wonders we shou'd act – upon a Stage.
"Why Ma'm, says *Coquetilla*, a Disgrace?
"Merit in any Form may shew her Face."

According to this satire, only the overly fastidious would disapprove
of Sir Francis' blackface. The judicious members of the audience,
Desdemona concludes, will judge without bias, responding to the
heroine's "Chastity unblemish'd and unbrib'd" and to the entire
cast's endeavors to bring them pleasure.[52]

Though the public display of Frank's mistress as Emilia may not fit
our definition of chastity, the Delavals had tried to insure a more
genteel crowd than was usual at Drury Lane. John Hill praised them
for carefully disposing of the tickets, so that "the women of the town,
who can very seldom be kept out of any place of entertainment"
would not be present. Betty Roach's upper-class prostitution was
allowable; ladies of the evening had to be excluded, if only for one
night. "The conductors of the plan," Hill continued, "knew that
every part of the house would be full of persons of the first fashion;
and they paid them the just and sensible compliment of keeping all
improper people from among them."[53]

Newspaper accounts confirm that the audience was composed of
the "best people"; in fact, the *General Evening Post* (7 March 1751),
the *London Evening Post* (9 March 1751), and the *Penny Morning Post*
(11 March 1751) pay more attention to the audience than to the
performance. The latter account begins:

On thursday Night their Royal Highnesses the Prince and Princess of Wales,
the Duke of Cumberland, Princess Aemelia, Prince George, and Princess
Augusta, with the greatest Number of the Nobility, Foreign Ministers, and
Gentry of both Sexes, went to the Theatre Royal in Drury-Lane, to see the
Play of Othello acted by several Gentlemen and Ladies for their Diversion.
The Company was the most brilliant ever seen in a Playhouse in this
Kingdom; the Streets and Avenues were so filled with Coaches and Chairs,
that the greatest Part of the Gentlemen and Ladies were obliged to Wade
through Dirt and Filth to get to the House, which afforded good Diversion
and Benefit for the Pickpockets, and other Gentlemen of that Trade. In

---

[52] Ibid., pp. 7–8.   [53] Hill, *The Inspector*, vol. I, pp. 10–11.

short, the Crowd was so great, that many Stars and Garters appeared in
Publick Houses adjacent to the Theatre, to wait for Entrance with the
greater Safety.[54]

The *London Evening Post* reported that the theatre was "crowded in
every part with the best Company, *even to the Upper Gallery*; which was
honour'd with *Beaux*, *Bells*, SENATORS, PRIVY-COUNCIL-
LORS, and *Titles*, Male and Female, of the FIRST RANK." The
Delavals placed no section assignment on their tickets; places in the
Boxes were obtained on a "first come / first serve" basis. This
subversion of the normal hierarchy of Box, Pit, and Gallery elicited
much comment. As John Hill noted, "by this means the whole house
was filled with equally good company; and half a dozen stars
glittered for the first, and probably for the last, time in the upper-
gallery." Part of the royal family filled the stage boxes, and every
corner of the house "glittered with diamonds and embroidery."[55]

Besides admiring each other's apparel and jewels and basking in
their collective wealth and power, what was this splendid audience's
reaction to the play? Horace Walpole's private correspondence is
probably more candid than newspaper acounts. He wrote of the
Delavals: "They really acted so well, that it is astonishing they
should not have had sense enough not to act at all ... " But like the
newspapers, Walpole seems to have been more fascinated by the
sociological phenomenon of a homogeneous, aristocratic audience.
"The rage was so great to see this performance," he wrote, "that the
House of Commons literally adjourned at three o'clock on purpose:
the footman's gallery was strung with blue ribbands! What a wise
people!"[56]

The play itself seems to have been acted competently but not
expertly. There were a few flaws onstage, perhaps from an understandable attack of nerves. Desdemona stumbled, but as John Hill
apologized, "the native modesty of the character made us rather
charmed than offended at it." Moreover, there were extenuating
circumstances:

The terrors of an audience, to persons not accustomed to speak in public, are
not to be got absolutely by all the resolution in the world. It was easy to see
that every one of the performers was affected by them; but it is amazing that

[54] Newspaper accounts are taken from the Burney Collection in the British Library.
[55] Hill, *The Inspector*, vol. I, p. 11.
[56] Horace Walpole, *The Yale Edition of Horace Walpole's Correspondence*, ed. W. S. Lewis (New
Haven: Yale University Press, 1960), vol. XX, pp. 230–31.

they were not all of them much more so. The management of the voice, in adapting it to the space it is to fill, is another circumstance of vast consequence to the player, and in another circumstance also, to which these performers must have been perfect strangers.

A public rehearsal would have helped them, Hill argued, to gauge the acoustics more accurately, for a filled house carries sound differently than an empty one. As mere amateurs the Delavals suffered from "infinite disadvantages" in contrast to "those whose nightly task it is to act." Despite these disadvantages, "the greater part of the play was much better performed than it ever was on any stage before."[57] In Hill's judgment, the amateurs had beaten the professionals at their own game.

Hill's explanation for this improbable situation was simple. The Delavals succeeded over "common players" because they were not imitating an action; they were in reality what they represented. They "felt every sentiment they were to express" and "were inspired by the sentiment to be the thing the author expected them to represent." Sir Francis' Moor is a case in point: "that in which he was peculiarly superior to every body, was the natural expression of the lover and the gentleman." When he asked pardon of Cassio in the final scene, his voice "had something in it so like the man of honour, and so unlike all that we see in imitation of it in the player, that we shall not easily be reconciled to the hearing it from any body else." In sum, Francis Delaval's Othello was to Hill, at least, "doubtless, the finest ever produced on a stage; his deportment in the whole was majestic, and his sense of the passions ... quick and exquisite."[58] Sir Francis embodied the eighteenth-century cultural forces that harnessed social tensions under a code of sentiment and civility. To the manor and the manner born, Delaval could portray Othello's nobility with *sprezzatura* because he, himself, was inherently noble in mid-eighteenth-century terms. Sir Francis' rank embodied more than social position; it represented a way of life that "common players" could only vaguely imitate.

John Delaval, Francis' brother, played Iago with the same easy grace, according to Hill: "his whole deportment" was "so much the gentleman, so perfectly adapted to every circumstance of the character, and so elegant in its propriety, that I think this audience

---

[57] Hill, *The Inspector*, vol. I, pp. 11–14.   [58] Ibid., pp. 12–13.

must forget him before they can see any other Iago with patience."
In short, "he was perfectly the thing that Shakespear drew." So too
with Edward Delaval as Cassio. Unconscious of his irony, Hill
praised the youngest Delaval's performance in the drunken scene:
Cassio's inebriation and sudden sobriety were "rendered natural by
his manner of performing it."[59] Clad in regimentals, the handsome
Delavals were brother officers. No non-commissioned officer, this
Iago; Othello could hardly be blamed for trusting him.

From the newspaper accounts, the Delaval *Othello* was a triumph.
But not everyone responded so enthusiastically. A broadside soon
damned the entire spectacle. Titled "A Satirical Dialogue Between a
Sea Captain and His Friend in Town," it included a prologue and
epilogue "more suitable to the Occasion than their Own." The
prologue, spoken by Ebeneazer Pentweazel (Smart's pseudonym),
begins:

> While *heedless Fops*, affecting to be Sage,
> With *awkward Attitudes* Disgrace the Stage;
> *Ours* be the Task to Paint the *Simple Elves*,
> And shew the Race of *Triflers* in *our Selves*.

Shakespeare is understandably horrified at the news of this production:

> behold the BARD advance,
> His eyes, Resentment's fiercer Rays elance;
> *Justice* before him wields her flaming Sword,
> [A]nd only waits the BARD's assenting Word!

With whips and stings, they advance on the players, particularly
Desdemona.

> Come on my Lads – nay hang me if I sham Her,
> And when WE'VE kill'd Her – let the AUDIENCE damn Her.

The Prologue is followed by a Dialogue between a Sea Captain
newly arrived to shore and his friend who reports the London news.
The Sea Captain learns that members of the gentry "Have *acted*, like
People *bereft of their Senses*, / For *Gentility's lost* when the *Player
commences*." The Sea Captain's friend reports that the audience

---

[59] Ibid., pp. 13–14.

applauded only out of good manners and that the production cost £1,500. Why couldn't the money have been donated to charity, wonders the Sea Captain? His friend agrees:

> Now *if* I was an Actor ...
> The *Stage* and its *Drudgery* both I'd *forsake*;
> Turn GENTLEMAN *now*, as the GENTRY *turn Players*
> *And exhibit a Taste* far *genteeler than* THEIRS.

The biting Epilogue concludes with a personal attack on Sir Francis for abandoning his wife, Lady Isabella:

> [I]t pleas'd me to the Life,
> To hear Oth – llo bawl so for his Wife.
>   ...
> Suppose he *had* lost her – *why* this mighty Pother,
> His *Monkey F – t* can help him to *another*.[60]

The author of this satirical broadside obviously disapproved of Sir Francis' private life and his public theatrics. Nobility had no business on the public stage. Not surprisingly, the professional actor and manager David Garrick agreed. Because of the gifts of nature and fortune – Sir Francis' height and aristocratic breeding – Delaval had succeeded where Garrick had failed and had filled the Theatre Royal with people who would not normally attend the theatre.

Foote apparently missed the play. Cooke recorded that "either from accident or design," Foote did not appear until after the performance was over and the players were taking refreshment in the greenroom. The company greeted him:

"Oh Foote! Where have you been? What have you lost! Such a play you'll never have another opportunity of seeing!" was the general buzz from one end of the room to the other. To all this the wit bowed contrition, disappointment, and so forth; when slily approaching the place where Garrick sat, he asked him, in a whisper loud enough to be heard by the whole company, "what he *seriously* thought of it?" – "Think of it," says Garrick, equally wishing to be heard, "why, that I never *suffered* so much in my whole life!" – "What! *for the author*? I thought so. Alas, poor Shakespeare!"

Sir Francis, observed Cooke, joined in the general laughter "with as much good humour as if he was not at all affected by the sarcasm."[61]

---

[60] Anon., *A Satirical Dialogue* (London: Printed for J. River, ?1751), pp. 1–7.
[61] Cooke, *Memoirs of Foote*, vol. II, p. 72.

The Delaval *Othello* remained a topic of conversation well into the next year. Charles Macklin referred to it briefly in his satirical afterpiece, *The Covent Garden Theatre, or Pasquin Turn'd Drawcansir*. Written in 1752, this farce burlesques theatrical follies and social pretensions. As its master of ceremonies, Pasquin, begins his pantomime, he receives advice from his fellow players. Bob Smart (a satire perhaps on Samuel Foote) suggests that he "treat the Public with the finest Pantomime that ever was seen, in Immitation of the Gentlemen Who Play'd Othello." Pasquin, of course, rejects the proposal.[62]

Whatever Garrick's suffering over the Delaval triumph, it was to last only one night. In the immediate future, he found his theatre closed when the Prince of Wales died thirteen days later. Garrick went on a summer tour to Paris and returned with schemes to improve his theatre. He enjoyed a long and successful career as actor and manager; he also was the well-spring for increasing bardolatry, particularly in his sponsorship of the Shakespeare Jubilee of 1769.

The amateur fared less well. Though Sir Francis' father died in 1752 and the son became a baronet, his life of dissipation continued. As Cooke observed, he employed his vast fortune "alternately as a means of dissipation and of generosity.... Though indolent in business, he was active in his pleasures;... he would be the leading *showman* of his day, whatever species of frivolity was the fashion." To this end he remained, in Cooke's words, "an agreeable gay companion," who "united generosity, affability, politeness, and good nature."[63]

Sir Francis died in 1771 as he had lived. Robert A. Smith describes the scene: "following a large venison dinner, a great deal of ice and a rummer of brandy, he collapsed in convulsions and died soon afterwards; he was forty-four years old and did not leave enough to pay for his own funeral."[64] His body traveled to Seaton accompanied by three coaches and two dozen black horses. Sir Francis, who always loved a good show, would have been gratified that his final journey from London was a lavish spectacle. He might have been even more gratified that his brother got stuck with the bill.

*   *   *   *

[62] Charles Macklin, *The Covent Garden Theatre, or Pasquin Turn'd Drawcansir* (Los Angeles: William Andrews Clark Memorial Library, 1965). Augustan Reprint Society, no. 116, p. 18.   [63] Cooke, *Memoirs of Foote*, vol. II, pp. 77–79.
[64] Smith, "The Delavals of Seaton," 480.

The Delaval *Othello* illustrates several facets of cultural life in mid-eighteenth-century London. First, it demonstrates the crucial role the public theatres played in reinforcing commonly held beliefs about proper deportment for members of the nobility. It also shows how those beliefs, in turn, affected interpretations of Shakespeare's plays.

Dougald MacMillan notes in an essay on David Garrick that "the Theatre Royal in the eighteenth century was a privileged institution under governmental protection and control."[65] Rank, as we see in the life of Sir Francis, had its privileges. Though he was by no means typical of England's aristocracy, his elevated social status enabled him the freedom to enact his passions with *sprezzatura*; his moral character was questioned by many, but he was nevertheless admired because he put up a good show.

What applied to Sir Francis' life applied to Othello onstage. He might murder his wife in a fit of rage, but what really mattered was that he was a noble gentleman who displayed the appropriate sentiments – love, pity, and honor. Thus, in John Hill's opinion, if no one else's, it was easier for Sir Francis to *be* Othello than for professional actors from the middle class. They could only *imitate* nobility.

The historical accounts are open about Sir Francis' appalling exploitation of women: Elizabeth Roach, Isabella Paulet, Ann Catley – all were victimized by a man of power and position. Yet few of the sources blame him for this behavior. Throughout his life, Sir Francis assumed that the right of property in women was one of the privileges of noble birth. It should not therefore be surprising that critical accounts of *Othello* from the eighteenth century never condemn Shakespeare's hero for his treatment of Desdemona. Like Claudio in *Much Ado About Nothing*, he sinned only in mistaking. Othello's attitudes toward women had nothing to do with it.

Nor did his race. While privately Garrick speculated that Shakespeare made Othello black because he wished to portray "jealousy in all its violence, and that is why he chose an African in whose veins circulated fire instead of blood,"[66] for actors and audience alike, race seems not to have been a controversial issue in public performance. Blackface might have hidden the actor's facial expressions, but it did not necessarily signify Otherness. Othello was

---

[65] Dougald MacMillan, "David Garrick, Manager: Notes on the Theatre As a Cultural Institution in England in the Eighteenth Century," *Studies in Philology*, 45 (1948): 630–46; quote from 646.   [66] Quoted from Hankey, *Othello*, p. 38.

conceived as an officer and a gentleman, not a representative of an alien culture. Beset by a villainous hypocrite, he is tempted from without, not from within.

The contrast between amateur and professional performances implies something about the state of the acting profession in 1751. The established actors of Drury Lane and Covent Garden – Macklin, Barry, and Garrick, among others – considered themselves a highly disciplined cadre of professionals entitled to a comfortable, even substantial, remuneration. After all, the Delavals were coached by Macklin. Their audience might be diverted by an amateur production for one evening, but the theatre belonged to the professionals, and during the Garrick years, they made it prosper.

The Delaval *Othello* also demonstrates the limits of eighteenth-century bardolatry. Shakespeare might be revered this side of idolatry, but his works were appropriated – both by textual cuts and by conventions of interpretation – in accord with eighteenth-century cultural assumptions. His words were perceived as elevated discourse, but also as an expression of tumultuous emotions. Such feelings were less threatening when considered as carefully categorized passions and represented on the public stage under an audience's surveillance. The hero, a gentleman to the core, knew how to express these passions through a series of signs that included manners of speech and body language. The greatest actors – Garrick and Barry – seemed natural because their representations of these codes were so fluid and energetic.

Finally, though the theatre audience in the eighteenth century contained many people of the "middling sort," legitimate theatre expressed, for the most part, conservative values. The Delaval *Othello* demonstrates that in 1751, long before Garrick's 1769 Jubilee, Shakespeare, England's patron poet, was already an instrument of cultural conservatism.[67]

---

[67] I borrow this term from Gary Taylor, who uses it in his discussion of Garrick's popular appeal. See *Reinventing Shakespeare: A Cultural History from the Restoration to the Present* (New York: Weidenfeld and Nicolson, 1989), pp. 120–21.

CHAPTER 7

William Charles Macready and the domestic Othello

[B]ut yet the pity of it, Iago! O Iago, the pity of it[.]

(*Othello*, 4.1.184–85)

The nineteenth century brought a new *Othello* to the stage. By the end of the eighteenth century, the Moor no longer appeared in a British army officer's uniform but wore an outfit that – according to English perceptions at least – represented the "custom of his country." Less the military hero, in the first half of the nineteenth century he became an adoring husband, a noble victim of an attractive but deceptive villain. The Moor was now, in many respects, the protagonist in a domestic melodrama.[1]

To capture the essence of the early Victorian *Othello*, this chapter focuses on actor-manager William Charles Macready. His theatrical activity spans the first half of the nineteenth century and represents the broadest range of experiences – from managing the sumptuous Covent Garden and Drury Lane theatres in London to touring the backwoods of America. Macready bridged classical and romantic styles of acting. Born in the age of Kemble and encouraged by Mrs. Siddons, he played Iago to Edmund Kean's Othello. As he matured,

---

[1] Joseph Donohue suggests that "the English fondness for melodrama could be traced even in the popularity of certain Shakespearean plays. *Richard the Third*, *Othello*, and *Macbeth*, being 'the most melodramatic,' were the most often performed." See *Theatre in the Age of Kean* (Totowa, NJ: Rowman and Littlefield, 1975), p. 128. George Taylor also describes *Othello* as "Shakespeare's nearest approach to domestic melodrama." See *Players and Performances in the Victorian Theatre* (Manchester: Manchester University Press, 1989), p. 122. Michael R. Booth defines Victorian melodrama as a form that contains "every possible ingredient of popular appeal: strong emotion, both pathetic and potentially tragic, low comedy, romantic colouring, remarkable events in an exciting and suspenseful plot, physical sensations, sharply delineated stock characters, domestic sentiment, domestic settings and domestic life, love, joy, suffering, morality, the reward of virtue and the punishment of vice." See *Theatre in the Victorian Age* (Cambridge: Cambridge University Press, 1991), pp. 150–51. While *Othello* does not contain all of these elements, it certainly shares many characteristics with Victorian melodrama.

he coached younger actors such as Helena Faucit and Samuel Phelps. He also left ample documentation of his acting concepts for others to emulate: The promptbook of his Covent Garden *Othello*, transcribed by George Ellis, was a major guideline for Charles Kean, Samuel Phelps, and Herman Vezin.[2] Through such borrowing, the shape of Charles Kean's or Samuel Phelps' *Othello* was essentially the same as Macready's. Moreover, the actor-manager's diary entries provide poignant insight into performances of Othello and Iago in the best – and the worst – of nineteenth-century acting conditions.[3]

Macready's personal lifestyle interfaced with his view of Othello's tragedy. He was known, contends Michael R. Booth, as "an actor outstanding in depicting the tenderness of domestic love." Such representations came naturally to "the father of a large family whom he adored, and for whom he endured the drudgery of acting; he held all the familiar ideals of his time."[4] To Macready, marriage meant "home endearments and domestic felicity."[5] Thus his Othello was primarily a loving husband whose domestic tranquillity becomes brutally shattered. As his friend, reviewer John Forster, wrote in 1836, Macready expressed his love for Desdemona "as that grand principle of virtue, tenderness, and affectionate admiration of beauty and good into which all the hopes and habits of an active life at length settled down, and which is to carry him happily and calmly and with a tranquil mind through the 'vale of years.'"[6]

Though Macready was never a great Othello, his career-long interaction with the role (and to a lesser extent with Iago) deserves attention. Booth argues the centrality of his managerial imprint:

Although he managed only briefly compared to others, his management is one of the most important of Victoria's reign. Coming early as it did, it set high standards in production and artistic integrity that all later manage-

---

[2] For a fascinating account of George Ellis's career, see Charles H. Shattuck, "A Victorian Stage Manager: George Cessal Ellis," *Theatre Notebook*, 22 (1968): 102–12.

[3] Thomas Postlewait warns that "theatre autobiographies cannot be read as straightforward historical documents." Macready's diaries, however, do reveal what his attitude toward his experience was in a particular time and place. See "Autobiography and Theatre History," in *Interpreting the Theatrical Past: Essays in the Historiography of Performance*, ed. Thomas Postlewait and Bruce A. McConachie (Iowa City: University of Iowa Press, 1989), pp. 248–72; quote from p. 259.   [4] Booth, *Theatre in the Victorian Age*, p. 133.

[5] Frederick Pollock, ed., *Macready's Reminiscences, and Selections From His Diaries and Letters* (New York: Harper Brothers, 1875), p. 216. The two editions of Macready's highly introspective diaries sometimes duplicate each other but often present different selections. I will also be using William Toynbee's edition, *The Diaries of William Charles Macready* (2 vols., London: Chapman and Hall, 1912).

[6] From Julie Hankey, ed., *Othello* (Bristol: Bristol Classical Press, 1987), p. 65.

ments of quality followed, influencing them particularly in the staging of Shakespeare, the use of stage crowds, the conduct of rehearsals, the illustrative value of scenery and spectacle and, in the largest sense, the sheer dedication to what was best in theatre.[7]

As his diaries show, Macready adhered rigorously to the work ethic. Even when a text had become standard in his repertoire, he continued to study it and insisted on long and frequent rehearsals. Helena Faucit Martin, who played Desdemona to Macready's Moor, recalled in later years that "Rehearsals began at ten in the morning, and usually went on until three or four. In the revival of an old, or the bringing out of a new play, these rehearsals were continued daily for three weeks at least, sometimes four or five."[8]

Macready decried the audience's penchant for "points" – moments like operatic arias, anticipated by the audience and highlighted by pauses for applause – aiming instead at a unified impression. J. C. Trewin praised this quality: "he saw a character always as a living man, not a dummy forced through a set of situations."[9] He wanted his characters to be consistent and sustained throughout the production. On 8 January 1835, he recorded in his diary:

Acted Othello with a feeling of having no sympathy from my audience; thought myself deficient in earnestness and spirit, but do not regret having done it, as it was a useful rehearsal to me. I never saw the "Senate" put so well upon the stage. I think I may play Othello well, but the prescriptive criticism of this country, in looking for particular points instead of contemplating one entire character, abates my confidence in myself.[10]

Othello's "farewell to his occupation" had been one of Kean's most memorable points: Kean's tremulous delivery was so famous that when Macready first played the Moor, he dropped the speech altogether. By the late 1830s, however, memory of Kean had faded somewhat and Macready could restore the "farewell" speech.[11]

Although Macready was necessarily influenced by Edmund Kean's passionate Moor, he was no mere disciple. He had his own conception of what Othello ought to be. On 28 October 1835, he

[7] Booth, *Theatre in the Victorian Age*, p. 44.

[8] Helena Faucit Martin, *On Desdemona* (London: For Private Circulation, 1881), p. 57.

[9] J. C. Trewin, *Mr. Macready: A Nineteenth-century Tragedian and his Theatre* (London: George C. Harrap, Co., 1955), p. 240.   [10] Pollock, *Reminiscences*, p. 326.

[11] Hankey argues that despite Hazlitt's reference to Macready's restoration of the speech, it was usually omitted in early Victorian performances. See Hankey, *Othello*, p. 253.

recorded in his diary that he was "particularly desirous of acting it [Othello] well," partly because he wished his wife Catherine to be pleased with it. He felt he had succeeded "in performing the *whole character* better – more grandly, deeply, and nobly – than I have yet done."[12] He intended the role to have a "*sustained reality.*"[13] Before a performance in 1836, he noted, "Employed my mind in thinking on Othello and endeavoring to fix in my thoughts the manly and chivalrous character of the Moor."[14] Macready's Othello was a gentleman, but at the same time he retained a large reservoir of repressed passion. He was, in short, much like Macready himself.

Yet Macready had difficulty solidifying this conception on stage. The entry for 12 September 1837, after a production at Birmingham, reads: "The great error of my performance of Othello was in the heavy, stately tone in which I pitched the part, instead of the free, bold, cheerful, chivalrous bearing of the warrior, the happy lover, and the high-born man."[15] Sometimes, however, he did feel successful, as on 1 November 1843: "Acted Othello in a very grand and impassioned manner, never better. The audience I thought cold at first, but I would not give way to the influence; I sustained the character from the first to the last."[16]

Besides consistent feeling and unity of effect, Macready strove for what Charles H. Shattuck describes as "a thorough emotional identification with whatever character he was performing."[17] Before appearing as Othello, Macready reread the play and pondered the character. On 15 April 1846, he wrote: "Acted Othello with great care, but suffering much from weakness and cold upon my voice and head. Thought that I never spoke the address to the Senate so directly and really as this evening, much too of the impassioned portions. I thought I acted as feeling it."[18] Helena Faucit Martin recalls Macready in the final scene after she, as Desdemona, had been strangled: "There was an impressive grandeur, an elevation even, in his ravings ... As I lay there and listened, he seemed to me to be like a soul in hell, whirling in the Second Circle of the Inferno. And there was a piteousness and a pathos in his reiteration of the loved one's name that went to my very heart."[19]

[12] Toynbee, *Diaries*, vol. I, p. 260.   [13] Ibid., p. 287.
[14] Pollock, *Reminiscences*, p. 384.   [15] Ibid., p. 415.   [16] Ibid., p. 513.
[17] Charles H. Shattuck, *Shakespeare on the American Stage* (Washington: The Folger Shakespeare Library, 1976), vol. I, p. 68.   [18] Pollock, *Reminiscences*, p. 560.
[19] Martin, *On Desdemona*, p. 92.

Othello's mind, torn between tender love and jealous rage, was akin in some ways to Macready's own. His relationship to the professional theatre was replete with tantrums, rage, and despair, while he sought peace and domestic happiness in his home life. The similarity between the Moor's mood swings and those recorded in Macready's diaries perhaps made the actor's impersonations more realistic and moving.[20] While Macready's Othello may not have ranked with Kean's and Salvini's, it was probably the best of his generation.

Macready's Iago appeared less often but was more successful. Macready studied the role intensely and argued that the Ensign should not be a traditional stage villain but an intellectual fascinated with the diabolic. Macready's diary entries are full of self-criticism whenever he succumbed to the easy gimmicks of stage villainy. His assessment on 21 February 1833, for example, reads: "There was a want of sustained earnestness and spirit; there was no proper direction of the sight, and, in consequence, a scowl instead of clear expression, besides a want of abstraction in the soliloquies."[21] The entry for 16 January 1834 echoes this motif:

Acted Iago very indifferently, indeed the habit of scowling or looking from under my brows, especially when an audience is close upon me, as in a small theater, is a direct prevention to good acting. I wanted reality and directness, indeed, a revision of the execution of the character, and strict attention to my general style.[22]

At his career's close, Macready believed he had at last succeeded. Following his farewell performance of Iago on 22 January 1851, he wrote:

Acted Iago with a vigor and discrimination that I have never surpassed, if ever equaled. I do not think I ever acted it so powerfully.

The last performance of Iago was, in my mind, a commentary on the text, an elucidation, an opening out of the profound conception of that great creative mind, that almost divine intelligence, Shakespeare, which has not been given before in the inward feeling of the part: the selfishness, sensuality, and delight in the exercise of his own intellectual power as I have never seen in Cooke or Young, nor read of in Henderson, as being so developed.[23]

[20] On 24 December 1839, for example, he bemoaned in his diary that he longed to quit "scenes where my mind is in a whirl of passion, intrigue, and tumult, where temptations to error are constantly before me and provocations beset me on every side." Instead, he "had hoped to retire to the serenity of a country life, to a slender establishment, and the society of my children." Pollock, *Reminiscences*, p. 465.   [21] Ibid., p. 262.   [22] Ibid., p. 296.
[23] Ibid., p. 625.

Macready's Iago needed no motivation besides delight in his own intellect. A reviewer in 1840 praised him: He "does not (as most actors do) make the performers engaged with him look fools, by making himself appear a complete villain, but, by his acting, makes us feel that had we been in Cassio's place, we should most likely have done as he did."[24] "Finally," concludes Marvin Rosenberg, "he cleared Iago's face of scowls, made him a blunt, honest soldier, and behind this sturdy mask of innocence merged intellect and passion into energetic purpose."[25]

Alan Downer, Macready's biographer, describes the tragedian's acting methods: "In the study and rehearsal of a part, Macready searched for character traits which an audience would recognize as natural, and by the skillful use of pause, transition, and colloquialism strove to convey the poet's meaning."[26] One technique was the "Macready pause," a slight hesitation within the speech in imitation of a natural speaking voice. Macready used these pauses to make Othello seem more realistic. On 1 November 1836, he recorded: "I think I acted Othello well with considerable spirit, and more *pause* than I generally allow myself, which is an undoubted improvement."[27] Again, on 7 November: "Acted Othello, not exactly well, but again derived great benefit from *taking time* between my sentences."[28] Macready also used specific stage business to achieve what he thought would be a more natural effect. Downer observes, for example, that "To further contribute to the reality of the senate scene in *Othello* he played with his back to the audience."[29]

The productions Macready mounted at Covent Garden and Drury Lane demonstrate his meticulousness over scenic design and costume. George Ellis prepared watercolor drawings of costumes and scenery from the Covent Garden *Othello* for Charles Kean; seven scenic drawings, now in the Folger Shakespeare Library,[30] show

---

[24] Quoted from Hankey, *Othello*, p. 197.

[25] Marvin Rosenberg, *The Masks of Othello* (Berkeley: University of California Press, 1961), p. 124.

[26] Alan Downer, *The Eminent Tragedian: William Charles Macready* (Cambridge: Harvard University Press, 1966), p. 80. See also Bertram Joseph, *The Tragic Actor* (London: Routledge and Kegan Paul, 1959), pp. 284–320, for a discussion of Macready's acting style and the traits of his competitors, including Vandenhoff, Phelps, and Kean.

[27] Toynbee, *Diaries*, vol. I, p. 354.   [28] Ibid., p. 357.

[29] Downer, *Eminent Tragedian*, p. 75.

[30] The promptbooks described below are listed in Charles H. Shattuck's *The Shakespeare Promptbooks: A Descriptive Catalogue* (Urbana: University of Illinois Press, 1965). This particular promptbook, Folger 14, is listed in Shattuck as no. 26 (p. 359).

THEATRE ROYAL, COVENT-GARDEN.

This Evening, MONDAY, Oct. 16, 1837,

Will be performed, Shakspeare's Tragedy of

OTHELLO,

MOOR OF VENICE.

Duke of Venice, - Mr. BARTLEY,
Brabantio, Mr. G. BENNETT, Gratiano, Mr. TILBURY, Lodovico, Mr. WALDRON,
Othello, - Mr. MACREADY,
Cassio, - Mr. ANDERSON,
Iago, - Mr. WARDE,
Roderigo, - Mr. VINING,
Montano, Mr. DIDDEAR, Antonio, Mr. YARNOLD, Julio, Mr. ROBERTS,
Marco, Mr. BENDER, Paulo, Mr. HARRIS, Luca, Mr. PRITCHARD.
Desdemona, - Miss HELEN FAUCIT,
Emilia, - Miss HUDDART.

IN THE COURSE OF THE EVENING,

Mozart' Overture to "Il Don Giovanni," and Rossini's Overture to "Le Italiani in Algieri."

After which, Dibdin's Comic Opera of

THE QUAKER.

Steady, - Mr. H. PHILLIPS,
(His First Appearance at this Theatre these Two Years.)
Easy, - Mr. AYLIFFE,
Lubin, - Mr. WILSON,
Solomon, - Mr. W. J. HAMMOND,
Cicely, Mrs. GARRICK, Floretta, Miss VINCENT,
Gillian, - Miss P. HORTON.

To conclude with the last new Farce (in One Act) of The

SPITFIRE!

Capt. Shortcut, R. N. Mr. ROBERTS. Lieut. Seaworth, R. N. Mr. ANDERSON,
Second Lieut. Mr. HARRIS, Midshipman, Mr. BENDER, Surgeon, Mr. C. J. SMITH,
Boatswain Bobstay, Mr. MEADOWS, Sam, Mr. YARNOLD, Seamen, Messrs. W. H. Payne, Becket, Paulo, Sharpe, &c.
Tobias Shortcut, - Mr. BARTLEY,
Margaret, Miss P. HORTON, Mrs. Fidget, Mrs. GARRICK.

BOXES—5s. Second Price—2s. 6d. PIT—2s. 6d. Second Price—1s. 6d.
LOWER GALL. 1s. 6d. Sec. Price, 1s. UPPER GALL. 1s. Sec. Price, 6d.
Second Price will be admitted at the End of the Third Act of the Tragedy.

Under the present regulation of the Prices of Admission, the system of nightly Orders, must be altogether discontinued, and no admittance behind the Scenes except on business.

The New Play of The

NOVICE

will be repeated To-morrow,—on Friday, and THREE TIMES A WEEK UNTIL FURTHER NOTICE

The New Farce of The

SPITFIRE!

Will be repeated EVERY EVENING UNTIL FURTHER NOTICE, Wednesday and Thursday next excepted.

The new Tragedy of The

BRIDAL, and the Opera of FRA DIAVOLO will be repeated EVERY WEDNESDAY.

Mr. PHELPS, Mr. WEBSTER, Mrs. GLOVER and Mrs. HUMBY

Are engaged at this Theatre, and will be duly announced.

To-morrow, (3rd time) the NEW PLAY in Three Acts, called The NOVICE.
After which, the Opera of The LORD OF THE MANOR. And the New Farce of The SPITFIRE.
On Wednesday, will be repeated the Tragedy of THE BRIDAL,
Melantius, Mr. Macready, Amintor, Mr. Anderson, Evadne, Miss Huddart.
Aspatia, Miss Taylor.
After which, the Opera of FRA DIAVOLO—Fra Diavolo, Mr. WILSON, Lorenzo, Mr. MANVERS, Lord Allcash,
Mr. ROBERTS, Matteo, Mr. LEFFLER, Giacomo, Mr. STRETTON, Beppo, Mr. RANSFORD, Zerlina, Miss
SHIRREFF, Lady Allcash, Miss P. HORTON.
On Thursday, the Comedy of The PROVOKED HUSBAND,——Lord Townly, Mr. MACREADY, Manly, Mr. WARDE,
Sir Francis Wronghead, Mr. BARTLEY, Squire Richard, Mr. MEADOWS, Count Basset, Mr. PRITCHARD,
John Moody, Mr. W. J. HAMMOND, Lady Townly, Miss HELEN FAUCIT, Lady Grace, Miss HUDDART,
Lady Wronghead, Mrs. W. CLIFFORD, Miss Jenny, Miss TAYLOR. After which will be produced A NEW
MELO-DRAMATIC ROMANCE, to be called The

AFRANCESADO,

The principal characters by Mr. WARDE, Mr. ANDERSON, Mr. LEFFLER, Mr. DIDDEAR, Mr BARTLEY,
Mr. MEADOWS, Miss VINCENT, and Miss TAYLOR.
On Friday, (4th time) the last New Play of The NOVICE.
On Saturday, Lord Byron's Tragedy of WERNER; OR, THE INHERITANCE.
Werner, - Mr. MACREADY, Ulric, Mr. ANDERSON, Gabor, Mr. WARDE, Baron Stralenheim, Mr. DIDDEAR,
Idenstein, Mr. MEADOWS, Josephine, Miss HUDDART, Ida, Miss TAYLOR.

A GRAND OPERA is in Preparation.

All Applications respecting the Play Bills of this Theatre to be addressed (post paid) to Mr. E. HARRIS, at the Stage Door.
Vivat Regina. No Money returned. W. S. JOHNSON, "Nassau Press," 6, Nassau Street, Soho.

Figure 8: The playbill for William Charles Macready's 1837 Covent Garden *Othello*.

careful attention to detail. The first is a wash of the Rialto that was also used for *The Merchant of Venice*, complete with bridge, canal, gondola, and Renaissance buildings in the background. The second scene is the citadel of Famagusta on the isle of Cyprus. It consists of three layers: the front panel shows the castle wall and cannons pointing out to sea; the middle panel portrays a castle turret, while the back panel opens to a prospect across the harbor. The third scene is a gateway leading from outside the castle to the inside. The drunken revels of *Othello*, Act 2, scene 3 would be staged before these gates. The fourth watercolor is an ornate chamber in the castle, suitable for the temptation scene, the fifth an antechamber in the castle, ornamented with carved scrolled walls. The sixth set is a piazza outside an Italian Renaissance building, flanked by columns. Last, of course, is the bedchamber. The bed, hidden in the center back alcove, is ornately decked with labial curtains. At first the bed's upstage location seems to marginalize Desdemona, but three sets of brightly colored curtains draped above lure the eye inward toward the recess. The entire set, in contrast to the grim action of the murder, is brightly colored in shades of blue, pink, and yellow.

Macready's elaborate scenery was symptomatic of his efforts to produce Shakespeare in historically accurate settings. Shattuck demonstrates the tragedian's meticulous attention to historical detail when he produced *King John*.[31] This concern was not confined to the history plays, however. For *Othello* accuracy meant realistic scenes from Renaissance Venice (the Rialto, bridge, canal, gondolas, and Doge's Palace) and Cyprus (the citadel at Famagusta). Though they were painted after the fact, these watercolors demonstrate the extravagant beauty of Macready's 1837 Covent Garden *Othello*, a beauty that set a high standard for subsequent spectacular, historically based productions.

Macready's quest for scenic harmony included detailed attention to costumes. For London productions no expense was spared. Watercolor sketches of the Covent Garden costumes[32] are just as detailed and colorful as the scenic designs. They too may have been used, where appropriate, in *The Merchant of Venice*. Brabantio wears a red robe trimmed with ermine over a black doublet. Gratiano, in contrast, appears in a black robe with red doublet. Othello's red tunic is fringed with gold to match his gold cape. Iago is dressed in a

[31] See Charles H. Shattuck, *William Charles Macready's King John* (Urbana: University of Illinois Press, 1962).   [32] Folger Promptbook 15, Shattuck 27. (See note 30 above.)

Figure 9: William Charles Macready as Othello.

buff doublet with a green vest and gold trim. He wears red hose and black shoes. Later, he changes to buff leggings and a blue jacket. Cassio is foppish. He sports a plumed hat, green vest, and a gold doublet slashed to show red beneath. Lodovico is more decorous in silver and blue, with hat, cape, doublet, and hose. Montano wears a

Figure 10: George Ellis' costume drawing for Iago in William Charles Macready's Covent Garden *Othello* (1837).

long white gown trimmed in red with a gold sash. The Venetian guard appears in sixteenth-century armor, while servants are appareled in rough brown jackets and doublets. White lace signifies Desdemona's purity, whereas black (with a red underskirt) suggests Emilia's earthiness. Tissue of gold or silver bespeaks an exalted station.

Red, black, gold, white, and blue – the colors create that harmonious effect Macready so cherished. Othello's red aligned him with the Venetian Senators, figures of law and authority. Emilia's red petticoat picks up the color scheme, but her scarlet indicates easy virtue. Each scene is chromatically planned, even the bed curtains' labial folds – the shapes and colors like the acting, should suggest the emotions represented onstage.

The grandeur of Macready's Covent Garden *Othello* is best conveyed by the Senate Council scene (1.3). Macready's promptbook notes:

> The Senators are discov'd seated on an elevated platform, up the sides, and aX the back of the stage. Ten in Red Gowns-/ including the Duke-Gratiano-and Brabantio / aX at back-Thirty-/ including Lodovico /- in Black Gowns, with large open ermin'd sleeves, -at sides R & L. - The Duke's seat is slightly elevated above the others.- The Secretary is seated, -writing, and faces the duke.[33]

This scene was the culmination of Macready's search in *Othello* productions for historical accuracy; this was the Doge and his Council as he envisioned it from historical research and his own visits to Venice. Macready even covered the walls of the Doge's Hall with Titians and Tintorettos.[34] He was pleased with the result: his diary of 16 October 1837 exudes that "The Council of Forty was a scene of beautiful effect, one of the most real things I ever saw.[35]

Productions in the provinces and the United States could never be this elaborate, but traveling stars could carry their costumes with them; the Moor, at least, could be seen in appropriate splendor. Even through the swamps of Georgia, from Savannah to Mobile, Macready carted mammoth trunks of resplendent costumes so that he could represent his characters as he envisioned them.

Costumes aside, Macready's careful preparation was often wasted when he left London to play with provincial casts or journeyed to the

---

[33] Folger Promptbook 13, Shattuck 25.   [34] See Hankey, *Othello*, p. 153.
[35] Pollock, *Reminiscences*, p. 416.

backwoods of America. Although he was a difficult, egocentric man who often upstaged his fellow actors, as Kean had before him, one can sympathize with the meticulous actor faced with inadequate theatres and poorly prepared casts. In Liverpool, 31 January 1850, Macready found that "The Roderigo, Mr. Brown was *drunk*!"[36] Later that year in Birmingham, Macready acted with an Othello who "actually *belaboured* [him] in the third act; it was so bad that at last [he] was obliged to resist the gentleman's 'corporal chastisement' and decline his shaking and pummelling!"[37] Perhaps such treatment was Macready's just punishment for rough handling of Desdemonas like Helena Faucit Martin. The wonder is that the perfectionist Macready could act at all with provincial and American casts too reluctant to rehearse and rather short on theatrical talent.

That Macready traveled from city to city, cast to cast, and performed Shakespeare's *Othello* night after night testifies to the uniformity of mid-nineteenth-century productions. As manager at Covent Garden and Drury Lane, Macready supervised his ideal *Othello*, a carefully designed performance in which scenery, costumes, blocking, and acting created a harmonious experience. In the provinces or outside New York and Philadelphia, the council scene might have two Senators instead of forty, but the blocking was substantially the same. So was the text.

A collation of the 1839 Macready acting edition with its pre-decessors – Mrs. Inchbald's (ca. 1808), Kemble's (1814), and Ox-berry's (based on Edmund Kean's performances, 1819) – shows that Macready's Covent Garden *Othello* was somewhat more chaste and sensitive to the delicate feelings of his audiences than his predecessors'. Like Oxberry, but unlike Kemble and Inchbald, Macready's Iago makes no reference to "making the beast with two backs." Macready's Senate scene is by design much grander, requiring forty Senators rather than his predecessors' seven. Othello's cannibals and anthropophagi are quietly eliminated in keeping with the hero's dignity. On the Cyprus quay Macready drops Iago's reference to wives as "Players in your housewifery and housewives in your beds" (2.1.132). Iago's observation that Othello "hath not yet made wanton the night with her ... " (2.2.32–34) is also removed. Instead of "Happiness to their sheets!" Iago cries, "Happiness to them!" In the temptation scene, lines 463–67 are cut, whereas Inchbald and

---

[36] Toynbee, *Diaries*, vol. II, p. 446.   [37] Ibid., p. 463.

Kemble had retained them. Macready and Oxberry also root out the kisses from Cassio's dream. The major cuts from the eighteenth century – clown, Bianca, fit, willow song scene – persist. Macready's fastidiousness climaxes in Act 4, scene 2, where he removes "Oh thou weed ... That the sense aches at thee" (77–79) and "Was this fair paper ... made to write whore upon" (82–83). He also substitutes the tame "one" for "strumpet" and "whore." In the next scene, Desdemona is not allowed to ask for her nightly apparel. Macready restores the original "Let me the curtains draw" (5.2.131), probably in reference to stage business. Hankey notes contemporary accounts of Macready's "thrilling effect" of thrusting his dark face through the curtains at Emilia's knock.[38] He closes the play – as Kean had done in performance – with Othello's last words.

Macready's purified text drops, in other words, all references to sheets, beds, going to bed, adultery, and sex. The bed behind half-closed curtains perhaps symbolizes the hidden sexuality underlying the play. While nothing remains in the revised language to offend a Victorian, the subject – adultery – was indeed salacious. Yet *Othello* was popular among all audiences, and no one apparently condemned the plot as immoral.

* * * *

Macready's London *Othello* was more sumptuous than other productions, but it nevertheless typifies a flexible production scheme shared by nearly all traveling players. As Charles H. Shattuck observes in his introduction to Macready's *King John*:

a production of *Othello* in those days might have been handsome or might have been shabby, but in the essentials of "the book" – the text and basic stage business – it would not stray far from the forms established by the histrionic tradition and community. The book of *Othello* was quite rigidly fixed, precisely because it was played so often and because every aspiring tragedian had to be ready on call to perform either of its leading roles. It was also fixed, one must note, in conformity with the *moral* tradition and community.[39]

With minor variations Macready's pristine text was used in Victorian productions throughout England and America.

A comparison of Macready promptbooks[40] with those of his contemporaries (including some from provincial theatres where

[38] Hankey, *Othello*, p. 317.   [39] Shattuck, *King John*, p. 3.
[40] Folger promptbooks 13, 14, and 15 (Shattuck 25, 26, and 27).

Macready performed) shows that blocking and staging were similar in most performances. One promptbook (Folger promptbook 26, Shattuck 32) was the property of the Edinburgh theatre and includes blocking for all the eminent Othellos who played there – Edmund Kean, Edwin Forrest, Macready, J. W. Wallack, and Edwin Booth. The following is a composite description of performances from *ca.* 1830–50, drawing on extant promptbooks at the Folger Shakespeare Library.[41] Two promptbooks come to us from American theatres where English actors frequently performed: the Tremont Theatre in Boston and the Park in New York. Despite the ocean between these theatres and Drury Lane, *Othello* in Boston and New York was much the same as it was in London.

The opening scene begins on a Venetian street, usually with painted canal and gondolas in the background. Roderigo "enters pettishly taking Stage L. then R." (PB26). When he calls to Brabantio (who appears in his nightgown at a window aloft), Iago stands "behind or in the shadows of the columns." Roderigo "restrains him by a motion of the hand" (PB26) from insulting Brabantio too bluntly. Brabantio enters, accompanied by two servants with torches and one with a sword. The servants range across the back of the stage while Brabantio and Roderigo talk.

The second scene is generally the same set or a similar one. Servants with torches flank the back of the stage. Othello takes his position at center stage between Brabantio's servants and his own men (including Iago and Cassio) – the blocking monumentalizes the Moor, focusing audience attention squarely on him. When they exit, "Othello as he is going, stops and turns towards Cassio who is R. H. and gently beckons him towards him – and Exits with his hand on Cassio's shoulder" (PB26). Or, "Brabantio first, followed by Othello, who turning offers his hand to *Cassio*. Exeunt together" (PB11). Thus the soldierly bond between Cassio and his general is stressed through gesture and blocking.

The basic set for the Senate scene consisted of a throne for the Duke, a table covered with papers, a chair for Brabantio, and perhaps seats for the other Senators. This varied according to location; as the Edinburgh promptbook notes, "This may be a council of 40 or of 10 or of 5." As the scene begins, the Messenger enters, delivers his letters to a Senator, who hands them to the Duke,

---

[41] The promptbook (PB) numbers will be indicated within the text by their Folger number.

"kneeling on the steps. then retires backwards to his place/" (PB13). All bow to the Duke on their entrance. Desdemona curtsies to the Duke as she enters, and Brabantio comes downstage to greet her. Once he is resolved that she has freely chosen to marry Othello, Brabantio takes Desdemona's hand and places it in Othello's. Then he retires to his seat. Desdemona kneels as she begs to accompany Othello; he, in turn, raises her up. As the scene concludes, "The Duke rises, and comes down LC. All the Senators rise, at the same time, -uncover their heads,-and follow him – those with 'Red Gowns', -nearest the person of the Duke,-the Black D's after him" (PB13). As in past productions, when Desdemona kneels to her father as he leaves, "he puts her from him. Othello raises her" (PB26). Or, more pathetically, "Des. kneels to Bra. seizes his hand! he throws her off, Oth. raises her" (PB30). Iago and Roderigo remain behind for their second conversation.

Act 2 begins at the Famagusta citadel on Cyprus. All the promptbooks include directions for voices, trumpets, and cannon in the background. The Edinburgh PB even states "Have band ready for march. Time near sunset" (PB26). The gentlemen kneel when Desdemona enters. Then Cassio takes Desdemona by the hand and introduces her to the gentlemen of Cyprus. Othello enters, sometimes from city or castle gates at the back of the stage. At the scene's conclusion, Roderigo begins to follow the rest but is detained by Iago. In the Edinburgh promptbook, Roderigo is at first incredulous at Iago's suggestion that Desdemona will be unfaithful; then, at the thought of attacking Cassio, "Rod. starts back a little alarmed" (PB26).

The drinking scene is staged outside the city or castle gates (usually they appear at the back of the stage in front of an alcove). The gates are flanked by soldiers and torchbearers. At Iago's insistence, Cassio brings on servants with wine. As he drinks, "Officers look at each other and begin to remark [on] his behavior. [Cassio] Turns and perceives Officers laughing at him – They shrink a little away – [Cassio] Feels for his sword to determine his R. Hand" (PB26). After Montano is wounded, Othello enters through the gates. According to Folger Promptbook 24, when he begins his exit up center stage, Othello "stops short, – looks with pity and regret at Cassio, – then Exits LC / followed by the attendants & Torch Bearers who entered with him." Or, "Oth. sighs is sorry for Cas. disgrace" (PB30). At the end of the scene, Cassio and Iago shake hands.

Surprisingly, there are fewer stage directions for the temptation scene (Shakespeare's Act 3, scene 3 but Macready's Act 3, scene 1) than any other in the promptbooks. Since the scene consists largely of interplay between two starring roles, each Iago and Othello would work out his own blocking in rehearsal. The *mise en scène* varies. Most promptbooks indicate a chamber in the castle, but two refer to a garden. Properties include chairs and a table. Charles Kean's property list calls for "Couch, or Sofa R. Scrolls for Othello. Table & Chair L. Footstool in front. Book on Table. Strawberry spotted H Kerchief for Desdemona" (Folger PB T.b.15). Othello sometimes enters reading a paper. Folger promptbook 30 suggests "Iago should watch this scene [the interplay between Othello and Desdemona] very attentively standing apart as he speaks of it – to Oth." Then, "At Cassio's Exit Desdemona retires up with Emilia and advances R at 'Twas he'" (PB26). The temptation is choreographed with Othello moving to and fro as he listens to Iago. The prompter for Folger PB 12 writes, "mind O.P Proscenium wing is firm for Mr. [Charles] Kean to lean against." Concerning Othello's "I'll know thy thoughts," Promptbook 30 cryptically observes, "Great point – Keans – hands on head – first time jealous, very low." At Iago's, "O, beware, my lord, of jealousy," promptbook 26 states, "[Othello] Recoils as if aware that he is getting jealous – and looks toward the place where Desdemona went off."

The handkerchief business is fairly standard. Desdemona lifts it to bind Othello's head; he stops her, and it falls. After their brief conversation, there is a poignant moment; according to promptbook 30, a "Long pause – Oth. looks at her – burst – embraces her very tenderly – exits in her arms, very slowly." Emilia picks up the handerchief, taunts Iago while holding it behind her back, and then he snatches it from her hand. When Othello asks for the ocular proof, he seizes Iago by the throat. Afterward, he "throws Iago off, – goes up L, – back to R, – up R, – and sinks in R. Chair" (PB24). The scene concludes as Iago joins the kneeling Moor in his vow to seek vengeance.

The next scene occurs in the same or another apartment.There is little stage business except for Emilia's exit to leave Desdemona and Othello alone – presumably she does not realize how important the handkerchief is because she is not present when it is discussed. After she returns, Desdemona creates a moment of special pathos by praying that jealousy be kept from Othello's mind: "Desdemona both hands raised to Heaven. Emilia with R. hand on Des[demona's] shoulder. The L. hand extended upwards" (PB26). The effect is reminiscent of melodrama, where the innocent heroine moves the audience to sympathetic tears.[42]

Trumpets announce Lodovico's arrival in the next scene. As he and Desdemona converse in center stage, Othello stands stage left and reads the letter recalling him to Venice. He strikes Desdemona "as he X'es to R. / She weeps" (PB13). He exits, and Lodovico, Emilia, and Iago escort Desdemona off.

The brothel scene is staged in another apartment. A door with a key in it is situated at the rear of the stage. The text is severely cut – all references to Desdemona as whore are emended or dropped. Emilia "places chair forward for Desdemona," then exit. As she goes, she should "Close and keep door fast. Des. approaches as if to comfort him" (PB26). Othello throws a purse at her feet as he leaves. Promptbook 30 reads, "throws purse a little up stage. goes to door, pause, looks at Des. for a moment, then dash open door, exit, slams it – after him." After she kneels to protest her innocence, Iago and Emilia raise her up and escort her offstage.

Nearly all promptbooks cut Shakespeare's Act 4, scene 3 and rush onto the murder of Roderigo. Promptbook 5 notes, "Green cloth down next act / Mr. McCready." The scene is a street; props include a lighted candle and nightgown or dressing gown for Iago's second entrance. Iago cuts Cassio in the leg, then reenters as if aroused from sleep. Gratiano and Lodovico raise Cassio and carry him off.

The set for the murder scene is usually an ornate bed chamber with the bed in the rear alcove carefully draped, an elaborate toilet table, a sofa and chairs.[43] The Edinburgh promptbook is most poignant: "Desdemona's shoes seen at side of bed. A Rosary and Missal in her hand which is out of bed." Othello enters, kisses Desdemona, sits down, then rises and paces to and fro. In promptbook 24 he "Goes up to bed, – touches the side of the drap'y curtains, they descend, and enclose them from the audience." Then he smothers Desdemona, finishing her off with a dagger. The prompters instruct Emilia to wait for a count of six, sixteen, or twenty before entering. Othello parts the curtains and listens, then closes the curtains and opens the door.

[42] Booth contends that in most melodramas, the heroine carries the burden of pathos. See *Theatre in the Victorian Age*, p. 157.
[43] James R. Siemon, "'Nay, that's not next': *Othello*, V. ii in Performance, 1760–1900," *Shakespeare Quarterly*, 37 (1986): 38–51 provides an invaluable overview of various ways of staging the murder scene.

Figure 11: George Ellis's drawing of the setting for the murder scene in William
Charles Macready's 1837 Covent Garden *Othello*.

Protesting her mistress' honesty, Emilia "Sinks on her knees. Othello
goes to table R. for sword. Montano perceives and follows him.
Throws his L arm over Othello's R – and takes sword from him –
Iago stabs Emilia and rushes out. Others run to assist Emila. All
rather rapid" (PB26). Emilia's body is either draped on the sofa or
carried offstage – neither action complies, of course, with her request
to be laid by her mistress' side. When Othello finally realizes the
truth, he makes some gesture to Cassio, sometimes taking him by the
hand. Often – but not always – Cassio wears the handkerchief
wrapped around his leg. At Othello's query, "Are there no stones in
heaven?" promptbook 30 reads, "Great point – the truth of Iago's
villiany [*sic*] at last dawns on him." Othello then rushes at Iago, but
Montano once again disarms him. Promptbook 24 describes the
Ensign: "Iago quietly retires up stage, gazing on the body of
Desdemona. Iago advances L. after looking with malignant satisfaction at the corse of Desdemona and the prostration of Othello.

Exits with an assumption of great bravado followed by Officers."
Promptbook 26 notes that "Iago smiles and looks triumphantly at
Othello." Promptbook 30 is even more graphic: "Iago surveys Oth
from head to foot – very slowly! then points to him with R. hand.
moves it to the Bed – strikes his breast three (3) times – 'I did it' folds
arms. Exit slowly – dashing door open."

This extended recognition allows time for the melodramatic
climax. This moment, contends Taylor, occurred with the "public
recognition of virtue after it had been forced into exile or disguise by
the menace of evil ... The audience shares the relief of the ritualistic
climax, when the characters on stage are forced to acknowledge what
the audience has known all along."[44] Here Iago makes Othello and
the Venetian onlookers recognize his responsibility for Desdemona's
death.

Othello's suicide, which in all promptbooks ends the play, is
usually blocked with the hero struggling to join Desdemona on the
bed. Promptbook 26 states that he "Endeavors to reach Desdemona's
hand which is hanging down from bed – Falls dead. Curtain slow.
With Mr. Anderson, When Othello stabs himself, Montano catches
him round the waist and prevents him from sinking quite down – He
then makes an effort to reach the bed staggers and falls." PB 13
directs, "Stagger up the side of stage, towards the bed, – and falls on
the stage, at back, C, – close in front of bed."

*   *   *   *

This was the *Othello* Macready brought to London, the English
provincial theatres, and America. Though he acted in drafty or
overheated halls with local supporting casts of abysmal talents, he
struggled to achieve the same melodramatic effects. Sometimes he
was extremely successful, appreciated by the audience and lionized
by high society. On other occasions he felt unappreciated and
homesick for his "dear Catherine" and children.

Macready made three tours to the United States. The first, from
September 1826 to June 1827, was successful. On this trip Macready
premiered his *Othello* in New York on Shakespeare's birthday (23
April 1827). But, since the actor did not begin to record the events of
his daily life until the fall of 1827, we have little evidence of his acting
and the American response to it.

---

[44] Taylor, *Players and Performances*, p. 121.

Macready's second journey to the United States, from October 1843 to September 1844, was more extensive, and his diaries reveal his reflections on American culture. While visiting Charleston, the tragedian wrote:

We went to the jail – ... I saw the negro crew of a ship locked up together until the sailing of the vessel, the law of the State not allowing them to be at liberty ... [and] some negroes below who were kept in the premises of the jail till they could be sold! Good God! is this right? They are an inferior class of man, but still they are man ... The world is a riddle to me; I am not satisfied with this country as it at present is. I think it will, it must, work out its own purification.[45]

Macready's social conscience surfaced in the North as well. Soon after his arrival in Boston, he visited the Colored Orphan Asylum. His diary reads, "I saw about seventy of these little human beings of a degraded caste eating their dinners together[.] I could not bear it."[46] Later, when Macready saw slaves being transported, he wrote, "I cannot reconcile this outrage on every law of right; it is damnable,"[47] and after seeing a sale of slaves in Mobile, he mused, "I should neither wonder nor blame if I saw these black and dusky men strike their knives into the brutal bosoms of those who assert the right of might over them."[48]

Although Macready was obviously appalled by the conditions of slavery, the diaries indicate no sense of connection between what he saw and the play he performed so often. Othello, a mighty black warrior, had in his youth been sold into slavery, yet as far as we can tell, Macready never thought to place the fictional character in the context of the slavery he saw around him. This dissociation between life and art would be less surprising if Macready – like Kean – had selected a light hue for his Moor. The actor-manager's Othello was, however, much darker than those of his contemporaries. George Vandenhoff described his colleague's Othello as "less the noble Moor ... than an enraged and desperate African, lashed into madness, and roused to thirst for blood by vindictive wrath, and implacable revenge."[49] Macready's biographer William Archer even claims that the decision to play Othello in blackface explains the actor's lack of success: "He made the initial mistake of giving him the complexion

[45] Pollock, *Reminiscences*, p. 518.   [46] Toynbee, *Diaries*, vol. II, p. 227.
[47] Ibid., p. 254.   [48] Ibid., p. 260.
[49] George Vandenhoff, *Leaves from an Actor's Notebook* (London: T. W. Cooper, 1860), pp. 232–33.

of a negro rather than a Moor."[50] Yet Macready portrayed a dark Othello not just in New York, but in Charleston, New Orleans, Mobile, and St. Louis.

Nor does there seem to have been any overt negative reaction from Macready's white, slave-owning audiences. Examination of extant newspapers in the Library of Congress from Charleston, Mobile, New Orleans, and St. Louis reveals that while papers throughout the South advertised Macready's *Othello*, they did not discuss it. Significantly, perhaps, *The St. Louis Democrat* for 17 April 1844, includes a full review of all roles Macready had performed in town – Hamlet, Richelieu, Virginius, and Werner – except Othello. In any case, the lack of controversy over Macready's *Othello* may support Charles B. Lower's argument that antebellum audiences in the United States regularly "regarded theatrical performance as Art, quite distinct from life."[51] They could accept a black Othello onstage where they would not welcome a genuine Negro.

Macready came to America seeking opportunity, fame, and wealth. He frequently toyed with the idea of resettling in the United States, partly because he sympathized with republican principles, partly because he believed America would provide a better financial base on which to support his family. As he toured the country, however, he became disillusioned with the American character. Though his earlier diaries record frequent disgust with English audiences that failed to appreciate him, such outbreaks are minor compared with his reaction to touring the United States. On 13 March 1844, he wrote from Mobile:

Acted Othello – if I may compare myself with myself, or trust to the reality and grandeur of my own feelings – *splendidly* for the first three acts. The apathy and vulgar applause of the audience – bestowed may I not say, on every one *except* myself, made the two last very laborious to me.[52]

He felt similarly unappreciated a month later in St. Louis:

Acted Iago, taking much pains with the part. The audience did not *notice* me on my appearance. ... Throughout the play, too, they really bestowed as much, if not *more*, applause upon the unmeaning rant and gabble of these people than they gave to me; and really I *tried* to act Iago in my old earnest,

---

[50] William Archer, *William Charles Macready* (London: Kegan Paul, Trench, Trubner, and Co., 1890), p. 202.

[51] Charles B. Lower, "Othello as Black on Southern Stages, Then and Now," *Shakespeare in the South: Essays on Performance*, ed. Philip C. Kolin (Jackson: University of Mississippi Press, 1983), pp. 199–228; quote from p. 216.   [52] Toynbee, *Diaries*, vol. II, p. 266.

"honest" way, but the difference is not of importance to them. In my last scene, which I was acting in a very true manner, as I was taking my departure from the room, the *continued* vulgar speeches, ejaculations, and laughs of some ruffians in the second tier quite overcame my patience. I threw up the attempt and walked right off.[53]

Later that month he declared, "I am sick of American audiences; they are not fit to have the language in which Shakspeare wrote."[54] Despite the troubled relationship between actor and audience, Macready's Othello and Iago, like those of other touring actors, brought the standardized British *Othello* onto the American frontier.

*   *   *   *

If imitation is a form of flattery, William Charles Macready (who lived until 1873) must have been flattered, for his Covent Garden *Othello* determined the play's form well into the last half of the nineteenth century. Using Ellis' promptbooks, Charles Kean took his version of the Macready *Othello* on several tours of the United States. Samuel Phelps also used Macready promptbooks to stage *Othello* at Sadler's Wells in 1844 and again in 1860.[55] In later years, Edwin Booth continuously honed his Iago, sometimes restoring the epileptic fit and the eavesdropping scene.[56] But for him, as for the later Victorian era's most famous Othello, Tommaso Salvini, the basic production scheme was still that of Macready.[57]

Along with *Macbeth, Hamlet,* and to a lesser extent, *King Lear, Othello* was one of the four cornerstones of nineteenth-century Shakespearean repertoires. As Gary Taylor persuasively argues, in the cultural environment of Victorian England (and America), "Shakespeare's artistic supremacy had ceased to be debated; it was simply assumed."[58] But even though *Othello* was recognized as a classical play, it also had tremendous audience appeal. During the first half of the nineteenth century, *Othello* appeared to a broad range of English and American audiences that encompassed all classes. In

---

[53] Ibid., p. 269.   [54] Ibid., p. 270.
[55] See Shattuck, *The Shakespeare Promptbooks*, pp. 359–60.
[56] See Daniel J. Watermeier's "Edwin Booth's Iago," *Theatre History Studies*, 6 (1986): 32–55.
[57] Salvini's Othello will be discussed at length in chapter 8. For now it should suffice to say that examination of Salvini's promptbook (an 1876 Italian–English acting edition), Folger promptbook 32, Shattuck 64, indicates that, except for Salvini's restoration of part of the willow song scene, the English text is practically identical to Macready's. There is no clown, no Bianca, no trance, and no bawdy language.
[58] Gary Taylor, *Reinventing Shakespeare: A Cultural History* (New York: Weidenfeld and Nicolson, 1989), p. 168.

a way that is perhaps difficult for us to understand today, the book of *Othello* was embedded in popular culture and parodied in minstrel shows.[59]

Othello's manly dignity appealed to Victorian conceptions of masculine honor. He was a true gentleman: noble, dignified, loving, openhearted. Desdemona's innocent beauty also suited Victorian standards of the female heroine – she should be modest and dependent. Desdemona's lines, drastically reduced from Shakespeare's script, indicate her innocence and powerlessness. Moreover, the many times she kneels to the men in authority shows her dependent position in a patriarchal society.[60]

Like many Victorian novels and plays, *Othello* flamed with sexual passion yet was eminently respectable. Macready's text muffled the drama's sexual undertones under elevated poetic language. No character uttered an indecent word; erotic passion was implied but not enacted.

Macready valued *Othello* for its domestic pathos and melodramatic terror – "the pity of it." Though his Covent Garden production sought historical accuracy in its representation of Venice and Cyprus, global politics were not the issue for Macready. Nor were racial or military concerns. *Othello* instead was interpreted in accord with Macready's own values: the most important dynamics of the play were the relationship between a husband and his wife and the bond between a gentleman and his friend. The Macready *Othello* portrayed a loving husband, beset by a scheming but appealing villain who destroys the hero's domestic and psychological harmony and causes an innocent wife to suffer and die. Iago's personal venom thus constituted a threat to what could have been a stable and happy family unit, the ideal building block of Victorian culture.

[59] See, for example, Maurice Dowling's *Othello Travestie: An Operatic Burlesque Burletta* (London: J. Duncombe and Co., n.d.), published in the 1830s. The text parodies Shakespeare's language while the action is basically the same as the Macready book. Only in the final scene is there a major change. Desdemona's ghost "rises between the lights and the bed LH." Seeing the ghost, Iago confesses and Othello repents – the final chorus shows the entire cast alive and in harmony. The burletta's satire relies heavily on the audience's knowledge of the generic *Othello* I have described above.

[60] For an intriguing discussion of Desdemona on stage, see Irene Dash, *Wooing, Wedding, and Power: Women in Shakespeare's Plays* (New York: Columbia University Press, 1981), pp. 103–30.

CHAPTER 8

Salvini, Irving, and the dissociation of intellect

[W]e have reason to cool our raging motions, our carnal stings, our unbitted lusts.

(*Othello*, 1.3.322–23)

When A. C. Bradley published his lectures on Shakespeare's major tragedies in 1904, he affirmed conceptions of Othello and Iago that were to dominate critical discourse for much of the twentieth century. To Bradley, Othello was a noble hero who "comes before us, dark and grand, with a light upon him from the sun where he was born." He is "by far the most romantic figure among Shakespeare's heroes," because

He does not belong to our world, and he seems to enter it we know not whence – almost as if from wonder-land. There is something mysterious in his descent from men of royal siege; in his wanderings in vast deserts and among marvellous peoples; in his tales of magic handkerchiefs and prophetic Sibyls; in the sudden vague glimpses we get of numberless battles and sieges in which he has played the hero and has borne a charmed life; even in chance references to his baptism, his being sold to slavery, his sojourn in Aleppo.[1]

This description exudes no overt prejudice against Othello because of his racial origins. But it does reflect late Victorian stereotypes about the passionate, exotic nature of Africans.

Bradley's view of Iago was in direct opposition to his romantic conception of the Moor. The Ensign should not be portrayed, he argued, as smouldering with a passionate desire for vengeance. The villain, in fact, has no passions. "None: that is the very horror of him. He has *less* passion than an ordinary man, and yet he does these frightful things."[2] By the time Bradley wrote these words, a

---

[1] A. C. Bradley, *Shakespearean Tragedy* (London: Macmillan, 1904), pp. 152–53.
[2] Ibid., p. 183.

dissociation between Othello's emotion and Iago's intellect had seeped into conceptions of Shakespeare's text, a dissociation that was fostered, in part, by public performances of the 1880s.

Late Victorian representations of Shakespeare's Moor powerfully influenced conceptions of *Othello* for several generations, not simply for literary critics like Bradley, but also for theatre professionals like Constantin Stanislavski.[3] Moreover, they mark a radical shift in attitudes toward Shakespeare's Moor, who could no longer be conceived in terms of similarity – the officer and gentleman of the Restoration and eighteenth century or the doting husband of Macready's productions. Now Othello was described primarily in terms of difference, the exotic Oriental or African whose nobility cloaked the passionate fury of an uncivilized savage.

Many cultural forces contributed to this shift: the aftermath of the Civil War in the United States and the expansion of the British Empire throughout the world no doubt influenced a play built around the marriage of a black man and a white woman. Within these larger forces, however, was the personalized influence of the public performances of the 1880s, particularly the widespread acclaim accorded to Tommaso Salvini for his rendition of the lead role. Iago's rationality, too, was shaped by performance during the late Victorian period. Marvin Rosenberg has commented at length about various Victorian Iagos;[4] my focus here is on one of the most influential, Henry Irving.

* * * *

The *Othello* that appeared on English and American stages during the first half of the nineteenth century – the paradigmatic touring performance outlined in the last chapter – was comparatively benign. While Othello was no longer dressed in the regalia of a British army officer (from Kemble onwards various Oriental costumes were adopted), his Otherness had not been institutionalized. In his nobility, honor, and manly dignity, he could be conceived, as Macready seems to have viewed him, as a gentleman very much "like us."

[3] See Constantin Stanislavski, *My Life in Art*, trans. J. J. Robbins (New York: Meridian Books, 1956), pp. 265–76 for a memorable account of Stanislavski's reaction to Salvini's performance.

[4] Marvin Rosenberg, *The Masks of Othello* (Berkeley: University of California Press, 1961), pp. 120–34.

By the 1870s, however, much had changed. In the United States, Civil War, Emancipation, and Reconstruction had hardened conceptions of racial difference. As Lynda E. Boose observes, the American coinage "miscegenation" didn't enter the language until 1864 when there suddenly seemed to be a need "for special taboos to mark out" any mixed sexual relationship.[5] *Othello* had been performed frequently in the American South during the first half of the nineteenth century, but after the Civil War it was seldom seen except in parodies. When he did appear, Othello was deliberately whitened, and "despite the whitening and orientalizing of the main character," contends historian Tilton G. Edelstein, "the fear of one drop of black blood in the men whom white daughters married continued to haunt and fascinate Americans with the tenacity of a morbid compulsion."[6] No matter how white the actor made Shakespeare's Moor, the character transgressed what were increasingly rigid sexual taboos.

Across the Atlantic other cultural forces altered British conceptions of *Othello*. By the 1880s the British Empire spanned the globe. Orientalism had become a respected academic discipline, as philologists and historians sought to understand the "Oriental mind." The desire to classify animals, plants, and human beings led to pseudoscientific theories of racial difference. By the time Salvini began touring as Othello in the 1870s, "Orientalism was such a system of truths that every European, in what he could say about the Orient, was consequently a racist, an imperialist, and almost totally ethnocentric."[7] Orientalism was superimposed onto theories about the biological determination of racial inequality. Influenced by Darwin's theory of natural selection, scientific writers promulgated the validity "of the division of the races into advanced and backward, or European-Aryan and Oriental-African."[8] Before the 1860s, black strangers to England were treated largely in accord with their social

---

[5] Lynda E. Boose, "The 'Getting of a Lawful Race': En-Gendering the Racial Discourse of Early Modern England," in *Women, "Race," and Writing in the Early Modern Period*, ed. Patricia Parker and Margo Hendricks (London: Routledge, 1994), pp. 35–54; quote from p. 46.

[6] Tilton G. Edelstein, "*Othello* in America: The Drama of Racial Intermarriage," in *Region, Race, and Reconstruction: Essays in Honor of C. Vann Woodward*, ed. J. Morgan Kousser and James M. McPherson (New York: Oxford University Press, 1982), pp. 179–97; quote from p. 187. For specific discussion of *Othello* in the South, see Charles B. Lower, "Othello as Black on Southern Stages, Then and Now," *Shakespeare in the South: Essays on Performance*, ed. Philip C. Kolin (Jackson: University of Mississippi, 1983), pp. 199–228.

[7] Edward W. Said, *Orientalism* (New York: Pantheon Books, 1978), p. 204.

[8] Ibid., p. 206.

standing; afterwards, contends historian Christine Bolt, it was no longer conceivable that a black man could also be a gentleman.[9] Rigid categorization of peoples of the world into "them" and "us" necessarily affected conceptions of Shakespeare's Othello.

As the century neared its close, such notions were increasingly widespread and were frequently used to justify Britain's colonial expansion and its mission to bear the "white man's burden" to other races. Race, charges Bolt, also "became a useful tool in distinguishing between the ostensibly similar white peoples of Europe, for the differences between the various racial components of Britain and Europe could assume as much significance in the Victorian mind as those between the white and coloured races."[10] Victorian racialism is further defined by Kwame Anthony Appiah as the belief that all human beings could be divided into groups

called "races," in such a way that all the members of these races shared certain fundamental, biologically heritable, moral and intellectual characteristics with each other that they did not share with members of any other race. The characteristics that each member of a race was supposed to share with every other were sometimes called the *essence* of that race; they were characteristics that were necessary and sufficient, taken together, for someone to be a member of the race.[11]

A logical consequence of racialist thinking was what historian Stuart Anderson terms "Anglo-Saxonism." Even more rigid than European ethnocentricism, Anglo-Saxonism maintained

that the civilization of the English-speaking nations was superior to that of any other group of people on the planet; and that the primacy of English and American civilization was largely due to the innate racial superiority of the people who were descended from the ancient Anglo-Saxon invaders of Britain.

People of Anglo-Saxon heritage were not simply characterized by light skin and hair, but also by traits of "industry, intelligence, adventurousness, and a talent for self-government."[12] The English-

[9] Christine Bolt, "Race and the Victorians," *British Imperialism in the Nineteenth Century*, ed. C. C. Eldridge (London: Macmillan, 1984), pp. 126–47, esp. p. 133. See also Bolt, *Victorian Attitudes to Race* (London: Routledge and Kegan Paul, 1971) and D. A. Lorimer, *Colour, Class and the Victorians* (Leicester: University of Leicester Press, 1978).

[10] Bolt, "Race and the Victorians," pp. 130–31.

[11] Kwame Anthony Appiah, "Race," in *Critical Terms for Literary Study*, ed. Frank Lentricchia and Thomas McLaughlin (Chicago: Chicago University Press, 1990), pp. 274–87. Quote from p. 276.

[12] Stuart Anderson, *Race and Rapprochement: Anglo-Saxonism and Anglo-American Relations, 1895–1904* (Rutherford, NJ: Fairleigh Dickinson University Press, 1981), p. 12.

man and his American cousin were "naturally truthful, logical and patient, as well as considerate of others and loyal to friends and country." The Anglo-Saxon was morally upright, hard-working, practical, and self-controlled; he kept his passions in check and lived a productive and moderate life.[13] Because other races were unfit for self-government, Anglo-Saxon nations had a moral imperative to take control.[14]

The emergent ideology of Anglo-Saxonism marked a shift, according to Bolt, from the ill-defined prejudices of earlier years.[15] The main factor behind this change was racial Darwinism, the belief that there was inevitable competition for supremacy among the nations of the earth.[16] That Britain controlled so much of the world proved its superiority. Because of that superiority, the Anglo-Saxons had a duty to bring their culture to the less fortunate peoples of the earth. They had a mandate to reign supreme.

It is no surprise, therefore, that the newspaper that announced Salvini's debut in the United States also reported, under the headline "FAITH IN THE ANGLO-SAXON RACE," an interview with Governor C. Walker of Virginia, in which he affirmed "the most abiding CONFIDENCE IN THE FREEDOM-LOVING AND INDEPENDENT SPIRIT of the Anglo-Saxon race" (*New York Herald*, 3 September 1873). Britons and Americans were determined never to be slaves, whether to a despotic dictator or to carnal passion.

These complex cultural forces – the establishment of tight anti-miscegenation laws in the United States, the expansion of Britain's overseas empire, and widely disseminated theories of racial Darwinism – mark a major shift from the eighteenth and earlier nineteenth centuries. Lines of difference between Othello and his white audiences had always existed, but now they were more rigidly defined and codified. Audiences continued to respond to the humanity of Shakespeare's tragic hero, only now their sense of his Otherness was stronger than it had been before.

* * * *

As a sophisticated and well-read European, Salvini perhaps represented some of these cultural forces. While preparing for the role

---

[13] Ibid., p. 20.   [14] See Bolt, "Race and the Victorians," p. 139.
[15] Bolt argues that racial attitudes, inchoate before the 1860s, changed and hardened during the later Victorian period. See ibid., p. 127.
[16] Anderson, *Race and Rapprochement*, p. 36.

of Othello, he partook of what Said describes as academic Orientalism. In his *Autobiography* the actor described how his conception of Othello was shaped:

When I took up *Othello*, I pored over the history of the Venetian Republic and that of the Moorish invasion of Spain: I studied the passions of the Moors, their art of war, their religious beliefs.[17]

This interest in historical accuracy extended to costume: according to theatre historian Marvin Carlson, Salvini took all his costumes for *Othello* "from Venetian paintings of the fifteenth century depicting Moorish officers."[18] Later in the autobiography he expressed his admiration for their physique:

At Gibraltar I spent my time studying the Moors. I was much struck by one very fine figure, majestic in walk, and Roman in face, except for a slight projection of the lower lip. The man's color was between copper and coffee, not very dark, and he had a slender mustache, and scanty curled hair on his chin.[19]

Salvini saw himself as a sophisticated European, different from the exotic Moors he studied so assiduously. But to his English and American audiences, he was equally different and exotic. Salvini never mastered English pronunciation; he performed Othello in Italian. Except for his 1873–74 tour with an Italian-speaking cast, his renditions of *Othello* were necessarily bilingual – he recited his lines in Italian while the rest of the performers spoke English, although the audience could buy the libretto in which his words were translated. The difference in language reinforced a focus on Salvini at the expense of the other actors[20] and emphasized not simply the actor's differentness from his audience but also Othello's differentness from the other characters in Shakespeare's play.

Though to many in the audience Salvini's passionate acting of Othello's most famous speeches recalled the fiery style of Edmund

[17] Tommaso Salvini, *Leaves from the Autobiography of Tommaso Salvini* (London: T. Fisher Unwin, 1893; repr. New York: Benjamin Blom, 1971), pp. 80–81.

[18] Marvin Carlson, *The Italian Shakespeareans: Performances by Ristori, Salvini, and Rossi in England and America* (Washington DC: The Folger Shakespeare Library, 1985), p. 61. See pp. 60–79 for an overview of Salvini's Othello.   [19] Salvini, *Autobiography*, pp. 139–40.

[20] It is perhaps symptomatic of the "star" quality of Salvini's *Othello* that Edward Tuckerman Mason did not bother to report on any scene in the play unless Salvini appeared in it. Thus, it is very difficult to reconstruct from the available evidence just how the other roles were played. See *The Othello of Tommaso Salvini* (New York: G. P. Putnam's Sons, 1890). Newspaper reviews also focus on Salvini, though from time to time they do mention the actors playing Iago and Desdemona.

Figure 12: Tommaso Salvini as Othello.

Kean,[21] other responses were shaped in part by cultural and racial assumptions. Theatre critic William Winter thought that Salvini represented "the Italian ideal of the part."[22] Henry James agreed, arguing that "We read [Shakespeare] in light of our Anglo-Saxon

[21] George Henry Lewes, for example, concluded from his own experience of both actors that Salvini's representation "as a whole was of more sustained excellence." See *On Actors and The Art of Acting* (London: Smith, Elder and Co., 1875), p. 267.

[22] William Winter, *Shakespeare on the Stage* (New York: Moffat, Yard and Co., 1911), p. 287.

temperament, and in doing so it is open to us to believe that we read him in the deepest way. Salvini reads him with an Italian imagination, and it is equally natural to us to believe that in so doing he misses a large part of him."[23] An American who saw Salvini perform Othello in Rome reported that, "Nothing is European in his embodiment of Othello; it is the inflammatory passion of the east bursting forth like fire, and consuming a noble and tortured nature – it is the Moor himself as Shakespeare drew him."[24]

Whether it was termed "Italian" or non-European, Salvini's performance was characteristic of what Carlson defines as an Italian school of acting that included Ernesto Rossi and Madame Ristori as well as Salvini.[25] Italian performances broke from the more restrained pattern of English acting: Italian actors seemed less studied and more flexible than their English counterparts, allowing for rapid shifts in tone. Among Italian performances, Salvini's *Othello* was judged superior to Rossi's because it seemed the most "natural," with the right combination of heroic dignity and animal furor.[26]

As Salvini's Othello gained its international reputation, it became what the late Bernard Beckerman defined as a show of skill; it featured the famous actor "*doing* something quite extraordinary," much like a magician or a gymnast.[27] And, like a magician sawing a lady in half, Salvini's performance was indefinitely repeatable.[28] Reviews from his five tours to the United States frequently comment on the same gestures and actions. Similar to opera fans waiting for their favorite aria, audiences came to Salvini's *Othello* after the first tour *expecting* the collaring scene or the suicide to be enacted in the same graphic manner. Salvini did not disappoint them.

The "show of skill" focused on the hero because whenever Salvini

[23] Henry James, *The Scenic Art: Notes on Acting and the Drama* (New Brunswick: Rutgers University Press, 1948), p. 173.

[24] William W. Story, *Roba di Roma*, quoted from David H. Fennema, "The Popular Response to Tommaso Salvini in America," *Theatre History Studies*, 2 (1982): 103–13; quote from 104.

[25] Carlson, *Italian Shakespeareans*, pp. 60–79.

[26] Henry James, for example, found Salvini compelling in the role, whereas he did not care for Rossi's representation. After a performance by Rossi, James wrote in his journal, "The interesting thing to me was to observe the Italian conception of the part – to see how crude it was, how little it expressed the hero's moral side, his depth, his dignity – anything more than his being a creature terrible in mere tantrums." From 10 April 1873, in *Italian Hours* (New York: Grove Press, 1959; repr. Westport, CT: Greenwood Press, 1977), p. 211.

[27] Bernard Beckerman, *Theatrical Presentation: Performer, Audience and Act*, ed. Gloria Brim Beckerman and William Coco (New York: Routledge, 1990), p. 15.

[28] Though the overall direction of his Othello remained stable, Salvini did sometimes try new business. Mason notes six places where he had observed variations during the many times he watched Salvini's performances. See Mason, *Salvini*, pp. 4, 14, 53, 56, 77, and 95.

appeared (except in 1886 when Edwin Booth served as his Iago), he surrounded himself with lesser known, less skillful actors.[29] Their roles, moreover, were severely reduced; as one reviewer put it, the characters of Cassio, Emilia and Roderigo "have been cut down to the merest sketches" (*Boston Globe*, 27 November 1873). Another reviewer in *Vanity Fair* (8 March 1884) wrote that "Very little can be said for Signior Salvini's supporters ... [T]he interest in the play flags woefully save when the hero is on." Salvini's version of Shakespeare's text began with Othello's entrance in Act 1, scene 2 and ended with his death in Act 5, scene 2. Even the egotistic Macready had emphasized ensemble acting; Salvini's *Othello* was very nearly a one-man show.

Whether the conditions of production were deliberate or the result of necessity, they threw the spotlight squarely on Salvini. Audiences thronged to see him, not the rest of the cast, and they were enthralled by his facial expressions, physical gestures, and emotional tone, even if they couldn't understand the Italian he was speaking. Contemporary reviews repeatedly stress the *visual* qualities of Salvini's performance. The *New York Herald*, for example, reported after the premier of 1873 that during the Council scene, "Every sentence was a picture; the speech in its entirety was a brilliant rhetorical panorama" (17 September 1873). Similarly the *Boston Globe* remarked during Salvini's 1880–81 tour that, "Prompted by the inspiration of his genius, every gesture was a study for a painter or a sculptor, and the passions of the soul animating his noble countenance verified the ideal personator ... [T]here is a striking resemblance to the antique sculptures in the contours of his splendid figure" (14 December 1880). Not understanding Salvini's words, the auditors relied on what they saw. And because Salvini, in turn, could not rely on language to convey his conception of Othello, he used a brilliant vocal range and broad gestures instead – pointing to his heart or his head if they were mentioned in the text. The result was an Othello far more physical than that of English-speaking actors.

The physicality of Salvini's conception was stressed most clearly in reactions to two controversial (and consequently memorable) episodes: the collaring scene and the Moor's suicide. The former emphasized the extreme contrast between the Moor's initial restraint

---

[29] Reviewers frequently noted the inferiority of the rest of the cast. The *New York Tribune* (20 February 1883) noted, for example, that "this was as bad an *Iago* as could be imagined outside of a country barn."

– his refusal to let Iago's insinuations upset him – and the animal fury he displayed later in the scene. At first, according to Edward Tuckerman Mason (who described the Italian actor's performances in detail from his own observations), Salvini showed "no personal feeling stronger than that of impatience at his friend's reticence."[30] Once aroused, however, Salvini's wrath was awesome. At Othello's words, "Be sure thou prove my love a whore," the actor seized Iago by the throat. Years later Stanislavski vividly recalled the scene:

He throws Iago to the floor and is on him in one leap, pressing him to the ground, leaps up, lifts his foot above Iago's head to crush it like a snake's, remains in that pause, becomes confused, turns away, and without looking at Iago offers him a hand, lifts him, and falls himself on a couch, crying like a tiger in the desert when he has lost his mate.[31]

George Henry Lewes described the same scene in less romantic, more Victorian terms:

seizing Iago and shaking him as a lion might shake a wolf, he finishes by flinging him on the ground, raises his foot to trample on the wretch – and then a sudden revulsion of feeling checks the brutality of the act, the *gentleman* masters the *animal*, and with mingled remorse and disgust he stretches forth a hand to raise him up.[32]

Here Lewes establishes an opposition between gentlemanly behavior and animal fury. In the collaring scene, moreover, Lewes found Salvini to be "emotionally perfect in expression ... [H]is whole being vibrating, his face aflame, the voice becoming more and more terrible, and yet so completely under musical control that it never approached a scream."[33] Stanislavski summarized his response succinctly: "At that moment the likeness of Salvini's Othello to a tiger was self-evident."[34] Note that both Stanislavski and Lewes chose predatory animal images – snake, tiger, and lion – to describe Salvini's body language.

The American press was less articulate but equally enthusiastic. According to the *New York Herald*, "when finally Othello, wrought to the last point of rage, lays Iago prostrate and raises his foot as though to crush him, the tableau acquired a demonic picturesqueness, a lurid and savage intensity" (17 September 1873). The *Boston Globe* gasped that "in a whirlwind of passionate anguish," Salvini hurled Iago "to the ground, and rais[ed] his foot to trample the life out of him" (27 November 1873). A reviewer for *Galaxy* described Salvini in this

[30] Mason, *Salvini*, p. 39.   [31] Stanislavski, *Life in Art*, p. 271.
[32] Lewes, *On Actors*, p. 269.   [33] Ibid., p. 269.   [34] Stanislavski, *Life in Art*, p. 271.

scene: "He counterfeits a wild beast. He crouches like a tiger in his hostile advances on Iago" (December 1873).[35] When the actor repeated this business during his 1880–81 tour, the *Boston Globe* proclaimed it as "the most terrifically realistic piece of acting ever seen" (14 December 1880).

Salvini's rendition of the murder scene also sparked heated reactions. It curiously combined extreme reticence in the enactment of Desdemona's murder with extreme exhibitionism in Othello's suicide. The actor argued that the strangling should be veiled from the audience: "The violent contortions of the executioner and the victim are more powerful if left to the imagination. Committed in the seclusion of an inner chamber, the strangling ... is intensified when hidden from the actual gaze."[36] Consequently, in Salvini's performances, Desdemona's bed was positioned behind curtains at the rear of the stage. Othello entered, delivered his opening speech ("It is the cause"), drew the curtains, and then retired to sounds of thunder in the background. Desdemona, aroused once again from her slumber, came downstage. Mason described the scene's culmination:

After saying "Weepst thou for him," etc., he drags her to her feet as she kneels, facing him; he then clutches her right arm with his right hand, and grasps her neck and head with his left hand, knotting his fingers in her loose hair, and pulling back her head, as if to break her neck. Holding her thus, he swiftly forces her up the stage, and through the curtains, which close behind them, concealing the alcove.[37]

Reactions were mixed. Henry James loved it; he considered Salvini's "tiger-like pacing at the back of the room," while "he strides to and fro, with his eyes fixed on her and filled with the light of her approaching doom" to be an "ineffaceable" theatrical moment.[38] The *Boston Globe* agreed; its critic bemoaned that from behind the curtains, Desdemona's "shrieks and groans, mingled with his hoarse and maniac cries, tells with terrible effect the frightful scene that is enacting there. It is almost too horrible to endure" (27 November 1873). William Winter, not surprisingly, hated it, complaining that Salvini's Moor was "over-sensual in his love" and "a raging fiend in his act of retribution" (*New York Tribune*, 27 April

---

[35] Quoted in Barnard Hewitt, *Theatre U.S.A.: 1668 to 1957* (New York: McGraw-Hill, 1959), p. 228.

[36] Tommaso Salvini, "Impressions of Some Shaksperean Characters," *Century*, Nov. 1881: 117–25; quote from 118.   [37] Mason, *Salvini*, p. 95.

[38] James, *The Scenic Art*, p. 174.

1886). The reviewer for the *Galaxy* concurred, charging that "The tragedy ... loses in Salvini's hands its internal grace, its precious sweetness, its spiritual depth. He makes it little else than a vulgar murder, such as is done in the Fourth and Sixth Wards where a common ruffian, believing his wife untruthful, cuts her throat, curses her corpse, and is carried drunk and raving to the station-house."[39]

While Desdemona's murder was hidden from the audience, Othello's suicide was open and palpably violent. After a moving delivery of Othello's "Soft you" speech, Salvini stepped a few paces backward. Then, in Mason's words, "he seizes the point of the curved sword with his left hand, grasps the blade, just below the hilt, with his right hand, and, leaning backward as he says 'thus' ('così'), he draws it violently across his throat, sawing backward and forward." Then he dropped the sword and staggered toward Desdemona's alcove. Before reaching her bed, he fell backward, dying "in strong convulsions of the body and the legs. Quick curtain."[40]

Salvini justified this method of suicide on the grounds of authenticity: "[T]his manner is more in accordance with the custom of the people of Africa," he claimed, "who usually execute their criminals and enemies in this way; then the arms used by these people are of a curved form, and, as such, are more adapted to this mode than to any other."[41] But such a suicide was also consistent with the tone of Salvini's overall interpretation of the role. The *Boston Globe* (27 November 1873) praised the play's final moments in which Salvini stood "like a madman at bay, full of the energy of despair, of wild anguish, unavailing remorse, and savage defiance, which culminate when he seizes himself by the throat and saws at it with his curved dagger, falling, at last, and attempting to crawl toward the body of Desdemona, while his whole frame quivers in the agony of death." Termed both "realistic and revolting" by the *Boston Globe* (16 November 1882), this suicide held audiences spellbound.

Theatre critic Joseph Knight took issue with Salvini's interpretation of Othello's death: "In the concluding scenes of the last act," he contended, "the conquest of the civilised being by the barbarian is carried out at the sacrifice of Shakspeare's intentions and at that of Art."[42] Though the suicide is "terribly realistic," it is "directly

---

[39] Quoted from Hewitt, *Theatre U.S.A.*, p. 229.   [40] Mason, *Salvini*, p. 107.
[41] Salvini, "Impressions," 124.
[42] Joseph Knight, *Theatrical Notes* (London: Lawrence and Bullen, 1893), p. 23.

opposed to Shakespeare."[43] George Henry Lewes had less trouble with Salvini's hacking his throat than with the rest of this scene: "My objection to Salvini's fifth act is that it is underfelt and overacted; ... He alternately raged and blubbered – and was never pathetic."[44]

Salvini's research into the methods of suicide commonly employed in Africa illustrates his Orientalist's approach to the role. This, he argued, was how "they" do it. Of course it strikes a civilized audience as barbaric and revolting, but it is *authentic*. Once again, Othello was associated in small but tellings ways with the uncivilized "races."

Stanislavski's reminiscences demonstrate the lasting legacy of Salvini's art. To the Russian actor/director, Salvini's performance "made a deathless monument of human passion, of jealousy, composed of a Romeo-like love, of endless trust, of hurt love, of noble honor and wrath, and of inhuman revenge ... The Othello of Salvini is a monument, a law unto eternity which can never change."[45] It was also the prototype of Bradley's romantic Moor.

Salvini's success at conveying Othello's fiery passion was often ascribed not simply to his brilliant acting skills but also to his southern Mediterranean origins. As an Italian, a man with a non-Anglo-Saxon temperament, he could convey the Moor's barbaric passions because he could also feel them. That ethnocentric English perception was illustrated by a reviewer in the *Gentleman's Magazine*, who contended in 1875 that "the nationality, the peculiar temperament, of an accomplished exponent may enable him to realise with greater truth certain of the master's conceptions – a southerner doubtless would give a more vivid and truthful colouring to Othello; and Hamlet is rather within the compass of a man of the north." Thus "Signior Salvini's southern blood serves him particularly well in the impersonation of the Moor."[46] Since the role of Othello lacked the "intellectual iridescence" of Shakespeare's other tragic roles, argued Henry James, it put "the character much more within Salvini's grasp." Othello was, after all, "a study of pure feeling."[47]

Salvini's nationality may have allowed him more scope in expressing Othello's sexuality than that enjoyed by respectable Victorians like Macready and Irving. Salvini was physical with Desdemona – he held her and kissed her – partly because that was the Italian way of displaying affection and partly because he relied

[43] Ibid., p. 24.   [44] Lewes, *On Actors*, p. 271.   [45] Stanislavski, *Life in Art*, p. 268.
[46] "'Mr. Irving and Signior Salvini' by a Parisian Critic," *Gentleman's Magazine*, NS, 14, (May 1875): 609–18; quotes from 609–10 and 617.   [47] James, *The Scenic Art*, p. 189.

on gesture rather than language for effect. Audiences seem to have
responded to Salvini's tenderness toward Desdemona. During the
Senate scene, for example, when Desdemona requested permission to
accompany him, the actor openly showed his pleasure. According to
Mason, "Othello's joy increases throughout Desdemona's speech,
and at its close he goes rapidly and impulsively to her, raising her
from her knees, and encircling her with his arm."[48] This "display of
tenderness and devoted love" was detailed by the *Boston Globe*
reviewer: "In the scene before the Senate, he gazes on Desdemona as
if his very life hung upon the sound of her voice" (27 November
1873). Emma Lazarus, too, hailed Salvini's affection in the opening
act: "The indescribable accent with which he utters the very name
of the '*divina Desdemona*' is in itself a revelation, and after the lurid
horror of the final catastrophe the music of the first tone comes back
with unforgettable pathos."[49] Twelve years later, "A Parisian
Critic" wrote in the *Gentleman's Magazine* that "In the manner in
which he, so to speak, devours Desdemona with his looks, Salvini
introduces strong touches of realism that may have taken his English
hearers by surprise, unaccustomed as they must have been to see such
manifestations on the English stage." However unprecedented, such
"realistic features" seemed "justified," especially given the Moor's
emotional temperament.[50]

Though William Winter was to interpret such effects as the display
of carnal rather than spiritual passion, Salvini claimed that Othello's

is not a sensual love; it is the pure affection of a soul which unites itself to
another, and without which he could no longer exist, – a sentiment so
profound, so intensified, and so wide that it embraces the affection of a
friend, of a brother, of a son, and of a father. It has become to him as the air
he breathes, an ever-present paradise.[51]

But despite Salvini's disclaimer, "the fierce tenderness" of his
greeting of Desdemona after arriving at Cyprus (*Boston Globe*, 16
November 1882) must have seemed surprisingly frank to a late-
nineteenth-century American audience. "Salvini, his majestic figure
set off by a suit of complete armor," recorded the 14 December 1880
Boston Globe, "rushes impetuously from the boat in which he has just
landed, into the arms of Desdemona, exclaiming 'O mia bella
guerriera,' in tones of such intense joy that the whole audience at

---

[48] Mason, *Salvini*, p. 17.
[49] Emma Lazarus, "Tommaso Salvini," *Century*, Nov. 1881: 110–17; quote from 114.
[50] "Mr. Irving and Signior Salvini," 617.   [51] Salvini, "Impressions," 123.

once seemed to enter the feeling." At the end of his speech, Salvini embraced Desdemona closely, kissed her, and stood "with his lips pressed to hers" while Iago spoke his "O, you are well tuned now" lines.[52] Before leaving the stage, he embraced her again. Clearly Salvini felt the best way to express Othello's love for his wife was through the physical gestures of kissing and touching. To some of his critics in the United States and England – William Winter, of course – this touching was too sensuous, too suggestive. Winter decried Salvini's display of "carnal passion. It lacks refinement; it lacks poetry; it lacks that feeling of awe which, commingled with human passion, is the invariable chief attribute of true love" (*New York Tribune*, 27 April 1886). Salvini's interpretation lacked, in other words, the self-discipline and refinement expected of a Victorian gentleman.

Though the role of Desdemona remained passive in comparison to Salvini's physical activity, the actor's interpretation allowed her to become more fully human, more expressive of her own passion. In the words of theatre historian Julie Hankey, Salvini brought Desdemona "back into it to be loved and hated, rather than used as a pretext for high-minded sorrow."[53] With Iago's, Cassio's, and Roderigo's lines so heavily cut, the focus was on Othello and Desdemona, caught in a tragic *Liebestod*. The lovers were transformed into more mature versions of Romeo and Juliet.

Winter's review of Salvini's performance with Edwin Booth best illustrates the binary opposition that began to dominate interpretations of the play at the end of the nineteenth century. Despite his problems with public displays of "carnal passion," Winter admitted that Salvini's Moor was "fraught with colossal force, both physical and emotional." Booth's Iago, in turn, was "vital with a splendid glow of intellectual light and brilliant with a wild lustre of monstrous wickedness" (*New York Tribune*, 27 April 1885). These opposing strengths were attributable, in part, to the actors' different styles. Nevertheless, Salvini could portray passion, Booth could convey intellect. When he played Othello to Ellen Terry's Desdemona, Booth could promise that "he would never make her black."[54] Salvini could not have made that promise, not just because his make-

---

[52] Mason, *Salvini*, p. 22.
[53] Julie Hankey, ed., *Othello* (Bristol: Bristol Classical Press, 1987), p. 87.
[54] Ellen Terry, *Ellen Terry's Memoirs* (New York: Benjamin Blom, 1969; rev. ed. of *The Story of My Life* [London, 1908]), p. 159.

up was heavier, but because his Othello was much too physical – he had to touch and embrace his Desdemona. Nor could Salvini switch roles, as Booth and Henry Irving did in 1881. By virtue of his southern temperament, he was fit to play the noble, passionate Moor, but not to portray the intellectual Ensign.

*   *   *   *

Cultural assumptions also affected late-nineteenth-century audience responses to Iago. By the 1880s the dissociation between passion and intellect evidenced in Bradley had begun. Four months after Salvini appeared as Othello in London, Irving mounted his first production of Shakespeare's tragedy at the Lyceum.[55] Unlike Salvini's one-man show, this production was carefully designed with new scenery by Hawes Craven, a musical score for the interludes, and brilliant new costumes.

To establish his hero's refinement (in contrast to Salvini's tigerish man of passion), Irving had to find the roots of his Othello in the outside world – it could not be the result of his own nature. Irving also tried, in theatre historian Alan Hughes' words, "to divert attention from the accident of race as the source of disorder."[56] To make Othello respectable once again, Irving changed the focus from the lone hero torn by passion to Othello, the good man victimized by a master deceiver. In short, he restored Iago to his full luster as the instigator of the hero's downfall.

The by-play between villain and victim was for Irving the key to Shakespeare's *Othello*. In a lecture on "The Art of Acting," delivered in Edinburgh in 1891, Irving described by-play as "the very essence of true art." He asked his audience to

Recall these scenes between Iago and Othello, and consider how the whole interest of the situation depends on the skill with which the gradual effect of the poisonous suspicion, instilled into the Moor's mind is depicted in look and tone, slight of themselves, but all contributing to the intensity of the situation.[57]

---

[55] See Rosenberg, *Masks*, pp. 73–79 and 126–28 for discussions of Irving's Othello and his 1881 Iago.

[56] Alan Hughes, *Henry Irving, Shakespearean* (Cambridge: Cambridge University Press, 1981), p. 142. In the discussion that follows I am greatly indebted to Hughes' analysis (pp. 140–51) of Irving's productions of *Othello*.

[57] Henry Irving, *The Drama: Addresses by Henry Irving* (New York: Tait, Sons and Co., 1893), p. 80. In his memoir of Henry Irving, Gordon Craig observed that "While he lived, his friend and secretary, L. F. Austin, wrote many of the lectures which have been handed down to us as by Irving." See *Henry Irving* (New York: Longmans and Green, 1930), p. 4. I am

Though Irving did not play Iago in 1876 as he did later in 1881, he selected a fine actor for the role and allowed him full scope in the part. The *Illustrated London News* (19 February 1876) responded favorably to this change: "Mr. H. Forrester's Iago is capital – thoroughly original and one of the best we have seen, besides being more natural than most. In the last act the concluding Iago-business is retained, and the villain remains on stage until the fall of the curtain." Iago had again come into his own.

Despite his careful preparation for the role, Irving's Moor was not the dignified hero he had hoped would eclipse Salvini's. He was, in fact, a colossal failure. First, Irving sought to lessen Othello's racial and cultural difference by appearing in light bronze make-up and by wearing the costume of a Venetian military officer (in contrast to Salvini's white turban). Second, his acting style – a calculated accumulation of discrete, seemingly trivial bits of business – could not convey the sustained moments of Othello's anguish. Audiences accustomed to Salvini's seemingly spontaneous emotive force did not want a mechanical Moor.

The *Illustrated Sporting and Dramatic News* (19 February 1876) commented:

Mr. Irving had evidently laboured to avoid any of the features of Salvini's performance. He has carried his eccentricity of both voice and gesture to the verge of the grotesque ... It is to be regretted that Mr. Irving's genius should select parts which by nature he is unfitted to play.

The Captious Critic agreed: "instead of giving a portrait of Shakspeare's Moor, he has produced a distorted and repulsive caricature. He has mistaken eccentricity for art, and has expended much labour and study to produce an utterly incorrect impersonation." The assumption underlying this critique is that there was a "correct impersonation," that Shakespeare's Moor was not English, let alone European. In the words of Joseph Knight, in Irving's Moor "there is more of European culture and refinement than of African imagination and heat of temperament."[58] Percy Fitzgerald, who admired Irving greatly, later recalled that the performance was "somewhat hysterical, and in his agitation the actor exhibited movements almost panther-like, with some strange

not sure what to make of such a cavalier claim, but in this chapter I cite material from Irving's lectures with the assumption that they reflect his public opinions if not his own words.   [58] Quoted from Hughes, *Henry Irving*, p. 142.

and novel notes." Moreover, Irving's physique was not suited to the role. "The ascetic face, too, was not in harmony with the dusky lineaments of 'the Moor'."[59]

But not all reactions were so negative. Some, especially those who found Salvini's Moor distasteful, fully approved of Irving's version. The *Illustrated London News*, for example, bemoaned the vulgar misconception that Othello "is a naturally jealous Moor, who because of his clime and colour, is predisposed to the dirtiest of all passions, the most debasing, and the most unjust." Irving, it argued, could not take the vulgar view, because he "is a thinking actor, and gives us in his delineations the fruits of his intelligence ... Mr. Irving's Othello is at present the best of all his impersonations" (19 February 1876).The prevailing view, however, was that Irving resembled "an infuriated Sepoy" in the role. The actor speedily ended the run and switched to a safer vehicle, Tennyson's *Queen Mary*.[60]

Irving's conception of Shakespeare's tragedy as the depiction of a harmonious world destroyed by a loveless and insecure villain – a melodramatic approach, if you will – also underlay the second production he mounted in 1881. In this version, the relationship between Iago and Othello was further emphasized by the actor-manager's decision to alternate the Iago/Othello roles with the respected American actor Edwin Booth. In addition, this version of *Othello* featured a third "star," Ellen Terry, as Desdemona. The result turned out to be good box office, but it also necessitated ensemble acting that was quite different from Salvini's one-man show.

Irving's Othello was judged an improvement over his 1876 rendition, but the actor's greatest success was his portrayal of Iago to Booth's Moor. Irving's study book, extant in the Harvard Theatre Collection, indicates his conception of both roles.[61] Moreover, Ellen Terry's study book, housed with all her personal playbooks at Smallhythe, reveals not just her business as Desdemona but her comments about the other roles, particularly Othello.[62] Drawing

[59] Percy Fitzgerald, *Henry Irving: A Record of Twenty Years at the Lyceum* (London: Chapman and Hall, 1893), p. 72.

[60] So says Madeleine Bingham in *Henry Irving and the Victorian Theatre* (London: George Allen and Unwin, 1978), p. 110.

[61] The quotes that follow are taken from Henry Irving's signed promptbook for the Lyceum, 1881, no. 65T-115 in the Harvard Theatre Collection (Shattuck no. 73). They consist of marginal comments and bits of stage business that appear in Irving's hand.

[62] The quotations from Ellen Terry that follow are from her handwritten marginal notes. I am grateful to the Curator at Smallhythe, who allowed me access to this valuable material.

upon marginal notations in both playbooks, one can reconstruct the basic lines of the 1881 production. My primary focus here is on Iago.

Irving differentiated his production immediately from Salvini's by beginning with Iago and Roderigo. When the Ensign completed his explanation with the statement "I am not what I am," his manner was to be "Reflectively sadly alone." This wistful pause broke with the admonition to "Call up her Father." The Iago pushed Roderigo forward: "Push Rod. Push Rod. Push. Iago leans against door standing bare with his hat. push Rod." As the scene concluded, Iago was to "smack hands. takes him L. Rod. stays him."

In the Council scene, Irving's Iago continued his nervous mannerisms. They were apparently intended to signify the Ensign's insecurity, but they were sometimes criticized by reviewers as distracting. The promptbook shows Irving's Iago, "Looking at fingers & biting them," even as he professes that "I hate the Moor." While the soliloquy progressed, he continued to look at his fingers and brushed "his hair back 2 or 3 times." In the final lines, he underlined his point by "shaking fingers."

The Cyprus quay scene began with Iago bowing to Desdemona and she to him. All sexual innuendo was cut from the Ensign's badinage, though the misogyny of his speech must still have been apparent. Ellen Terry's study book shows her attempts to be merry, indicating laughter at "is he not a most prophane and liberal counselor?" She also noted Othello's entrance, "all happy." Irving's playbook shows that his most famous piece of business in this scene was Iago calmly eating grapes. Ellen Terry recorded her response in her *Memoirs*: "Could one ever forget those grapes which he plucked in the first act, and slowly ate, spitting out the seeds, as if each one represented a worthy virtue to be put out of his mouth?"[63]

Ellen Terry's playbook notes that at the end of this scene Iago appeared "blunt & tough" to Roderigo. Irving's study book has the Ensign fiddling with his fingers again, "slowly finger to lip." He "commandingly" pushed Roderigo off, then spoke his soliloquy "standing still." As he reflected on his plot against Cassio, he "laughingly" played with his hat. Iago exited slowly, still "laughing ... hand behind him." Terry wondered at this point about Iago's desire to be evened with Cassio "wife for wife"; "Does it mean the beast makes up to Desdemona?" Apparently Irving's Iago did not.

---

[63] Terry, *Memoirs*, p. 161.

Mr. HENRY IRVING
(*Iago*).

Figure 13: Henry Stephen Ludlow's engraving of "Henry Irving as Iago."

During the temptation scene, the interaction between the Moor and his Ensign built gradually as Iago probed and parried. The Ensign's nervous mannerisms – all that business with his fingers – was calculated to show his introspective insecurity. Othello, in contrast, was initially confident, but by the time Desdemona reentered at line 279, he seemed doubt-ridden. Thus, when Irving's Moor murmured to his wife, "I am to blame," the stage business reads, "Faintly. Rubbing himself – hand to head. Suddenly stopping her. looks at her – smiles – goes off suddenly – she looks worried at Emilia & follows."

Iago's response to Desdemona at the end of the brothel scene indicates something of Irving's power as an actor. In her *Memoirs*, Ellen Terry recalled:

My greatest triumph as Desdemona was not gained with the audience but with Henry Irving! He found my endeavors to accept comfort from Iago so pathetic that they brought the tears to his eyes. It was the oddest sensation when I said, "O, good Iago, what shall I do to win my lord again?" to look up – my own eyes dry, for Desdemona is past crying then – and see Henry's eyes at their biggest, and most luminous, soft and full of tears! He was, in spite of Iago and in spite of his power of identifying himself with the part, very deeply moved by my acting. But he knew how to turn it to his purpose: he obtrusively took the tears with his fingers and blew his nose with much feeling, softly and long (so much expression there is, by the way, in blowing the nose on stage), so that the audience might think his emotion a fresh stroke of hypocrisy.[64]

The scene concluded, according to Irving's study book, with Iago taking Desdemona by the hand. He "Gives her to Em. who conducts her to door." Terry's Desdemona was later criticized for flinging herself upon the bosom of Iago and accepting "the consolation of his embraces and caresses. The wives of commanding officers should not be wont to accept comfort at the hands of subalterns."[65]

The study books reveal both the secret of Irving's success as Iago and his failure as Othello. Hughes aptly describes Irving's conception of the Ensign: he "seems to have played Iago as a vulnerable, insecure cynic who committed dreadful crimes, probably for the first time, when the promotion of an honest fool like Cassio threatened his anarchic vision."[66] The stage business outlined above – playing with his fingers or his hat – was no doubt intended to convey that

---

[64] Ibid., p. 160. [65] Bingham, *Henry Irving*, p. 169.
[66] Hughes, *Henry Irving*, p. 146.

insecurity, though nervous mannerisms were characteristic of Irving's acting style. While the business may seem disjointed as described in Irving's study book, overall it seems to have achieved the desired effect. The *Illustrated Sporting and Dramatic News*, for example, raved that

> Mr. Irving's Iago proves to be perhaps his finest Shakespearean impersonation ... The soliloquy in which the traitor thinks out his hellish plot is for the first time rendered unconventionally. It is the spoken contemplation of one who is piecing together a puzzle, and the very restlessness of the man, is characteristic of his mental activity. He constantly changes his attitude as he lounges by the table, slowly swings now one leg, and then another, passes his hand over his hair, and rubs his ear in meditation. The whole growth of this "monstrous birth" is indicated in all its stages with the rarest and most delicate art. (7 May 1881)

Everyone recognized that *thought* went into Irving's Iago. As Francis Marshall wrote in 1883, "His Iago, who speaks from brain to brain, comes as near perfection as anything he has done."[67]

Many years later, actor George R. Fosse discussed the discrepancy between Irving's Othello and his Iago; once again, the explanation is based partly on abilities but partly on racial characteristics:

> It is very difficult for an Englishman to simulate convincingly the blind rage and overwhelming passion of Othello, and almost impossible to fall into the swoon without being ludicrous; therefore the best Othellos have come to us from the south. Salvini, Rossi, Grassi, Paul Robeson.

Irving, Fosse concluded, made an interesting Othello, but unfortunately "In heavy tragic parts his mannerisms sometimes obtruded themselves at tragic moments with very comic effect." With Irving's Iago, on the other hand, "these peculiarities were of great assistance to him and helped him in his rapid changes from grave to gay."[68]

Irving's difficulties were not simply the result of his techniques, his style, or his angular physique, though certainly these were important in his failure at Othello.[69] His troubles were also the result of hardened lines of racial difference that had come to permeate British culture. When Irving first played Othello, he tried to minimize the

[67] Francis A. Marshall, *Henry Irving: Actor and Manager: A Criticism of a Critic's Criticism* (London: George Routledge and Sons, 1883), p. 76.

[68] George R. Fosse, *What the Author Meant* (London: Oxford University Press, 1930), pp. 78–80.

[69] Rosenberg attributes Irving's failure to physical qualities and mannerisms. See *Masks*, p. 77.

differences, but in 1881 he gave in, wearing heavy, black make-up and exotic Moorish costumes. Though he wore the guise of a "man of southern temperament," he could not doff his English sensibilities. Thus he succeeded as Othello in the play's early scenes when the Moor is in control, dignified, and restrained. From the temptation scene onward, he failed to convey the passionate fury audiences expected.

*   *   *   *

During the 1870s and 1880s, the heightened sense of racial division described earlier in this chapter coalesced with the disparate talents of two actors, Tommaso Salvini and Henry Irving, to affirm the expectations of English and American audiences that Othello should be passionate, Iago should be rational and controlled. It had been possible in the eighteenth century to play the Moor as a British military officer with dark skin, as a well-intentioned gentleman who succumbs to jealousy. A century later, Irving's attempt to restore Othello's "Englishness" and make him "one of us" was outdated. A radical shift, symptomatic of ideological changes in the larger culture, had taken place. At the height of the British Empire, Shakespeare's opposition between Venetians and Turks – the civilized man and the infidel – was subsumed in the split between Europeans and those races "without the law," to use Rudyard Kipling's phrase. Embedded, too, in the late-nineteenth-century assumption of racial difference was a bifurcation between thought and feeling that affected responses to Shakespeare's *Othello*. Long before Bradley wrote in 1904, the split had taken place.

Later, in the fourth decade of the twentieth century, audiences began to embrace a black Othello and find his racial difference a badge of honor, not a signifier of his propensity toward savage fury.

CHAPTER 9

"The Ethiopian Moor": Paul Robeson's Othello

Haply for I am black.

(Othello, 3.3.265)

Cultural assumptions – comprised of many forces, including Orientalism, racial Darwinism, and Anglo-Saxonism – were based on pejorative categories of racial difference, yet they made the debut of a black actor as Othello possible, if not inevitable. Once Othello had been identified as a role difficult for cold "Anglo-Saxon" temperaments and more suitable for those from southern climes, it was easier to conceive of a black actor in the role. Many potential viewers would still believe that no Negro could or should mix with white actors on a public stage; others rejected Salvini's approach, preferring English Othellos who were "high and chivalrous."[1] But some audiences were ready for a change, particularly when they watched a young African American actor enthrall audiences with his magnificent physique and singing voice in the 1928 production of *Showboat* at Drury Lane. Paul Robeson was not, of course, the first black man to enact Othello in a white cast to a white audience. During the nineteenth century, Ira Aldridge left the United States because of its segregated theatre and spent a long career acting Othello on the provincial stages of England and in Europe. But though Aldridge was acclaimed as the "African Roscius," he was barred from the United States and from the prime professional theatres of London, Drury Lane and Covent Garden.[2] It wasn't until 1930 that a black American actor would play Othello to a London

---

[1] See Julie Hankey, ed., *Othello* (Bristol: Bristol Classical Press, 1987), pp. 89–91 and 96–99 for a discussion of the white actors who portrayed Othello during the early part of the twentieth century.

[2] For a full biography of Aldridge, see Herbert Marshall and Mildred Stock, *Ira Aldridge: The Negro Tragedian* (London: Rockliff, 1958).

audience in a major theatre, and only in 1943 was the color barrier broken on Broadway; both of these firsts featured Paul Robeson.

Although the 1930 and 1943 Robeson productions of *Othello* were haunted by fear of public reaction to an openly sexual relationship between a black man and a white woman, they bravely and openly presented an African American Moor. Even so, the reactions from some participants in the productions and from the critics who saw them indicate how and deeply engrained white racism had become.

*   *   *   *

Paul Robeson's debut as Othello is usually treated by theatre historians – to use Macbeth's words – as a mere "prologue to the swelling theme," his Broadway triumph in Margaret Webster's production of 1943.[3] Whether the 1930 *Othello* succeeded as theatre or not (in many respects it seems to have failed), it made theatre history. The Savoy production lost money, but it established Paul Robeson, son of a former slave, as worthy of serious attention by London drama critics in the country of Shakespeare's birth. By working with trained English Shakespeareans (young though they were at the time) like Ralph Richardson (Roderigo), Peggy Ashcroft (Desdemona), and Sybil Thorndike (Emilia), Robeson was legitimized as an actor. Though he was doubly handicapped in London theatrical circles as an American and a black, Robeson's success in London made possible his later Broadway success.

The 1930 Savoy *Othello* is not only important for being Robeson's debut. The production itself displays difficulties the entire cast felt about breaking the color taboo to feature a black husband kissing a white wife in a public theatre. This was a concern to all, but especially to Robeson. After the opening performance, Robeson admitted in an interview that " 'I was a little disturbed ... when we started rehearsals, and rumors of an objection to a colored actor playing with a white girl came to my notice. I felt that in London trouble couldn't possibly arise on racial grounds. People here are too broadminded for that' " (*New York Times*, 22 May 1930). Fourteen years later he recalled the interview and his fears at the time:

When I set up as an actor, I didn't know how to get from one side of the stage to the other. When I started playing *Othello* – in London, that is, I was almost as bad. And I wasn't helped a bit when Hannen Swaffer – you know

---

[3] See, for example, Errol Hill's discussion of Robeson in *Shakespeare in Sable: A History of Black Shakespearean Actors* (Amherst: University of Massachusetts Press, 1984), pp. 120–30.

about Swaff, anything for a headline – brought up the question of how the public will take to seeing a Negro make love to a white woman and throw her around the stage. Now probably most people that didn't bother a bit – but it sure bothered me. For the first two weeks in every scene I played with Desdemona, that girl couldn't get near to me, I was backin' away from her all the time. I was like a plantation hand in the parlor, that clumsy. But the notices were good. I got over it. (*New York Times*, 16 January 1944, Drama Section)

While publicly Robeson expressed faith in the good will of his British audience, his later comment shows his fear of breaking the color barrier. He was not alone. In a memoir written to Robeson biographer Martin Bauml Duberman, Peggy Ashcroft remembered the run as her first experience in racism:

I had never encountered it or thought about it before... but there were many manifestations of it during this production. For example, Sybil [Thorndike] and I received several abusive letters and post-cards for appearing with Paul; and we were shocked to find that the actor who was playing Othello at the Savoy Theatre, was persona non grata in the Savoy Hotel.[4]

Robeson was only thirty-two years old at the time and naturally apprehensive. According to his 1967 biographer, Edwin P. Hoyt, "A few weeks before the opening, long after all was settled that he *would* open, he suggested to Maurice Browne that he was inadequate for the part and that the producer ought to find another actor. It was too late, even if Browne had been willing to make a change. Browne said so, as gently as he could."[5] Duberman's more recent biography takes a different stance, noting that "Robeson realized from the first that his director and his Iago were hopeless."[6] Whatever the explanation, Robeson's fears and ambivalence were not misplaced, for the reviewers – favorable or unfavorable – all allude to his race as the primary fact of the production. Moreover, whether the principals were conscious of it or not, fear of the audience's response and reticence about shocking its sensibilities seem to have shaped the entire production and guaranteed its financial failure. While the quality of acting is a primary factor in a production's success or

[4] From a memoir written to Martin Bauml Duberman, now in the Martin B. Duberman Collection at the Moorland-Spingarn Research Center at Howard University.
[5] Edwin P. Hoyt, *Paul Robeson: The American Othello* (Cleveland: World Publishing Co., 1967), p. 50.
[6] Martin Bauml Duberman, *Paul Robeson* (New York: Alfred A. Knopf, 1989), p. 134.

failure, the set contributes importantly to shaping audience response. Space can suggest relations between characters – hierarchical or equal – and it can incorporate (engage) or distance (detach) the audience. Most experienced designers are conscious of the semiotics of their craft and know that shapes, colors, props, furniture, and space itself signify a broad range of conventional meanings. The designer for the Savoy 1930 *Othello* had no experience with staging, however. James Pryde, as reviewers were quick to point out, was a successful artist who had never worked in the theatre. As Herbert Farjeon ruefully commented after the opening performance, "being a painter of pictures, he does all he can to emphasize the pictorial aspect of the production, with consequences which would kill the finest acting stone dead."[7] James Agate described the set's major drawback: "[N]early the whole of the play was produced up-stage and in remote corners, and we got the result that the tragedy appeared to be taking place not in our midst but in the next room."[8]

The Savoy's structure was part of the problem. Ashley Dukes reported that since the Savoy was "a house with a broad orchestral pit that apparently cannot be converted into an apron stage, the scenes for the most part were played too far from the audience."[9] Because of poor lighting, the lack of an apron stage, and pictorial set design, the actors were lost. And to make matters worse, the set was underlighted so that the Savoy's gaudy frame would not compete for audience attention with Pryde's designs.

Director Maurice Browne's souvenir promptbook[10] reveals that reviewers were right. Photographs show five steps leading up from the middle of the stage; the sets were designed for the area above these steps – the back of the stage. Entrances and exits were from center stage back. The opening scene, for example, presented Brabantio's balcony at the rear of the stage. According to the diagrams in the promptbook, the front stage area was used only for Cassio's entrance in Act 1, scene 2. Roderigo's and Iago's conversation took place upstage, hidden in the dark from the audience's view. The lighting was so dark, recalls Peggy Ashcroft, that "there

---

[7] Herbert Farjeon, *The Shakespearean Scene* (London: Hutchinson, n.d.), p. 165.

[8] James Agate, *Brief Chronicles: A Survey of the Plays of Shakespeare and the Elizabethans in Actual Performance* (London: Jonathan Cape, 1943), p. 288.

[9] Ashley Dukes, "The English Scene: Europe in London," *Theatre Arts Monthly* (August 1930): 645.

[10] Quotations are taken from *Othello* promptbook Fo. 2, which is extant in the Folger Shakespeare Library.

was not much Ralph could do as Roderigo – except for himself when, deprived of lighting by a director, who had a passion for the dark, he managed to light himself, hand on spear, and torch up his sleeve, for his long speech in Act 1!"[11]

The Council Scene was equally inaccessible. The Duke appeared on a raised throne at the back of the stage. The Senators entered from downstage but spent the bulk of the scene seated at the rear left and right. They reacted to Othello's eloquent speeches, notes the promptbook, but it is difficult to imagine how the audience could see, let alone share, their response.

The promptbook emphasizes this remote staging. Only three scenes permitted the actors to make good use of the downstage area: the herald's speech, the willow song scene between Desdemona and Emilia, and the last-act attack on Cassio. Presumably these scenes were played in front of the mid-stage curtain at the top of the steps so that the elaborate furnishings of Pryde's set could be changed. The effect, however, must have been to distance physical and emotional activity from the audience, keeping them as far as possible from the immediate experience.

In short, whether Pryde and producer Ellen Van Volkenburg intended to or not, the set contained the revolutionary impulses embedded in the production by keeping black Othello and white Desdemona far from the audience. Take, for example, the play's most inflammatory scene, the murder of Desdemona. As James Siemon has brilliantly shown, a production's use of space in this scene, particularly the placement of Desdemona's bed, tells us much about the emotional experience the audience is intended to share.[12] The promptbook's photograph of the final scene makes clear that in this production the audience was to be sheltered from the full brutality of the strangling. The bed is at the far back of the stage, the pillow toward the audience; implausibly tall bed-curtains dwarf the space where Desdemona must lie, monumentalizing the *idea* of the bed but obscuring its occupants from sight. If the viewers could see Peggy Ashcroft's recumbent form at all, they were not likely to see much of her face. The promptbook's comments on stage business show that she was allowed to sit up in bed, to "attempt to catch hold of Othello who draws back." At her exclamation, "Alas, he is betray'd and I

[11] From Peggy Ashcroft's memoir. See note 4 above.
[12] James Siemon, "'Nay, that's not next': *Othello*, V. ii in Performance, 1760–1900," *Shakespeare Quarterly*, 37 (1986): 38–51.

Figure 14: James Pryde's set for the murder scene in the Savoy Theatre's 1930 production of *Othello*.

undone!" the prompter states, "Othello's hands on Des throat pushes her down." Othello "Stifles Des with pillow." When she no longer moves: "Des relaxes fingers of Right hand." Then Othello must "move fwd. Sees Des hand which he folds across her breast draws curtain." Desdemona never left the shelter of that fortress-like bed. Aldridge and Salvini pulled their Desdemonas from their beds, dragged them across the stage by the hair, and brutally strangled them with bare hands. Peggy Ashcroft's Desdemona was politely and chastely stifled with a pillow.

Insecurity about the audience's willingness to accept him may also have affected Robeson's performance. He was particularly anxious about his American speech and worried whether he could adjust to the English accents of his supporting cast. Robeson's wife quoted him in her 1930 tribute, *Paul Robeson, Negro*, written during preparation for the production:

Paul was happy in his work. "When I do *Othello* they'll all expect a crusted American accent. I'll fool 'em. I'll do the role in good honest English, as pure as I can make it, because pure English will bring out the music of the text. Why, I might as well sing the Negro dialect of the spirituals with a correct Boston accent, as do Othello in 'American'." He was like a small boy in his enthusiasm and intense activity.[13]

[13] Eslanda Goode Robeson, *Paul Robeson, Negro* (New York: Harper and Brothers, 1930), p. 165.

Later, he thought that this concern about speech patterns had interfered with his impersonation; he confessed to Margaret Webster that he was "so overwhelmed at the thought of playing Shakespeare at all, especially in London, with his unmistakeable American accent, that he never reached the point of looking Othello in the eye."[14]

But if he was worried about his American accent, he also knew that his race might affect English audiences negatively. Julie Hankey quotes from an interview Robeson conducted with the *Observer* (18 May 1930); *Othello*, he noted, "is a tragedy of racial conflict; a tragedy of honour rather than of jealousy ... [I]t is because he is an alien among white people that his mind works so quickly, for he feels dishonour more deeply."[15] As a victim of racial prejudice throughout his life, Robeson saw Othello as an underdog, a stranger in someone else's culture whose experience was by definition akin to his own. Othello, he contended,

in the Venice of that time was in practically the same position as a coloured man in America to-day. He was a general, and while he could be valuable as a fighter he was tolerated, just as a negro who could save New York from a disaster would become a great man overnight.

So soon, however, as Othello wanted a white woman, Desdemona, everything was changed, just as New York would be indignant if their coloured man married a white woman.[16]

This conviction informed his representation of Othello. For biographer Hoyt, "The secret was that his success, his power, lay in *his* representation of the tragedy and pathos of a black man in a white world ... He would concentrate, Paul said, on portraying the suffering of the Negro in the role of the Moor."[17]

Robeson also felt alienated from his producer and director. Duberman reports that both Robeson and his wife Eslanda concluded that Ellen Van Volkenburg was a racist. She not only approved a set designed to Robeson's disadvantage, but she also "pasted a disfiguring beard and goatee on Robeson and until the final scene dressed him in unsuitably long Elizabethan garments (including tights, puffed sleeves, and doublets), instead of Moorish robes, which would have naturally enhanced the dignity of his performance."[18]

---

[14] Hankey, *Othello*, p. 100.   [15] Ibid., p. 100.
[16] Paul Robeson, "My Fight for Fame. How Shakespeare Paved My Way to Stardom," *Pearson's Weekly*, 5 April 1930, p. 1100.   [17] Hoyt, *Robeson*, p. 51.
[18] Duberman, *Robeson*, p. 136.

Robeson's understandable lack of confidence was noted by reviewers and assessed according to their various preconceptions. Ashley Dukes wrote with a mixture of praise and reservation that

Robeson brings to his part the special and sensational appeal of a Negro actor; he brings also a noble voice, a tremendous presence, and an infinite simplicity that is of the elemental forest and not at all of the world of Renaissance Europe as seen through the mind of Stratford. He brings an infinite humility, too; and that must detract from the rank and prestige of the man Othello, who will never lose an audience's affection from having his own share of vanity.[19]

James Agate argued in his review that Robeson "did not trust his power *as an actor* sufficiently; he certainly did not take the risk, with the result that all that Othello ought to be throughout the first two acts he was not." Agate then extended his critique beyond language to Robeson's stage presence: "He walked with a stoop, his body sagged, his hands appeared to hang below his knees, and his whole bearing, gait, and diction were full of humility and apology: the inferiority complex in a word." Agate summed up the performance in overtly and offensively racist terms: "This was nigger Shakespeare."[20] Herbert Farjeon noticed a similar lack of command: "He was the underdog from the start. The cares of 'Old Man River' were still upon him. He was a member of a subject race, still dragging the chains of his ancestors." "Shakespeare wrote this part," Farjeon concluded, "for a white man to play."[21] For Agate and Farjeon the color line had been violated; by definition Robeson was not fit to play the noble Moor.

If racism pervades these critiques in obvious ways, it appears more subtly in the reviewers who praised Robeson's performance. Believing fully in the concept of "the romantic Moor," they lauded Robeson's performance because he succeeded in presenting Othello as the truly primitive man he was meant to be. As a Negro (primitive man), Robeson could convey Othello's true character more faithfully than a white (nonprimitive) actor. The *Illustrated Sporting and Dramatic News*' "Captious Critic" praised Robeson as an Othello who "looms majestic, larger than human." This is why

You may say that Robeson might fail with western and northern characters, that his triumph is merely because the simple nature of Othello is that of his

---

[19] Dukes, "The English Scene," 645.   [20] Agate, *Brief Chronicles*, pp. 285–87.
[21] Farjeon, *Shakespearean Scene*, p. 166.

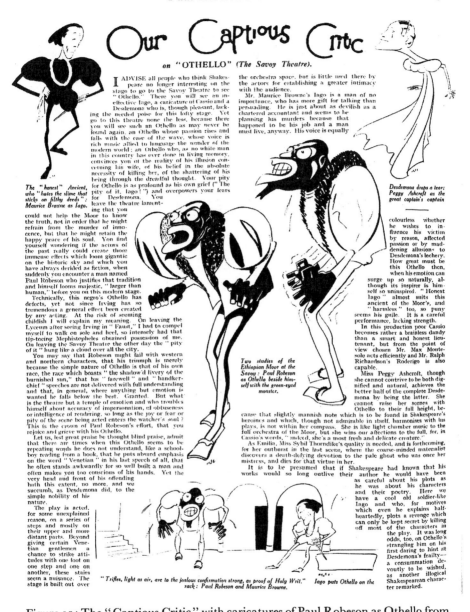

Our Captious Critic

on "OTHELLO" *(The Savoy Theatre).*

I ADVISE all people who think Shakespeare no longer interesting on the stage to go to the Savoy Theatre to see "Othello." There you will see an ineffective Iago, a caricature of Cassio and a Desdemona who is, though pleasant, lacking the needed poise for this lofty stage. Yet go to this theatre none the less, because there you will see such an Othello as may never be found again, an Othello whose passion rises and falls with the ease of the wave, whose voice is rich music allied to language the wonder of the modern world; an Othello who, as no white man in this country has ever done in living memory, convinces you of the reality of his illusion concerning his wife, of his belief in the absolute necessity of killing her, of the shattering of his being through the dreadful thought. Your pity for Othello is as profound as his own grief (" The pity of it, Iago!") and overpowers your fears for Desdemona. You leave the theatre lamenting that you

The "honest" Ancient, who "hates the slime that sticks on filthy deeds": Maurice Browne as Iago.

could not help the Moor to know the truth, not in order that he might refrain from the murder of innocence, but that he might retain the happy peace of his soul. You find yourself wondering if the actors of the past really could create those immense effects which loom gigantic on the historic sky and which you have always derided as fiction, when suddenly you encounter a man named Paul Robeson who justifies that tradition and himself looms majestic, "larger than human," before you on this modern stage.

Technically, this negro's Othello has defects, yet not since Irving has so tremendous a general effect been created by any acting. At the risk of seeming childish I will explain my meaning. On leaving the Lyceum after seeing Irving in "Faust," I had to compel myself to walk on sole and heel, so intensely had that tip-toeing Mephistopheles obtained possession of me. On leaving the Savoy Theatre the other day the "pity of it" hung like a cloud over all the city.

You may say that Robeson might fail with western and northern characters, that his triumph is merely because the simple nature of Othello is that of his own race, the race which boasts "the shadow'd livery of the burnished sun," that his "farewell" and "handkerchief" speeches are not delivered with full understanding and that, in general, where anything but emotion is wanted he falls below the best. Granted. But what is the theatre but a temple of emotion and who troubles himself about accuracy of impersonation, of obtuseness or intelligence of rendering, so long as the joy or fear or pity of the scene being acted enters the watcher's soul? This is the crown of Paul Robeson's effort, that you rejoice and grieve with his Othello.

Let us, lest great praise be thought blind praise, admit that there are times when this Othello seems to be repeating words he does not understand, like a schoolboy reading from a book, that he puts absurd emphasis on the word "Venetian" in his last speech of all, that he often stands awkwardly for so well built a man and often makes you too conscious of his hands. Yet the very head and front of his offending hath this extent, no more, and we succumb, as Desdemona did, to the simple nobility of his nature.

The play is acted, for some unexplained reason, on a series of steps and mostly on their upper and more distant parts. Beyond giving certain Venetian gentlemen a chance to strike attitudes with one foot on one step and one on another, these stairs seem a nuisance. The stage is built out over

Two studies of the Ethiopian Moor at the Savoy: Paul Robeson as Othello beside himself with the green-eyed monster.

the orchestra space, but is little used there by the actors for establishing a greater intimacy with the audience.

Mr. Maurice Browne's Iago is a man of no importance, who has more gift for talking than persuading. He is just about as devilish as a chartered accountant and seems to be planning his murders because that happened to be his job and a man must live, anyway. His voice is equally

Desdemona drops a tear; Peggy Ashcroft as the great captain's captain

colourless whether he wishes to influence his victim by reason, affected passion or by maddening allusions to Desdemona's lechery. How great must be this Othello then, when his emotion can surge up so naturally, although its inspirer is himself so uninspired. "Honest Iago" almost suits this ancient of the Moor's, and "harmless" too, so puny seems his guile. It is a careful performance, lacking strength.

In this production poor Cassio becomes rather a brainless dandy than a smart and honest lieutenant, but from the point of view chosen Mr. Max Montesole acts efficiently and Mr. Ralph Richardson's Roderigo is also capable.

Miss Peggy Ashcroft, though she cannot contrive to be both dignified and natural, achieves the better half of the complete Desdemona by being the latter. She cannot raise her scenes with Othello to their full height, because that slightly mannish note which is to be found in Shakespeare's heroines and which, though not admirable in itself, harmonises with his plays, is not within her compass. She is like light chamber music to the full orchestra of the Moor, but she wins our affections to the full, for, in Cassio's words, "indeed, she's a most fresh and delicate creature."

As Emilia, Miss Sybil Thorndike's quality is needed, and is forthcoming, for her outburst in the last scene, where the coarse-minded materialist discovers a death-defying devotion to the pale ghost who was once her mistress, and dies for that virtue in her.

It is to be presumed that if Shakespeare had known that his works would so long outlive their author he would have been as careful about his plots as he was about his characters and their poetry. Here we have a cool old soldier-like Iago and who, for motives which even he explains half-heartedly, plots a revenge which can only be kept secret by killing off most of the characters in the play. It was long odds, too, on Othello's strangling him on his first daring to hint at Desdemona's frailty—a consummation devoutly to be wished, as another illogical Shakespearean character remarked.

"Trifles, light as air, are to the jealous confirmation strong, as proof of Holy Writ." Iago puts Othello on the rack: Paul Robeson and Maurice Browne.

Figure 15: The "Captious Critic" with caricatures of Paul Robeson as Othello from the *Illustrated Sporting and Dramatic News* (7 June 1930).

own race, the race which boasts "the shadow'd livery of the burnished sun," that his "farewell" and "handkerchief" speeches are not delivered with full understanding and that, in general, where anything but emotion is wanted he falls below the best. Granted. But what is the theatre but a temple of emotion and who troubles himself about accuracy of impersonation, of obtuseness or intelligence of rendering, so long as the joy or fear or pity of the scene being acted enters the watcher's soul? This is the crown of Paul Robeson's effort, that you rejoice and grieve with his Othello. (7 June 1930)

This praise is accompanied by cartoon drawings of "The Ethiopian Moor" that caricature a black man with grossly thick lips and bug-eyes, a monkey-like figure who surely suggests the "primitive." The subsequent page provides black and white illustrations from the production, but these are well-lighted close-ups, depicting Robeson and Ashcroft on intimate terms. They hardly reflect what must have been the actual visual experience of the Savoy production.

John Dover Wilson saw the 1930 *Othello*, and later argued on the basis of that performance in his 1957 New Cambridge edition that Othello had to be black. His rationale stemmed from his recollection of Robeson:

I felt I was seeing the tragedy for the first time, not merely because of Robeson's acting, which despite a few petty faults of technique was magnificent, but because the fact that he was a true Negro seemed to floodlight the whole drama ... [T]he trustfulness and simplicity which Bradley among others notes as Othello's seem his by nature when he is played by a Negro gifted with all the winning integrity of that race.[22]

In sum, despite some generous praise, the reviews reveal that although Robeson hoped that his appearance on the London stage as Othello would overcome at least one barrier of racial prejudice, his performance confirmed rather than contradicted many of the racial stereotypes embedded in traditional literary criticism and cherished by his white British audience.

A contributing factor was director Maurice Browne's performance as Iago. Van Volkenburg and Browne, observes Duberman, both homosexual themselves, were "fascinated with the 'psychological dimensions' of the play and urged on Paul the theory ... that Iago's motivation was best explained as a result of his having fallen in love with Othello. When Paul asked for specific direction, he got instead

---

[22] John Dover Wilson and Alice Walker, eds., *Othello* (Cambridge: Cambridge University Press, 1957), pp. x–xii.

patronization. "[23] It was clear to Robeson early into rehearsals that Browne was unsuitable both as a director and in the role of Iago. The reviewers agreed.

The Captious Critic of the *Illustrated Sporting and Dramatic News* wrote:

Mr. Maurice Browne's Iago is a man of no importance, who has more gift for talking than persuading. He is just about as devilish as a chartered accountant and seems to be planning his murders because that happened to be his job and a man must live anyway.

Dukes described Browne's Iago as well thought out, but "it wants the physical vitality, the mercury of the character that should run through every scene and leave no trace, and yet should run and glisten and poison the whole. "[24] Farjeon lamented, "I have rarely seen a less conspicuous or impressive Iago than that of Mr. Maurice Browne who, looking rather like Hamlet, appeared to be cut out for anything but villainy. He spoke his part without a trace of relish. "[25] Agate, predictably, was more vivid: "He trotted through the play like Jack Point in a temper, some schoolboy whipping a top, some incommensurate gnat. "[26]

The critics implied the synergistic relationship between Iago and Othello, but they never stressed it, although the relationship is the foundation of the play. If Othello is felled by a mere gnat, how can he win our respect? Making matters worse, the Savoy production cut the bulk of Iago's soliloquies. Ten lines of his remarks in Act 1, scene 3, for example, are cut, as are the last seventeen lines Iago speaks after the Senate scene. Gone is Iago's desire to even himself with Othello wife for wife. Gone is the poison that gnaws his entrails. Similarly, his ironic comments after the brawl on Cyprus are lopped; from the twenty-seven-line soliloquy, only four remain. Instead of a spider relentlessly weaving a web to enmesh them all, Browne fashioned a perfunctory and mechanical villain.

The emasculation of Iago has inevitable effects on Othello. If Iago is not perceived as having a powerful influence on the protagonist, his fall becomes the inevitable outpouring of his own passionate nature. What the critics sensed but never openly stated is that Browne's gnat-like Iago necessarily made Robeson's Othello seem obtuse; the noble hero became a simple primitive quickly yielding to his inherent

---

[23] Duberman, *Robeson*, p. 134.
[24] Dukes, "The English Scene," 645
[25] Farjeon, *Shakespearean Scene*, p. 167.
[26] Agate, *Brief Chronicles*, p. 289.

barbarism. If Robeson did not seem intellectual, there was little in Browne's Iago to be intellectual about. Passion was the only available route into the character. The more "English" Browne was in his reticence, the more passionately "African" Robeson seemed by contrast.

Despite its financial loss, the 1930 Savoy *Othello* helped make Robeson's 1943 performance possible. His success in Eugene O'Neill's *The Emperor Jones* had established him as an actor of great power; *Othello* provided credentials from the classical theatre. The critical notice he received made the debut a success, criticism of the production notwithstanding. As Hoyt concluded, "With all its imperfections, the London *Othello* was magnificent. ... The success of *Othello* changed Paul Robeson's life in several ways. First of all, he was recognized as an important actor as well as a curiosity."[27] Such recognition was clearly important to Robeson. "Othello has taken away from me all kinds of fears," he proclaimed, "all sense of limitation, and all racial prejudice. Othello has opened to me new and wider fields; in a word, Othello has made me free!"[28]

Soon after the Savoy production closed, in theatre historian Errol Hill's words, "negotiations were begun to take the production across the Atlantic. Sentiment against mixed casting ran high in America, however, and the idea of a transfer to Broadway was shelved."[29] A less public but more important reason may have been Browne's refusal to relinquish rights to the production.[30] When Margaret Webster later asked Browne to enact Iago in an American *Othello*, he refused, arguing that feelings against miscegenation ran too strong in the United States. In order to raise money and support for her production, Webster had to repeat again and again that an American audience indeed could and would allow a white woman to be kissed by a black actor.

*　　*　　*　　*

The obstacles Paul Robeson faced at the Savoy Theatre in 1930 could not overshadow his victory for African Americans in general and for himself as an actor. His triumph was in London, however, not his native land. There segregation was not only a way of life, but legally institutionalized. In 1924, when Robeson appeared with a

[27] Hoyt, *Robeson*, pp. 52–53.　　[28] Quoted from Duberman, *Robeson*, p. 137.
[29] Hill, *Shakespeare in Sable*, p. 124.　　[30] See Duberman, *Robeson*, p. 138.

white actress in O'Neill's *All God's Chillun Got Wings*, she required an escort from the theatre each evening to prevent racist attacks.[31] Crossing the color barrier in the United States took great courage.

By 1942, however, Robeson had teamed with the British actor-director Margaret Webster. At the suggestion of Eva Le Gallienne, they selected two relatively unknown actors for the roles of Desdemona and Iago: Uta Hagen and Jose Ferrer. To economize on rehearsal time and money, Webster decided to portray Emilia herself. Roderigo was portrayed by George Keene, Cassio by Ernest Graves, and Lodovico by Phillip Huston.

Webster and Robeson could not at first find backing for their production. Broadway producers were too frightened of taboos against miscegenation. As Webster later recalled in her autobiography, "Stars wouldn't play Iago, nor, of course, Desdemona. It had been all right, they said, for Peggy Ashcroft to do it in London, but she was English and that was London. In America – a white girl play love scenes with a *black* man ... they were appalled."[32] Webster settled for a trial run in two academic venues, Harvard and Princeton, where the audience would, presumably, be more tolerant.

Margaret Webster's *Othello* opened cautiously at the Brattle Theatre on 10 August 1942, where it received an uproariously positive response; then it continued to Princeton, New Jersey, where it again received rave reviews. Only after these successes were Broadway producers willing to bring Robeson's Othello to New York. After some delays, the play opened 19 October 1943 on Broadway, under the sponsorship of the Theatre Guild, where it ran for 296 performances.[33] Later the production toured forty-five cities and returned to Broadway for a final two weeks. At that time it was the longest running and most successful Shakespearean production ever mounted in the United States.

The details of the 1943 New York *Othello* have been chronicled by Webster herself in her autobiography. Writing nearly thirty years

---

[31] For a full account of the difficulties surrounding Margaret Webster's 1943 production of *Othello*, see Susan Spector, "Margaret Webster's *Othello*: The Principal Players Versus the Director," *Theatre History Studies*, 6 (1986): 93–108 and Duberman, *Robeson*, pp. 263–79. The following analysis is heavily indebted to both accounts.

[32] Margaret Webster, *Don't Put Your Daughter on the Stage* (New York: Alfred A. Knopf, 1972), p. 107.

[33] For a marvelous array of photographs from the production, see Susan Robeson, *The Whole World in His Hands: A Pictorial Biography of Paul Robeson* (Secaucus, NJ: Citadel Press, 1981), pp. 143–51.

Figure 16: The program cover from Margaret Webster's 1943–44 production at the Shubert Theatre, New York, featuring Paul Robeson as Othello.

later, she expressed reservations about Robeson's acting ability,[34] an attitude that was caused, according to Duberman, by a profound difference about acting techniques. "Webster superimposed surface effects, and what Robeson most needed and wanted was inner exploration. Her formalistic gifts and perceptions came out like prose essays, the content impressive and difficult for an actor to dispute – but equally difficult to translate into performance skills." Duberman concluded that "It was not, for Robeson, a fruitful way."[35] Despite their cultural and conceptual differences, Webster and Robeson both worked extraordinarily hard to make their *Othello* work.

Margaret Webster's repeated insistence that *Othello* was meant to be portrayed by a black man helped make possible Robeson's greatest triumph in the role. It did not, however, mean that she escaped the late nineteenth century's racial thinking about Othello. In her book of commentary on Shakespeare's plays, she underscored her belief in the Moor's primitive qualities:

He is more somber, profound and dangerous, primitive in simplicity, primitive also in violence, alien in blood. The gulf which divides him from Desdemona, once their first concord has been broken, is much more than a difference of pigmentation, though this is an essential part of it. It is a gulf between two races, one old and soft in the ways of civilization, the other close to the jungle and the burning, desert sands. It divides him from his officers and men, from his Senatorial superiors, from the whole society by which he is surrounded, its religion, morals, conventions and habits of living ... The conviction of difference must be instant and all pervasive.

Robeson, an African American, was best able to convey these qualities:

When Paul Robeson stepped onto the stage for the very first time, when he spoke his very first line, he immediately, by his very presence, brought an incalculable sense of reality to the entire play. Here was a great man, a man of simplicity and strength; here also was a black man. We believed that he could command the armies of Venice; we knew that he would always be alien to its society.[36]

No white actor could meet this fundamental requirement.

Robeson, too, was deeply aware of his race as a factor in the production. Duberman concludes, for example, that the actor intended "to make of his portrayal a political statement beyond the

[34] Webster, *Don't Put Your Daughter*, pp. 109–11. [35] Duberman, *Robeson*, p. 271.
[36] Margaret Webster, *Shakespeare Without Tears* (New York: Capricorn Books, 1975; orig. pub. 1955), pp. 178–79.

purview of art – while preserving the integrity of his performance as art."[37] Through Othello, Robeson hoped to convey the dignity and humanity of his people. Later, he analyzed Othello in an interview with theatre historian Marvin Rosenberg:

Shakespeare meant Othello to be a "black moor" from Africa, an African of the highest nobility of heritage ... But the color is essentially secondary – except as it emphasizes the difference in *culture* ... Shakespeare's Othello has learned to live in a strange society, but he is not *of* it – as an easterner today might pick up western manners and not be western. Othello's personal, racial dignity is involved in his love. He might have been much slower to suspicion if his wife had been of the same background. But he is intensely proud of his color and culture; in the end, even as he kills, his honor is at stake, not simply as a human being and as a lover, but as Othello. The honor of his whole culture is involved.[38]

To Robeson, who actively researched the history and culture of Africa, Othello was not "primitive" at all, but a noble warrior of great accomplishments. This conception accorded with his overall view of his world, for in Duberman's words, "Unlike many black leaders of the subsequent generation, ... Robeson continued to stress the success rather than the pathology of black life."[39] Robeson also used his success as Othello to speak out for racial equality, for a world where there is "no high and no low, no superior and no inferior – but equals, assigned to different tasks in the building of a new and richer human society."[40] The House Committee on Un-American Activities' revocation of his passport during the 1950s for supposedly Communist leanings is but one indication that such egalitarian aspirations were to remain unrealized during his lifetime.

Robeson appeared as Othello again in a Royal Shakespeare Company production at Stratford during 1959. Directed by Tony Richardson, the production featured Sam Wanamaker as Iago and Mary Ure as Desdemona and ran for seven months. Once again, Robeson played a "romantic Moor – steadfast, dignified, honorable, put-upon, loving –" but this time he was at odds with the flashy effects of a production that also featured "rock-and-roll drumbeats, Great Danes dashing across the footlights, a deathbed scene enacted on an elevated platform."[41] Peggy Ashcroft, who saw this *Othello*,

[37] Duberman, *Robeson*, p. 273.
[38] Marvin Rosenberg, *The Masks of Othello* (Berkeley: University of California Press, 1961), p. 195.   [39] Duberman, *Robeson*, p. 267.
[40] Paul Robeson, "Some Reflections on *Othello* and the Nature of our Time," *The American Scholar*, 14 (1945): 391–92; quote from 392.   [41] Duberman, *Robeson*, pp. 476–77.

commented in her memoir, "I think that his performance could be said to have dimmed and one felt again that he had been directed in a production that did not suit his particular genius."[42] Despite his difficulties with Margaret Webster, only she, it seems, was able to bring out the full power of Robeson's Othello.

*   *   *   *

Paul Robeson's Othello had tremendous repercussions for the twentieth-century's understanding of the play and the title role. It not only influenced the efforts of black actors such as James Earl Jones (who saw and admired Robeson's Moor),[43] but also white actors such as Sir Laurence Olivier. But if Robeson's interpretation of Othello had a lasting impact, it by no means closed the issue of race in *Othello*.

As theatre historian Martin L. Wine wrote in 1984, "The initial impression of natural strength and dignity that Robeson brought to Othello gave rise to the much debated, though ultimately pointless, question of whether white actors should attempt the role at all."[44] Pointless or not, the debate continues. When Sir Laurence Olivier chose total black body make-up for his National Theatre production in 1964–65, the decision aroused understandable controversy. The BBC/Time-Life production's casting of Anthony Hopkins in the title role also sparked negative reactions. And in 1987 I heard Sir Ian McKellen state in an interview with Michael Kahn at the Folger Shakespeare Theatre that he had no plans to essay the role of Othello, and that in our time, no white actor should. Two years later he attained great acclaim as Iago in an RSC production at The Other Place in Stratford.[45]

Othello's blackness also became an issue in 1987 when Janet Suzman directed the first professional production of *Othello* in South Africa with a black actor in the title role. The Market Theatre production featured John Kani as Othello and Richard Haddon Haines as Iago. According to a newspaper report, Kani and Suzman believed that *Othello* "with its focus on the destruction of an interracial marriage, contains important messages for South Africans." In the program notes Suzman wrote: "The overtones, undercurrents and reverberations for our country are hauntingly

---

[42] From Peggy Ashcroft's memoir. See note 4.   [43] See Duberman, *Robeson*, p. 279.
[44] Martin L. Wine, *Othello: Texts and Performance* (London: Macmillan, 1984), p. 47.
[45] See chapter 11 below.

evident" (*Washington Post*, 6 September 1987). Whatever its success as theatre, staging *Othello* in the context of apartheid was a strong political statement; the videotaped stage play, shown at the 1992 convention of the Shakespeare Association of America, is understandably more moving to an audience who knows *where* the performance was staged and *why* it was symbolically important.

Multiracial casting, now prominent in the urban theatres of England and the United States, is likely to affect *Othello* productions in the future. During the 1989–90 Folger Shakespeare Theatre season in Washington DC two African Americans – Andre Braugher as Iago and Avery Brooks as Othello – changed the racial dimensions of the play. The presence of a black Iago, for example, explained Othello's absolute trust in his Ensign; it became logical that he should believe a black comrade in arms before a white wife. But at the same time, it removed the issue of race as a factor in Iago's motivation, blurring the obvious racism the Ensign displays under Brabantio's window. In an interview director Hal Scott, himself an African American, argued,

"I have always believed in casting the best actor for the role, but in the past, producers would prejudge the casting of a part solely on the basis of someone's skin color. I don't believe you have to be forced to cast anyone – just give an equal opportunity for any actor to be seen for a role regardless of his race."[46]

Now that multiracial casting is increasingly prevalent in the theatres of England and America, the interpretation of Othello's character along racial stereotypes and cultural assumptions is likely to change too.

As the twentieth century closes, we remain far from Scott's goal. The color prejudice Shakespeare depicted in Renaissance Venice still thrives. Still, the increasing prevalence of multiracial casting indicates that much has changed since Paul Robeson's "Ethiopian Moor" first spoke the Othello music in 1930. In the words of James Earl Jones, "Just by his presence, he commanded that nobody play him cheap. And that was astounding to see in 1943."[47] Paul Robeson opened up *Othello* to new resonances, forcing audiences and critics alike to debate – if not to solve – the racial issues embedded in Shakespeare's text.

[46] Christopher Olsen, "The dynamic duo from *Othello*: Avery Brooks and Hal Scott," *Intermission* (January 1991): 4–6; quote from 4.

[47] Quoted in Duberman, *Robeson*, p. 279.

CHAPTER 10

Orson Welles and the patriarchal eye

Would you, the supervisor, grossly gape on? Behold her topped?
(*Othello*, 3.3.396–97)

Paul Robeson's Othello was informed by the racial prejudice he experienced throughout his life: race was the most important dynamic of the play, what fueled the actors' dramatic conflicts and the audience's response. When Orson Welles filmed his cinematic adaptation of *Othello* in the late 1940s, however, he minimized race as an issue. Though he is best known for his idiosyncratic cinematic style in a handful of experimental films, Orson Welles began his career in the theatre, first at school and then at the Gate Theatre in Dublin. In both venues Welles was exposed to Shakespeare as a classical icon of English culture. *Othello* was special to him not because of its racial themes, but because it was one of Shakespeare's greatest tragedies. "Othello's blackness does not count for much in Welles," contends Peter S. Donaldson. "He is played as very light-complexioned, not at all rude or exotic in speech or manner, and little emphasis is given to lines that evoke his strangeness or cultural alterity."[1]

Welles focused instead on the emotional relationship between Othello and Iago, displaying Desdemona as the object of masculine exchange, the pawn in an intense psychological struggle between the men who surround her. Barbara Hodgdon has perceptively suggested the outlines of such an interpretation. In Welles' *Othello* she finds Desdemona transformed into a "textual body which is signified upon in order to legitimate or resist strategic, shared cultural assumptions, fantasies, and obsessions concerning male subjectivity and female

[1] Peter S. Donaldson, *Shakespearean Films / Shakespearean Directors* (Boston: Unwin Hyman, 1990), p. 118. As will be apparent, this chapter relies heavily on Donaldson's psychoanalytic reading of Welles's *Othello*.

objectification."[2] Constructed by a male auteur who was known to have difficulty in his own relationships with women, Welles' *Othello* fetishizes the female body and demonstrates the tyranny of the male gaze. My purpose here is to pursue these dynamics in greater detail and to relate them to the history of *Othello* interpretation and appropriation explored in this book.

A close examination of Welles' ninety-minute film reveals, moreover, that though much of the text is cut (making this film an adaptation rather than a straightforward representation), Welles draws upon concepts that are embedded within the text (outlined in chapter 4), that construct Desdemona as the object of masculine sexual anxiety. As a filmic adaptation, Welles' *Othello* exploits this aspect of Shakespeare's tragedy, translating the dramatist's poetic imagery into visual signifiers.[3] While other filmic treatments of Shakespeare's play emphasize a variety of elements (race is highlighted, for example, in Stuart Burge's film of Olivier's National Theatre *Othello*), Welles' *film noir* version centers squarely on the female body and the camera functions as a patriarchal eye.

While it may seem incongruous to switch to film this far along in a study of theatrical representations, my goal is to situate *Othello* within the culture at large. From the mid-1940s – starting with Sir Laurence Olivier's wartime *Henry V* – to the present – Franco Zeffirelli's *Hamlet* and Kenneth Branagh's *Much Ado About Nothing*, for example – Shakespeare's texts have reached their largest audiences through film. While Welles' *Othello* was never a popular film in the same sense, it has probably been seen by more people than any contemporary theatrical production and its visual imagery reflects some mid-twentieth-century western stereotypes.

*   *   *   *

Orson Welles lived the life of a celebrity whose escapades were avidly charted in the popular press. Since his death, two substantial biographies have recounted in detail the ups and downs of his frenetic life.[4] A *Wunderkind* from his youth, Welles scored his greatest successes

---

[2] Barbara Hodgdon, "Kiss Me Deadly: or, The Des/Demonized Spectacle," *Othello: New Perspectives*, ed. Virginia Mason Vaughan and Kent Cartwright (Cranbury, NJ: Fairleigh Dickinson University Press, 1991), pp. 214–55, esp. pp. 222–28; quote from p. 217.

[3] Jack Jorgens brilliantly analyzes Welles's use of visual imagery in his discussion of the film. See *Shakespeare on Film* (Bloomington: Indiana University Press, 1977), pp. 175–90.

[4] Barbara Leaming's *Orson Welles* (New York: Viking, 1985) was in press when Welles died in 1985 and it draws heavily on interviews Leaming had with the director over a period of

(*Citizen Kane* in particular) early in life. He was a whirling dervish – frantically planning new projects, desperately trying to finish those already half-completed, enthusiastically meeting people, gorging himself on food and drink, exploring new places, and pursuing a variety of women. In the first half of his life, his gargantuan appetites focused on sexual conquest, but in his later years – as his girth proclaimed – on food and wine.

Welles' relations with women were difficult, to say the least. He married three times: the first at twenty years of age to Virginia Nicholson, the second to Rita Hayworth (a marriage that broke up just as Welles began planning his *Othello*); the third to Italian actress Paola Mori. Each marriage produced a daughter and ended in divorce or, in the case of Paola Mori, estrangement. Welles also engaged in countless affairs, but sustained few sexual relationships for more than a few years.[5]

His notoriety prompted repeated interviews about his attitudes toward women. The comments he made, whether flippant or serious, reveal a man who viewed woman as inalterably Other and, therefore, opaque and difficult to understand. In 1947, shortly before *Othello* began, he told interviewer John Ralph that no woman could be an idealist. "'There never was such a woman.' He sat down again. 'Idealism,' he said, 'is entirely masculine.' He was emphatic, final." Women, moreover, were to Welles ineluctably different. "'They are practical. They are more sensible. They are more realistic. But they have no sense of humour and they do not dream.'" Nor could they love as intensely as men, though Welles admitted, "'when a woman loves successfully it is certainly a love more mature than any man is capable of.'" Woman, claimed Welles, "'used to be what men wanted her to be ... She was an ideal defined by man.'"[6] Four years later, when *Othello* was in its final editing, Welles repeated this theme. Women, he declared, "are practical, sensible, realistic. But they cannot love deeply, they have no sense of

several years. More recent is Frank Brady's *Citizen Welles* (New York: Charles Scribner's Sons, 1989).

[5] Leaming quotes Welles's secretary, Shifra Haran, who explained the actor-director's womanizing: "I always felt that he was trying to prove his virility" (italics deleted). See Leaming, *Orson Welles*, p. 296. Brady criticizes Leaming for focusing on Welles's affairs, but he admits that between Welles's first and second marriages, at least, "he freely engaged in one extramarital affair or brief encounter after the other in rapid succession" (*Citizen Welles*, p. 226).

[6] *Sunday Graphic*, 3 August 1947. Newspaper clipping from the British Film Institute.

humour and they cannot dream. There never was a woman who was an idealist. "[7]

These conversations suggest that in Welles' personal life, woman was the object of desire, the focus of romantic quests, and a bitter source of masculine anxiety and rivalry. Once she became known, the mystery disappeared, the tension and desire dissipated. Yet the ego depended upon her for validation. An episode at the time he began *Othello* (recounted by biographer Barbara Leaming) is illustrative. He had fallen in love with an Italian actress with a "face like a spoon" (presumably Lea Padovani), but she refused his advances, which only increased his desire. Welles recalled that

I knew perfectly well that I was acting like an idiot. I couldn't help it! The reason is so egotistical and unspeakable. You see, I have been blessed by some kind of interior sexual mechanism, where if a girl is not ever going to say yes, something clicks, and I don't want it. This had given me the impression that no woman in the world would refuse me if I tried hard enough ... It was the total novelty: I had everything to offer her and she wouldn't have anything to do with me.

Finally, Welles successfully bedded this Italian actress, only to discover that she had been sleeping with a member of his *Othello* film crew. "'What happened was that I slowly realized that she was going to bed with him all the time, and had been from the beginning. It slowly dawned on me that I was the biggest cuckold in Italy.'"[8] So for Welles in this period, life mirrored art. Othello's desire to possess a woman exclusively and his discovery of her infidelity were paralleled in Welles' own sexual saga, but fortunately with less drastic results.

Life mirrored art for Welles' relationships with the men of *Othello* as well. When he cast the film, he called on Micheál MacLiammoir to play Iago and his partner, Hilton Edwards, for Brabantio. The three men were an odd triangle, for though Welles' sexual drives were directed toward women, he held Hilton Edwards in high esteem. MacLiammoir was jealous. Welles recalled the ensuing psychological tension: "'He was always *on* – ferociously *on* –' says Orson of MacLiammoir, 'not to show his jealousy about Hilton, you see. Because Hilton loved me – I think Hilton genuinely did – at the moments when he was not under Micheál's influence.'"[9] Welles, like

---

[7] Paul Holt, "Orson Welles: Born to Genius," [no title] 30 May 1951. Newspaper clipping from the British Film Institute.　　　[8] Leaming, *Orson Welles*, pp. 360–61.
[9] Ibid., p. 367.

Othello, had the upper hand in this psychological tug-of-war; he was not only the financier who paid MacLiammoir's salary but the film's star and director. He shaped MacLiammoir's representation of Iago with the concept of impotence, a concept the Irish actor tried to disprove in real life by seducing members of the Mogador police force.[10]

MacLiammoir, understandably, omitted such details from his memoir of the production. He did, however, recount Welles' directions for Iago:

no single trace of the Mephistophelean Iago is to be used: no conscious villainy; a common man, clever as a waggonload of monkeys, his thought never on the present moment but always on the move after the move after next; a business man dealing in destruction with neatness, method, and a proper pleasure in his work.[11]

One can't know whether MacLiammoir played upon his jealousy of Welles in his representation of Iago, but as film critic Peter Cowie notes, he "gives Iago a lean and hungry look. He appears forever to be harbouring resentment, not merely against the Moor but against the world in general. A terrible loneliness exists within him." Cowie also describes MacLiammoir's appearance: "Time after time the wind blows his hair about his face, making him look like some predatory animal; his headgear resembles a vulture's straggling hood."[12]

As MacLiammoir's memoir reveals, he, like Iago, was obsessed with his male partners in *Othello*: Edwards and Welles. The Desdemonas were of passing interest but not important to his emotional life. The film shows Iago more often than any other character, usually as the onlooker who gazes from aloft or aside at Othello as much as at Desdemona. In the interface between life and art, the casting of MacLiammoir as Iago added an extratextual charge to the film, highlighting homoerotic dynamics of Iago's motivation that many critics have identified as inherent in Shakespeare's text.[13]

---

[10] Ibid., pp. 370–71.

[11] Micheál MacLiammoir, *Put Money in Thy Purse* (London: Methuen and Co., 1952; repr. London: Columbus Books, 1976), p. 27.

[12] Peter Cowie, *The Cinema of Orson Welles* (New York: Da Capo Press, 1983; repr. of *A Ribbon of Dreams: The Cinema of Orson Welles* [South Brunswick: A. S. Barnes, 1973]), p. 119.

[13] See, for example, Stanley Edgar Hyman, *Iago: Some Approaches to the Illusion of His Motivation* (New York: Atheneum, 1970); Robert Rogers, "Endopsychic Drama in Othello," *Shakespeare Quarterly*, 20 (1969): 205–15; and Jean Melon, "Etude sur la psychopathologie du mariage interethnique," *Feuillets psychiatriques de Liège*, 5 (1972): 5–14.

It is not surprising then that Welles' 1978 documentary, *The Making of Othello*, reveals the three men – at a dinner table – recalling the events that happened thirty years earlier. No women appear, though Suzanne Cloutier (Desdemona) was still alive and could, presumably, have contributed a woman's perspective. During their table talk, Welles openly refers to his film as "monumentally male," and to its hero's story as a "monumentally male tragedy."[14] As the conversation continues, the men speak of Desdemona as the locus of masculine passion. In Welles' art, as in his life, the female was an object to be discussed, not a subject to speak for herself. Or, as Peter Stallybrass remarks of Shakespeare's *Othello*, "woman's body could be imagined as the passive terrain on which the inequalities of masculine power were fought out."[15]

*   *   *   *

While the male members of his cast were easily selected, Welles had trouble finding a Desdemona. He began filming in Venice with Italian actress Lea Padovani, despite her inability to speak English. Welles insisted to MacLiammoir that this linguistic deficiency was no problem, for her voice could be dubbed.[16] As long as the body was right, someone else could speak for her. But when Welles' affair with Padovani ended, he sought a substitute female body. He turned to a French actress, Cécile Aubry, described in MacLiammoir's memoir as "Small, delicate, long hair like pale sunshine, looks about sixteen, irrepressible and heart-breaking smile. Obviously not a dry eye in the house when Othello starts knocking her about."[17] Aubry, described by MacLiammoir as the "true ingenue," left after one day's rehearsal to take another film role. Welles continued work on the film, shooting scenes in which Desdemona did not appear.[18]

A third Desdemona was soon found in Betsy Blair; MacLiammoir

---

[14] I was reminded of this phrase by Kathy Howlett's insightful but as yet unpublished essay, "Voyeurism in Orson Welles' *Othello*," which is part of a longer project she is completing on Shakespearean films. While our examinations of Welles's *Othello* overlap somewhat, my focus is more directly on Desdemona than is hers.

[15] Peter Stallybrass, "Patriarchal Territories: The Body Enclosed," in *Rewriting the Renaissance: The Discourses of Sexual Difference in Early Modern Europe*, ed. Margaret W. Ferguson, Maureen Quilligan, and Nancy J. Vickers (Chicago: Chicago University Press, 1986), pp. 123–42; quote from p. 141.   [16] MacLiammoir, *Money*, p. 12.   [17] Ibid., p. 33.

[18] On 7 April 1992, *USA Today* featured a story by Stephen Schaefer, "Orson Welles' 'Othello' Restored." It includes a photograph with the caption, "Cloutier: of the '52 'Othello' cast, only the fair Desdemona remains." But the still is of some other actress, presumably Aubry, not Suzanne Cloutier. Such is the lasting confusion caused by Welles's procession of Desdemonas.

characterized her as having "longish lovely face crowned with light hair, and a performance full of gentleness and understanding," but worried that she would be too "modern" for Desdemona: "[T]hat is what she is, with an undisguised frankness in her eyes and free loose-limbed gestures and walk. Would cast her unhesitatingly for Jo in *Little Women* or equally for any girl who walks straight and alone into life, but cannot feel the Renaissance, the Latin world of the fifteenth century."[19] Blair began work on the production when it moved to Mogador in Morocco, and she actually appears in the final film on the castle walls of Cyprus, eager to greet Othello. But before long, Welles, too, found her to be too modern. Two weeks later she left and he began the search for a fourth Desdemona.

The final Desdemona (and the one who received credit when the film was finally released) was Suzanne Cloutier. MacLiammoir thought she had a voice "warm, flexible and soft; her face a Bellini with large grey eyes that bestow lingering and slightly *reproachful* glances, perfect nose and mouth, chin a little too broadly modelled, age just twenty, figure good ... [S]he is by all appearances a genuine Renaissance type."[20] Cloutier had to have her hair, originally "a dark, smokey brown," dyed blonde. Otherwise, she was just what Welles wanted.

Cultural critic John Collick believes that "The protracted search for an actress to play Desdemona hints at an indecisiveness on Welles' part and an inability to come to terms with the sexual implications of the Othello-Desdemona relationship in the film."[21] But it also illustrates Welles' desire to find a woman who fit his *visual* conception of what Desdemona should be. The perfect Desdemona as he and MacLiammoir defined her was a sum of various parts. She required a good figure, angelic grace, purity of expression, a gentle voice, and an aura of innocence. Women who shared these traits – Aubry and Cloutier – could fill the space provided for her. A "modern" woman like Blair could not.

Biographer Brady explains one source of tension between Welles and Cloutier: "Orson, filled with puissance and at his most charming, spent months attempting to seduce her, but she was inflexible ... Because of her rejection of him, he could be brutal toward her."[22] The desire to efface Cloutier/Desdemona – to render her voiceless –

---

[19] MacLiammoir, *Money*, pp. 39, 76.   [20] Ibid., p. 126.
[21] John Collick, *Shakespeare, Cinema and Society* (Manchester: Manchester University Press, 1989), p. 96.   [22] Brady, *Citizen Welles*, p. 226.

was perhaps expressed later, when Welles hired Scottish actress Gudrun Ure to dub some of her lines:

"Wouldn't it be fun to dub her completely?" Welles asked [film editor] Morton mischievously. Morton couldn't believe what he was hearing. "But Orson, there's no need to do more than just a few tracks," he replied. "Nonsense," boomed Orson with a Bacchic laugh. "We'll have Ure dub the entire Desdemona. I can't wait to see what Cloutier's reaction will be when she attends the première and finds out it's not really her, at least not her voice, and in many shots not her body – on the screen."[23]

Welles' relationships with his Desdemonas demonstrate, therefore, that his conception of Desdemona as a sexual object whose *to-be-looked-at-ness*, to borrow a term from film theorist Laura Mulvey, could be "coded for strong visual and erotic impact." Mulvey explains that the woman displayed in scopophilic films serves "as erotic object for the characters within the screen story, and as erotic object for the spectator within the auditorium, with a shifting tension between the looks on either side of the screen." Within film, woman stands much as she does in patriarchal culture, "as a signifier for the male other, bound by a symbolic order in which man can live out his fantasies and obsessions through linguistic command by imposing them on the silent image of the woman still tied to her place as bearer, not maker, of meaning."[24] Whatever discredit has been cast on Mulvey's conceptions of visual pleasure and the male gaze since 1975,[25] her analysis is strikingly apropos of Orson Welles' *Othello*, not only in the film that was produced but in the physical procession of substituted bodies selected to represent the space called Desdemona.

*   *   *   *

Welles' *Othello* is best known for its fragmented film imagery. Composed of 500 separate shots, the film features only one long take,

[23] Ibid., p. 440.

[24] Laura Mulvey, "Visual Pleasure and Narrative Cinema," first published in *Screen*, 1975; repr. in her collection of essays, *Visual and Other Pleasures* (Bloomington: Indiana University Press, 1989), pp. 14–26; quotes from pp. 19 and 15.

[25] Mulvey has since modified her theory, allowing for a female gaze as well as the masculine. See "Afterthoughts on 'Visual Pleasure and Narrative Cinema' Inspired by King Vidor's *Duel in the Sun*," *Framework*, nos. 15–17 (1981), reprinted in her collection of essays, *Visual and Other Pleasures* (Bloomington: Indiana University Press, 1989), pp. 29–38. Teresa De Lauretis argues in *Alice Doesn't: Feminism, Semiotics, Cinema* (Bloomington: Indiana University Press, 1984) that cinema audiences cannot be characterized as either identifying with masculine or feminine perspectives because they oscillate between the two. See pp. 142–43. In a more recent essay, Jane Gaines explains how racial difference complicates the spectator-object relationship. See "White Privilege and Looking Relations: Race and Gender in Feminist Film Theory," *Screen*, 29 (1988): 12–27.

Iago and Othello walking on the battlements during the temptation scene. It is also known for Welles's highly stylized use of light/dark imagery. Jack Jorgens sets the context for this repeating pattern:

From the torches lit by Brabantio's hopeful followers to Othello's sustained speech before the Duke in which he moves from light to shadow to light as he speaks, from the flashes of lightning in the Cyprus night to Desdemona's white handkerchief and dress, from the emblem of the sun on Othello's black cloak to the lighted window in the huge fortress tower and the repeated extinguishing of the light towards the conclusion, the conflict and interpenetration of these opposites are stressed.[26]

Within this brilliant manipulation of light and dark contrasts,[27] Desdemona appears almost uniformly as light, in the light, her face shining with a glow that visually embodies Othello's orient pearl and perfect chrysolite. Her hair lit like a golden halo (no wonder Cloutier's hair had to be dyed!), her dress of white gossamer, her shining white handkerchief, her luminous eyes – all reify the association between Desdemona and "fairness" embedded in Shakespeare's text. But as light she is also empty space that must be filled, covered, written upon. The camera's gaze does the writing.

The substitution of the camera for the patriarchal eye begins as the film opens. Borrowing from Eisenstein's *Alexander Nevsky*, Welles first displays Othello's face (upside down) upon a funeral bier that is slowly carried along the top of the fortress walls. A procession of monks follows the body, holding a cross aloft. The camera lingers next over the pale face of Desdemona under a transparent shroud. As her bier passes, the camera shifts first to Iago, who gazes down upon her body from the cage where he has been hoisted; then we see the faces of her male countrymen, Lodovico and Cassio, who might have been her lovers but were not. They cross themselves as they watch her body pass. Even before the film's title appears, Desdemona is represented in all her *to-be-looked-at-ness* as a silent, inert body, the passive object of male fantasies and desires.

Iago also studies Othello's corpse from his lofty cage. Thus from the film's opening shots we have Desdemona and Othello identified as what film critic Judith Mayne describes as sites of "ambivalent

---

[26] Jorgens, *Shakespeare on Film*, pp. 182–83.
[27] Welles's set designer, Alexander Trauner, should also be credited here. An important figure in French filmmaking in the late 1930s and during the Occupation, Trauner was known for contrasts of light and dark, characteristic of what later became known as *film noir*.

positions of desire."[28] Desdemona's body, repeatedly serves as the locus for Othello's desire, while Iago's gaze is directed at Othello and fraught with homoerotic overtones.

Images of Desdemona's body repeat throughout the film. Aroused from her marital bed after the drunken brawl, for example, Desdemona appears aloft in a shining, white dress. As she descends to Othello's side, the camera pans to the men assembled about her, and in a reverse angle shot we see what she would see, a host of men staring at her. Once the temptation begins, she appears in bright sunlight on the battlements, and then the camera jumps to a darkened Othello below, gazing up at her. Light haloes from her face when she speaks for Cassio. Later in the same sequence, after she realizes something is wrong with Othello, her figure is again highlighted in whiteness. Anthony Davies contends that in this scene she appears as the object of the camera's gaze, not as a speaking subject:

Instead of giving the expressive work to the actress, Welles articulates the complexity of her confusion and her powerlessness through camera angle, lighting angle and frame composition. Desdemona is seen in a high-angled shot, as a small figure dwarfed by two tall, dark-shadowed pillars which extend upwards beyond the top of the frame. Between these dark, upward thrusts, Desdemona walks on to a sunlit courtyard whose surface is decorated by a continuous pattern of white semi-circles resembling a boundless network of chain.[29]

A small speck of white space between two dark, phallic pillars, Desdemona physically represents the object of male anxiety, the emptiness that must be filled, the force that must be chained.

Similar psychosexual dynamics are at play in Welles' repeated use of mirror images,[30] a motif that has been perceptively discussed in psychoanalytic terms by Donaldson. Once Othello is in the throes of jealousy, he turns his gaze (and the camera follows) to Desdemona. First he sees her in a mirror; then he

returns to her, and stares into her eyes, holding her face in his hands. Thus, twice her eyes replace the looking glass where he seeks an answer. He forsakes the mirror finally only when she appears there, reduced to a

---

[28] Judith Mayne, "Feminist Film Theory and Women at the Movies," *Profession* (1987; pub. Modern Language Association): 14–19; quote from 17.

[29] Anthony Davies, *Filming Shakespeare's Plays: The Adaptations of Laurence Olivier, Orson Welles, Peter Brook, and Akira Kurosawa* (Cambridge: Cambridge University Press, 1988), p. 111.

[30] Again, Alexander Trauner, the set designer, may deserve much of the credit for these brilliant scenes.

minuscule reflection. His own image cannot be seen clearly or steadily, and a tiny image of the other replaces it ... From this troubling interrogation of self and other, of face and mirror, Othello flees to the bedchamber, parting its curtains.

As Othello's "inquiring gaze" turns to the marriage bed, he finds it, too, to be false. The "lesson of the mirrored gaze," Donaldson concludes, "is one of alienation and lovelessness," because Desdemona, the maternal object, fails to satisfy.[31]

While Donaldson's psychoanalytic reading of Welles's film focuses on Oedipal conflicts and maternal loss, other readings focus mainly on Iago and Othello. Jack Jorgens, for example, traces two cinematic styles: "Othello's nature is embodied in Welles' low angles, vast spaces, monumental buildings, crowds of soldiers, and processions of mourners." Iago's style is refracted in "dizzying perspectives and camera movements, tortured compositions, grotesque shadows and insane distortions."[32] Othello's style dominates the stately architecture of Venice, site of the film's opening scenes. Iago's takes over in Cyprus where images of cages, labyrinths, bars, and grills repeatedly appear.

Jorgens's analysis of Welles's cinematic imagery is certainly astute, but his division of the film into two styles – Othello's and Iago's – leaves Desdemona not only voiceless but styleless. One might argue that the absence of a distinct style is symptomatic of her objectification, that she appears only as Othello and Iago see her and is therefore refracted in their disparate gazes. But while Desdemona is repeatedly shot in reverse camera angles reflecting the gazes of others, certain themes are repeated whenever the camera is on her. The use of light on her hair, her face, her dress strikes me as a style, a technique that encodes the fetishization of her body.

Desdemona wears voluminous gowns throughout the film; for the most part, the physical reality of her body underneath is only suggested by a curve of the fabric, an angle of the arm. This voyeuristic effect teases the viewer. The desire to see Desdemona's body is only satisfied by close, well-lighted shots of her face and her hair (which, remember, Cloutier had to dye to the perfect shade of

---

[31] Donaldson, *Shakespearean Films*, pp. 103 and 107.
[32] Jorgens, *Shakespeare on Film*, pp. 176–77. See also Lorne M. Buchman, "Orson Welles's *Othello*: A Study of Time in Shakespeare's Tragedy," *Shakespeare Survey* 39, ed. Stanley Wells (Cambridge: Cambridge University Press, 1987), pp. 53–65. Buchman finds two opposing uses of time in the film and relates them to the Iago and Othello styles identified by Jorgens. For time, space, and style, there seems to be no place for Desdemona.

gold). Blonde hair was mandatory for the light/dark contrasts Welles planned for his film, but it was also consonant with the traditional Western association of female purity with fair skin and blonde hair, darkness with impurity. Thus Doris Dowling's Bianca sports dark hair that falls from a pert cap down to the nape of her neck. Her locks are loose, hanging freely. Fay Compton's Emilia, caught somewhere between the polar opposites of the virgin/whore dichotomy, is also a brunette; but unlike Bianca, she is inscribed by patriarchal marriage, a condition that is signified, in part, by hair that is braided and tightly bound.

As the film progresses, Welles' camera turns several times to Desdemona's golden hair. During the Senate scene she appears dressed in white, clutching an ermine cloak about her, with her hair richly bound with shining pearls. But later that night, when Othello comes to her chamber and closes the curtains, her tresses are unbound; the camera angle follows the bridegroom's gaze at her prone form and focuses on the golden hair spread in a circle around her face. Just as her marriage is to be consummated, her hair is free, unbound.

Note, too, that the camera angle in this scene approximates Othello's own gaze. He stands above her, looking down. This position denotes more than his power and control over her.[33] The gaze is fraught with erotic overtones, for, as the camera implies, he is about to "top" her – to use Iago's crude phrase. The higher vantage point signifies sexual mastery here, and in the murder scene, its repetition suggests rape.

Desdemona's appearances during the middle of the film also show her hair hanging down; when she is raised from her nuptial bed by the drunken brawl, we see the golden locks fall freely. But, beginning with the loss of her handkerchief – once Othello begins to be convinced of her infidelity – her hair must be confined. In subsequent scenes before her death, she wears a dark snood that covers her luxurious hair with a lattice-like net akin to the imagery of bars, cages, and grills featured in the castle's architecture. Iago's "mesh that will entrap you all" thus eventually finds its way to Desdemona's body, in particular to her hair.

[33] Although the disparity in elevation does not always imply an unequal relationship, most often the person standing (in a classroom, a church, or a board meeting, for example) is the one who is in charge. I am indebted to John O. Thompson for this idea; his unpub. paper, "Micro-Level on Screen: The Case of the Welles *Othello*," reexamines some of the assumptions repeated in standard criticism of Welles's film.

Entrapped not just by Iago's malevolent machinations but by patriarchy itself, Desdemona's unruly locks – a manifestation of her physicality – must be confined, bound up, controlled. From the love scene on, Welles associates Desdemona's hair with her sexuality; like the other parts of a woman's body, her hair "must be subjected to constant surveillance," in Stallybrass's words, or else it will betray more men.[34]

Welles' fetishization of Desdemona's hair climaxes in the murder scene. Here the camera follows Othello's gaze through iron-latticed windows into the bedroom to watch Desdemona let down her hair. The sight is unquestionably erotic, and its overtones are reinforced after the killing when her body lies much as it did during the love scene, with golden tresses spread out over the sheets, encircling her face. Welles' manipulation of Desdemona's hair thus demonstrates that, to borrow once again from Stallybrass, "woman's body could be both symbolic map of the 'civilized' and the dangerous terrain that had to be colonized."[35] The hair arouses desire, but it also "poisons sight," and as used by Welles, it reflects what Edward A. Snow has analyzed as Othello's psychological confusion between his own coition with Desdemona and the adultery he imagines she has committed.[36]

Visual images of enclosure, in fact, dominate the "Desdemona style" in Welles' film. Barbara Hodgdon summarizes the overall effect: "she moves from being enfolded by one patriarchal enclosure – represented by the formal stability of the Venetian state spectacle – only to be bound up within another – where the natural, but often vertiginously constructed spaces of Cyprus reveal patriarchal law but admit, and reveal, its most transgressive, psychotic manifestation."[37] Her subjection is represented in the monumentalized space that surrounds her – pillars, walls, grilled windows, arches, domed ceilings – and in the clothes she wears. In his memoirs MacLiammoir whimsically describes the costume designs that were used: "All is to be Carpaccio... Females also laced, bunched, puffed, slashed and ribboned."[38] Except when Desdemona appears in her diaphanous nightdress, her bust is held in check by tight bodices, her legs covered

---

[34] Stallybrass, "Patriarchal Territories," p. 126. [35] Ibid., p. 133.
[36] Edward A. Snow, "Sexual Anxiety and the Male Order of Things," *English Literary Renaissance*, 20 (1980): 384–412. Snow argues that Othello demonstrates a pathological male animus against sexuality; as a result, he becomes a "punitive onlooker in the primal scene of his own marriage" (395). [37] Hodgdon, "Kiss Me Deadly," p. 223.
[38] MacLiammoir, *Money*, p. 13.

with folds of material, her arms cloaked with capacious sleeves. Only her face is allowed to appear natural – the rest is "civilized" – to use Stallybrass's term – by the stylized confinements of Renaissance female clothing.

The Desdemona style is more difficult to characterize than that of Othello and Iago because it is not so much expressed by disjunctive editing, rapid changes in scale, and manipulations of space, as by moments of light and stillness. Desdemona's role is to be the object of masculine exchange; her *to-be-looked-at-ness* is conveyed through luminous close-ups of her face and shots of her diaphanous figure. Welles' filming of Othello's lines (from 4.2.46–63) best exemplifies Desdemona's objectification. Her lines are cut so that, instead of defending herself, she stands in silence. As Othello speaks, he (and the camera) work their way down her body. Donaldson summarizes the scene:

Othello's hand comes into the image as he touches her just below the bust ... As his hand moves downward in the folds of the gown along her belly, the camera moves downward with his hand, so that her face disappears from the shot ... [T]he gesture or caress begins below the breast and ends just below the genitals. At "dries up," the hand clutches the folds of the dress momentarily in a gesture of infantile dependence: Welles presents the failure of sexual connection as if it were a withholding of the breast, a failure of maternal nurture.[39]

Mouth, breast, genitals – these are the grotesque female openings that must be kept from others' uses. Whether the psychic dimensions are Oedipal – as Donaldson suggests – or something else, the camera's gaze reifies the masculine obsession with woman's body that is embedded in Shakespeare's text.

Desdemona's objectification in this film is softened several times. She is granted a voice before Brabantio and to speak for Cassio. But she is most humanized, most a subject, in her few scenes with Emilia. Welles apparently did not think much of Emilia; according to MacLiammoir, he explained her to an aspirant to the role as "a trollop,"[40] which perhaps reflects the virgin/whore dichotomy in Welles' own constructions of the female. But whatever his intentions for her, Fay Compton's Emilia comes through clear and strong in the film. Although Emilia is absent from the landing on Cyprus and does not appear until she filches Desdemona's handkerchief in the middle

---

[39] Donaldson, *Shakespearean Films*, p. 109.   [40] MacLiammoir, *Money*, p. 31.

of the temptation scene, Compton provides crucial moments of humanity in a film that mostly depicts alienation and isolation. Middle-aged and throaty in voice, Emilia is jarring in a film based on visual images, for she conveys a solidity, a physical presence, and a voice that few of the other characters achieve, certainly not Desdemona.

After the brothel scene, for example, Emilia shows human connection by physically embracing the sobbing Desdemona while Iago lurks in the distance. But most important is the truncated willow scene, which, unlike most of the dialogue that takes place on Cyprus, is filmed in an interior, domestic space – the sphere relegated by patriarchy to women. Desdemona enters humming the willow song and comments to Emilia, "Mine eyes do itch." As she talks to Emilia, she speaks from the other side of a latticed window, a repetition of the film's characteristic net/cage imagery.

As the scene continues, Emilia sits quietly, sewing. She exudes a quiet efficiency, suggesting the traits Welles associated with women in his conversation with John Ralph: "They are practical. They are more sensible. They are more realistic." Desdemona is the idealist here, and, as Welles told Ralph, "idealism is divine, but dangerous nonsense."[41] Her lines about Lodovico's attractiveness are cut; instead, she sighs, "These men," and asks Emilia if she would indeed do the deed. Emilia's response is thoughtful; she looks up from her sewing, and as she talks, Desdemona moves from the other side of the window to sit beside her. The moment is a rarity in this film, for here two human beings actually communicate, eye-to-eye, the one talking quietly and earnestly, the other listening intently. Desdemona blanches when Emilia mentions men that "strike us," as if remembering the blow Othello has just given her. Emilia appears in half-light; Desdemona's face is fully lit. But at Emilia's peroration, Desdemona suddenly rises. She doesn't want to talk anymore. She makes a conscious decision to go to Othello's bed, and the next time Emilia embraces her, she is dead.

Jorgens contends that Emilia's "shrill, ludicrous death scene detracts from the film."[42] The shrillness, however, is inherent in the lines given her by Shakespeare, for it is Emilia, as Kent Cartwright compellingly argues, who vents the audience's pent-up anger. "Reacting to the murder of Desdemona, so bloodless, so cold, and so

[41] *Sunday Graphic*, 3 August 1947.   [42] Jorgens, *Shakespeare on Film*, p. 186.

recent, spectators need the loud, commonsensical, aggressive, and heedless burst of outrage that Emilia provides."[43] Yet our annoyance with her "iteration" is dispelled with her death. Though her declamations may seem shrill, they provide an essential emotional ingredient in the complex passions of *Othello*'s denouement, an ingredient that is no less important to film than to live theatre.

While the objection to Emilia's shrillness is easily answered, the assertion that the manner of her death is ludicrous depends on one's expectations. Welles filmed the shot in a studio in Rome, a different locale from the murder of Desdemona.[44] The conditions of production, in short, necessitated that Emilia be killed in an antechamber, separated from Desdemona's dead body. As Emilia explains to Othello how she stole the handkerchief, Welles uses a reverse angle shot to show her in close-up as Othello would see her. The camera watches Iago approach from behind and, suddenly, Emilia doubles over, stabbed in the back. She collapses on the floor, her final words, "She loved thee," directed at Othello.

Is this, in fact, ludicrous? Welles used reverse angle shots throughout the film to simulate the patriarchal eye. Why should he change tactics at the finale? Iago's characteristic pose has been oblique – behind, below, aside, above his victims – seldom full-face. The killing is abrupt, but so is Othello's realization of his fatal error. But even more important, the sudden and graphic representation of Emilia's death underscores the parallel betwen Iago and Othello – husbands who murder their wives in an effort to contain them. Because in Renaissance discourse "the speech of a noble woman can be no less dangerous than the nakedness of her limbs," as Stallybrass astutely comments,[45] both women can be accused of violating patriarchal standards of behavior.

Yet there are subtle differences here. Desdemona's death is characteristic of the "Desdemona style"; Othello envelops her face in the sheet, masking her identity, absorbing her space. Emilia's final moments, in contrast, are full-face into the camera, a shot which situates her as a speaking subject who can only be contained by disruption of the frame.

*   *   *   *

---

[43] Kent Cartwright, "Audience Response and the Denouement of *Othello*," in *Othello: New Perspectives*, ed. Virginia Mason Vaughan and Kent Cartwright (Cranbury, NJ: Fairleigh Dickinson University Press, 1991), pp. 160–76; quote from p. 165.

[44] Brady, *Citizen Welles*, p. 437.   [45] Stallybrass, "Patriarchal Territories," p. 127.

Figure 17: A still from Orson Welles's 1952 film. Othello (Orson Welles) gazes at the body of Desdemona (Suzanne Cloutier).

Orson Welles can hardly be said to be representative of his era. He was *sui generis*, a bohemian behemoth, an independent director who mostly worked outside the Hollywood mainstream. But he never questioned the essential sexism of his chosen media, an art form that in the 1950s was controlled exclusively by powerful male directors and producers, and his depiction of Desdemona imbricates him in the Hollywood culture that produced pin-ups of Betty Grable, Rita Hayworth, and Marilyn Monroe – to name just three women who were victimized by the studio system. Like his contemporaries, Welles repeatedly made cinematic fetishes of women's bodies; he alone directed the camera's eye, and thus it is not at all surprising that he should focus on Desdemona's body and hair – whoever might be representing her at that moment.

Welles' cinematic treatment of Desdemona is symptomatic of popular representations of women in the mid-twentieth-century movie industry. But it also highlights patriarchal elements that are deeply embedded in Shakespeare's text. The dramatist's Othello, as we have seen in chapter 4, shares the male obsession with the physicality of Desdemona's body. He repeatedly describes her as an object, a "thing" to be possessed. When he loves her, she is a pearl, the "purchase made," or an "entire and perfect chrysolite." Once he is convinced of her infidelity, he then sees her as a "cistern for foul toads / To knot and gender in." She is the catalyst for *his* emotions, both for love and for hate. Welles' twentieth-century film, just like the sixteenth-century narratives that informed Shakespeare's text, is encoded with the conviction that a woman's body, just by provoking male desire, could become a locus of perturbation and violence. Though Laura Mulvey was the first to discuss the "male gaze" in the context of mid-twentieth-century cinema, a woman's *to-be-looked-at-ness* had already been represented in medieval and Renaissance texts as a source of both visual pleasure and physical aggression.

CHAPTER 11

Othello *for the 1990s: Trevor Nunn's 1989 Royal Shakespeare Company production*

> I will a round unvarnish'd tale deliver / Of my whole course of
> love.
> > *(Othello, 1.3.90–91)*[1]

Because the cultural historian depends upon general conceptions of a particular era's social and political ethos, she finds it far easier to contextualize the past than the present. Previous chapters examined a variety of *Othello* productions from the safe distance of long timespans; this chapter concerns a recent rendition of *Othello* and is necessarily more subjective. With that caveat in mind, I conclude my analysis of *Othello*'s stage history with Trevor Nunn's Royal Shakespeare Company *Othello*, a production that embodies several contemporary cultural concerns, at least in the United States and the United Kingdom.

The 1980s provided many memorable performances of *Othello*, including Jonathan Miller's BBC/Time-Life television production and Janet Suzman's pathbreaking South African version. Both are preserved on video, a prerequisite for widespread influence on school and college students and on society. Both sparked heated political debate: the BBC for casting white actor Anthony Hopkins in the title role, Janet Suzman's for breaking the South African color barrier and casting a black actor (John Kani) opposite a white Desdemona. Still, neither video strikes me as particularly representative of social and cultural trends. Trevor Nunn's *Othello*, now available on video in the UK, speaks more eloquently and poignantly to the world I read about in newspapers and watch on my television screen.

The analysis that follows is based on the Royal Shakespeare

---

[1] Because the RSC promptcopy was M. R. Ridley's Arden text, quotations from *Othello* in this chapter are taken from that edition (London: Methuen, 1958). Ridley used the Quarto text as his copy-text, but the promptbook also includes several emendations from the Folio. Quotations from the RSC promptbook will be noted by references to the specific line in the Arden edition where the stage business occurs.

Company's promptbook, assorted theatre reviews, and repeated screenings of the Primetime video which aired first on BBC television in June 1990. (I did not see, alas, the original Trevor Nunn production during its short run in August and September 1989.) The selective perspective of a video camera – with its framing, tracking, and close-up shots – does not provide the same experience as sitting in an audience in a live theatre. But a comparison of the promptbook and the video indicates that despite the inevitable differences between live theatre and video, in this case the blocking and stage business were virtually identical. The video, moreover, will be disseminated to college and university students in the United Kingdom and the United States and will consequently influence conceptions of *Othello* for the foreseeable future.

The most palpable characteristic of the Trevor Nunn *Othello* is its spareness. Like Othello's address to the Venetian Senate, it is a "round, unvarnish'd tale," performed on a simple square set surrounded at the upper level with grey wooden shutters. The original production's naturalistic design provided, according to Stanley Wells, "rare intimacy of communication and directness of emotional impact,"[2] an effect equally apparent in a video screening in the privacy of one's home. The switch from Venice to Cyprus is marked only by the removal of a carpet from the bare floor. There is consequently no Venetian grandeur – no Tintorettos and velvet gowns – and no Oriental exotica on Cyprus, except perhaps the *muzzein*'s morning call to prayer. Trevor Nunn deliberately reduces the play's global dimensions to the absolute minimum. His focus is the inner world of husbands and wives, minds and souls. In this production, evil is not satanic or cataclysmic; it is commonplace, banal, and integral to the texture of everyday life.

By underplaying the Venetian-Turkish conflict, Nunn deprived his *Othello* of an important dimension of Shakespeare's text – the global framework – but that in itself is symptomatic of the post-Cold War ethos. The rigid division of the Western world between communist and capitalist regimes has broken down, replaced by resurgent nationalism and ethnic conflict. More terrible than the old specter of atomic annihilation is the immediate dread of neighborhood drug wars, random shootings, and domestic violence.

---

[2] Stanley Wells, "Shakespeare Production in England in 1989," *Shakespeare Survey 43*, ed. Stanley Wells (Cambridge: Cambridge University Press, 1991), pp. 183–203; quote from p. 191.

While global conflict is not highlighted in this production, racial issues are emphasized, although they are not stressed as explicitly and forcefully as in other versions (Suzman's, for example). For Nunn, a black Othello was not a problem; it was a given. He chose Willard White, a Jamaica-born black opera singer who trained at the Juillard School of Music in New York, for his Othello. He also selected a black actress, Marsha Hunt, for Bianca. Iago's venom against her may bespeak his racist feelings as much as his misogyny; the way he (Ian McKellen) spits out the words "Moorship," and "Moor" also suggests racial hatred. The theme remains understated, however, throughout this production, as if it were implicit in the situation but not dominant.

Nunn's *Othello* emphasizes instead the search for meaning in human relationships, the struggle to find trust and intimacy in a world of appearances, the fragility of human bonds. This emphasis, too, strikes me as symptomatic of the 1990s, when each day's newspaper features the story of another battered woman murdered by her husband or boyfriend, and talk-show hosts probe people's most intimate secrets on nationwide television. Whether Nunn's concept of *Othello* was directly influenced by the feminist criticism of Shakespeare that proliferated during the 1980s, I cannot say. But this production is more nuanced in its treatment of gender relations than any I have seen, not just because the women's lines are uncut and the roles superbly acted, but because all human relations, man to man and woman to woman, as well as man to woman, are depicted as problematic within a patriarchal social structure. Nunn's *Othello* depicts the fear of women's sexuality embedded in Shakespeare's text and recently described by Susan Snyder as the "psychosocial web that ensnares men and women alike."[3]

Nunn's *Othello* makes gender relations even more difficult by emphasizing the play's military milieu – the struggle for advancement up the ranks, the coarse humor of the barracks, the fleeting moments of male intimacy interrupted by the bugle's blare and a return to protocol, and the exclusion of women from the business at hand. The entire production questions, in ways that seem strikingly contemporary, the impact of a military career on an individual's

---

[3] Susan Snyder, "A Modern Perspective," in *The New Folger Library Othello,* ed. Barbara A. Mowat and Paul Werstine (New York: Washington Square Press, 1993), pp. 287–98; quote from p. 296. I was pleased that the "modern perspective" provided for students in 1993 is so similar to my own.

ability to relate to others, especially in the United States where the recent Tailhook scandal revealed the sexism of military culture and where feminists and homosexuals are challenging traditional military regulations.

What makes this *Othello* compelling, then, is a link between the marital and the martial. Though they seem to represent disparate spheres of human activity, Nunn portrays them as joined by the human compulsion to create and, in Iago's case, to destroy, intimacy. The ensuing analysis will show how both areas of human concern are represented through stage business, blocking, and a uniformly high standard of acting.

*   *   *   *

Nunn chose the Royal Shakespeare Company's most intimate acting space for his *Othello*, the small tin-shed studio called The Other Place (since demolished and replaced by a more commodious, comfortable theatre). After six weeks in Stratford, he moved the production to the Young Vic in London, and, in the following spring, to the closed space of a small television studio. After an interview with the director, Peter Conrad reported that "Nunn chose these venues – a shed in a field, and a concrete bunker – because he believes that in *Othello* Shakespeare was writing an intimate drama about emotional corrosion, meant for a smaller theatre than the world-enclosing Globe. "[4] The effect of this decision was to create "a study in claustrophobic desperation" (*Guardian*, 26 August 1989).

The setting is the nineteenth century, but otherwise indefinite, variously described by reviewers as the American Civil War, the Franco-Prussian War, the Austro-Hungarian War, Venice of *Death in Venice*, or perhaps the worlds of Chekhov or Tennessee Williams. Except for the civilians, who sport summer suits, ties, and broad-brimmed hats (Brabantio, Gratiano, Roderigo in Act 1, Cassio after the cashiering), the men wear military uniforms vaguely styled after the Union army's during the American Civil War. The Duke is dressed as a commanding General, a red collar indicating his rank. Because of the bare stage and consistent military costuming, Venice is hardly distinct from Cyprus. The overall ethos is military, but the lack of ties to specific wars or places makes this ethos more symbolic than real. Cyprus becomes any colonial outpost where the men live

---

[4] Peter Conrad, "When Less Means Moor," *Observer Magazine*, 29 April 1990, pp. 24–26. Quote from p. 25.

closely confined in barracks, the heat is oppressive, and the women minister with lemonade and barley water. Sound effects enhance this atmosphere: bugles announce the changing of the guard, a harmonium plays hymns in the background, and cicadas chirp in the noonday sun.

This self-enclosed world has strict codes of behavior which Nunn exemplifies through specific details of business. The stage production's general effect impressed one reviewer as "the meticulousness of army life where each person and each object has a correct place and etiquette is to be followed exactly" (*Stratford Observer*, 31 August 1989). The video has similar business. Before entering and exiting, soldiers and officers stand at attention, click heels, and salute. Hats, coats, and swords are properly adjusted, beds are carefully made, luggage is stowed, and everything is ready for inspection.

The chief fusser among the military personnel is, not surprisingly, Iago, whose tidiness reflects an obsessive-compulsive personality who can never be satisfied. The promptbook is full of business for McKellen, who sometimes resembles a perpetual motion machine. In the drinking scene especially, Iago's fastidiousness is repeatedly demonstrated: he turns up the bottom of his blanket before lying down, ostensibly to keep his boots from muddying it; later in the scene (the promptbook notes), "I[ago] tidy up own bed + box" (2.3.251), "I[ago] wash out bowl + wipe with towel[.] replace" (2.3.260), and "I[ago] pick up blanket" (2.3.324). During the temptation scene, Iago is to "tidy desk + collect sword + cap" (3.3.243), "tidy papers to table" (3.3.440), and replace the furniture Othello has disordered. The ensign goes so far as to "brush him [Othello] down" and "brush hair with his handky" (4.1.68) after the epileptic fit. These compulsive bits of stage business form a pattern, described here by Anne Barton:

Psychotically unable to tolerate disorder, Iago is perpetually tidying up the barracks, righting overturned chairs, pouncing on litter. For this "model" NCO, the marriage of Desdemona and black Othello, an even more conspicuous irregularity in his world, naturally demands eradicating too.[5]

The *Sunday Times* repeated this theme: "He has the soul of a servant and the instincts of a destroyer: a trim vicious and compulsively tidy male mother-hen, whose manhood is sublimated in professional resentment and in keeping order in the army" (27 August 1989).

[5] Anne Barton, "Other Places, Other Customs," *Times Literary Supplement*, 8–11 September 1989.

McKellen's northern accent sets him apart from the rest of the cast, particularly Othello and Cassio (Sean Baker) who speak in traditional BBC tones. Baker's Cassio is, as Robert Smallwood wryly observes, reminiscent of "a public-schoolboy freshly graduated from military academy, conspicuously different from the officers of the Cyprus regiment, so that his agreement to carouse with them carried more than a hint of patronage."[6] Iago, by contrast, is the seasoned veteran, always solicitous of his fellow soldiers and providing for their needs; in the words of Harry Eyres, a *Times* theatre critic, "he is constantly attending to people and things – mixing punch, applying bandages, mopping brows. He is the person everyone instinctively turns to for practical help, advice, even consolation" (26 August 1989).

In his role as purveyor of goods and services, McKellen's Iago seems to share moments of intense bonding with his barracks fellows. Most often these are quiet moments of relaxation over a drink or a cigarette. In the play's opening scene, for example, Iago signifies his alliance with Roderigo by offering a drink from his hip flask. The other military men also turn to liquor and tobacco for solace. During the Senate scene, the Duke's table provides, along with the requisite maps and reports, a brandy decanter; as the discussion of Turkish warships proceeds, the first Senator is to "pour drink for self, look at Duk[e], pour him one" (1.3.18). Later, when Brabantio is overwrought at Desdemona's defection, the promptbook reads, "Du[ke] pour brandy for Br[abantio]" (1.3.201). Along with the brandy are cigars – the Venetian Council is, in effect, a smoke-filled room where political decisions are made amid male camaraderie.

Drink as a form of bonding and succor recurs as late as Act 5, when Gratiano offers his hip flask to the wounded Cassio. Drink thus becomes a sign of intimacy and temporary equality. The sharing of a flask provides comfort and communion between one soldier and another. That Cassio has so much trouble with this aspect of army life bespeaks his inexperience and alienation from his troops.

In Venice, Iago is excluded from the inner circle. At the end of the Council scene, when he suggests that, "The Moor is of a free and open nature, / That thinks men honest that but seem to be so" (1.3.382–83), the Ensign stealthily pockets the Duke's cigars. But after he arrives on the Cyprus quay, he creates his own inner circle.

---

[6] Robert Smallwood, "Shakespeare at Stratford-upon-Avon, 1989 (Part I)," *Shakespeare Quarterly*, 41 (1990): 101–14. Quote from 111.

Figure 18: Othello kisses Desdemona in the Cyprus quay scene from Trevor Nunn's
1989 Royal Shakespeare Company production.

He begins by magnanimously distributing the stolen cigars to his
fellow soldiers. The hip flask appears too. Wet and chilled from the
sea voyage, Iago drinks, shares his flask with Emilia, and then
distributes it to the soldiers. Only Desdemona and Cassio refuse.

Nunn uses the drunken barracks brawl to show that Cassio doesn't
fit comfortably in this rough masculine ethos, whereas Iago is its
perfect embodiment. After Othello and Desdemona retire, Cassio
and Iago lie on their cots, smoking and talking. Then, as if by
impulse, Iago "take[s] 2 bottles, mug + corkscrew from I[ago]'s
box" (2.3.26). He proceeds to mix punch in the washstand basin,
adding extra potency from his flask. Presiding over the singing and
frollicking, Iago is the manipulative host, quickly filling cups and
toothmugs, orchestrating the songs and gags. As the fun continues,
Iago pulls down a soldier's trousers. Cassio thinks this is great sport
until Iago heads his way. In a revealing moment, Cassio abruptly
ends the festivity by warning that "the lieutenant must be saved
before the ancient" and straightening the furniture. After an

interview with Nunn, Conrad wrote that this incident "is meant to show 'how soldiering unfits these men for marriage, for all human relations other than military ones'; how matey coarseness has overruled other feelings. "[7] The incident also conveys the ambiguities of military protocol; clearly Cassio feels that debagging a subordinate is a great lark, but once Iago moves toward him, a line is crossed that endangers his status within the hierarchy. Intimacy, carried too far, is threatening.

Intimacy can also be physical, and it is remarkable how often the promptbook calls for Iago to touch, caress, or "cuddle" his fellows. At the end of Act 1, for example, the promptbook directs the Ensign to "run fingers through R[oderigo]'s hair" (1.3.330), then Roderigo is to "hold I[ago]'s hand" and "I[ago] hit R[oderigo]'s hand gently" (1.3.362–64). When Cassio vomits in Act 2, scene 3, Iago holds his head and then gently tucks him in bed. Later in the same scene he "cuddles" Roderigo and bandages his wounds. When Desdemona is in despair after the brothel scene, Iago holds her hands and "cuddle[s]" her (4.2.132). In the video, this embrace, displayed in close-up, is particularly long and sensuous, as if Iago were receiving sexual pleasure from his comforting strokes.

Such intimate moments show why everyone trusts Iago. He is the consoler, the ministering angel, the one who makes everything right. They also show how illusory the quest for intimacy can be, especially if one of the parties is only pretending.

Despite the repeated emphasis on physicality as a form of human contact, Iago does not touch Othello, nor do they attain any sustained eye contact until the end of the temptation scene. Iago is only intimate with the other characters when Othello is offstage. Whenever the General enters, Iago snaps to attention, watching from the margins until ordered to action. After seeing the original production, Wells remarked that in Othello's presence, Iago "was always under iron control, though his eyes narrowed to slits in intense concentration as he observed anything that might serve his purpose."[8] The video camera's framing shots also reveal this pattern until the end of Act 2. Then, for the bulk of the temptation scene, Iago looks only obliquely at Othello. The two sit "side by side at a camp table," observed the *Times*'s Eyres of the stage performance, "pushing papers in the hot Cyprus sun. The way in which White's

---

[7] Conrad, "When Less Means Moor," p. 26.
[8] Wells, "Shakespeare Production," p. 194.

Figure 19: Othello (Willard White) beside Iago (Sir Ian McKellen) in the temptation scene from Trevor Nunn's 1989 Royal Shakespeare Company Production.

eyes, narrowing and turning inwards, mirror the clouding of his mind is riveting to watch" (26 August 1989). At the scene's violent conclusion, however, Iago stands close to Othello, facing him directly. The Ensign and the General search each other's faces, while, as the promptbook directs, "Ot[hello] take I[ago's] hand. I[ago] kiss Ot[hello]'s hand put his on top" (3.3.485). Iago has not simply become Othello's lieutenant; the men are bound, soul to soul.

Iago's bond with the jealous Othello is represented again after the eavesdropping scene of Act 4. Once Bianca and Cassio exit, Iago collects a stool and sits by Othello. At Act 4, scene 1, line 190 the promptbook reads, "I[ago] slowly raise US arm put around Ot[hello]." At line 193, he is to "cuddle him." This is the last time the two are seen alone onstage, and it signifies physically a union of two men that will only be destroyed by Emilia's revelations about the handkerchief in the final scene. And this union is rooted in an alliance against the common enemy, woman.

The military world of Nunn's *Othello* allows close and intimate bonds between man and man – on the battlefield, in the barracks, over a shared drink or smoke, and – in the eavesdropping scene – in shared jokes about prostitutes and camp followers. In such moments, made more intense because they are so often interrupted by the blare of bugles and a snap to attention, the protocols are temporarily set aside. The video also posits that male bonding is deeper and more intense than any relationship possible, in this milieu, between man and woman. Women are by definition excluded from the battlefield and barracks. Kept in the bedroom and at the dinner table, they share neither the same experiences nor the same intimacies. No wonder the husbands in this version of *Othello* relate more intensely to their fellows than to their wives.

*   *   *   *

Against this military backdrop, Nunn spotlights two marriages, one new and full of promise, one old and dysfunctional. For McKellen, Iago's motivation is more sexual than racial, though his contempt for Bianca may express a fusion of the two. Iago is eaten with jealousy to the point of madness, claims McKellen, and his soliloquies tell the audience, "'I don't like Cassio and I hate Othello, because I think they have fucked my wife. Even if they haven't, it *feels* as if they have.'"[9] Iago's jealousy, decried by Emilia as a "green-eyed monster, begot on itself," has destroyed any relationship he might have had with his wife.

During their performance, both McKellen and Zoë Wanamaker (Emilia) take pains to show a marriage run amuck. Smallwood raves at Wanamaker's success in the stage version:

Sad, pale, and watchful, she moves through the play observing its events, suspicious but bewildered until the truth finally dawns on her: ... On her first appearance she had watched the extravagant affection of the greeting between Desdemona and Othello with pained wonder, surprised to find her attention to their embrace interrupted by a rough, affectionless kiss from her husband.[10]

In the video version of the same scene, Emilia, shivering and coughing from the sea voyage, is beset by unwanted attentions from Cassio, who kisses her hand and cheek, and by Iago's pointed jibes

---

[9] Robert Gore-Langton, "A Round Unvarnished Tale," *Listener*, 1 February 1990: 36–37. Quote from 37.   [10] Smallwood, "Shakespeare at Stratford," 112.

about talkative women. When everyone leaves the stage, the breakdown in Emilia's marriage is conveyed by simple stage business: the promptbook notes "E[milia] xit USC look DS as I[ago] shut door on her – he looks DS all the time" (2.1.213). Iago dismisses and ignores her, and, since it is Roderigo (now dressed as a soldier) he stays to address, she must assume that military bonds matter more to Iago than marital relations.

Wanamaker's face expressively shows the pain of such repeated rejections. Similar glances occur later in the play, deepening the feeling of estrangement. Early in the temptation scene, for example, Othello embraces Desdemona in a passionate kiss. The promptbook reads, "I[ago] look at them. E[milia] look at I[ago] catch his eye" (3.3.88). Later, to please her husband's "fantasy," Emilia steals the handkerchief. When he enters, she insists, "Do not you *chide*" (3.3.305), as if Iago's regular practice is to berate her. Her reward for stealing the handkerchief is to be pulled into Iago's lap and kissed passionately. But this embrace is rough, not tender, and the promptbook has Iago "brake [*sic*] it + push her off" (3.3.324). He dismisses her abruptly – "Go, leave me" – to ruminate on his plans. While Iago finds the wife a source of aggravation, the pipe is a comfort: the promptbook directs, "I[ago] light pipe – long drag, put foot up on table" (3.3.325). "McKellen's invincible, unsleeping Iago," suggests Michael Ratcliffe of the *Observer*, is "so choked with tension he gulps at a narcotic for sweet, explosive relief" (27 August 1989).

Wanamaker conveys Emilia's pain most poignantly in the willow song scene, the only part of the video in which female bonding is privileged over male relationships. Emilia moves through the stage business of undressing Desdemona with a sorrowful expression and workmanlike precision. When Desdemona tries to hug her, she breaks away. Then Desdemona unlocks her desk drawer to take out the sweets Cassio had given her. Like the men's drink, the exchange of sweets signifies an informal, intimate moment, when women can share their views about particular men (Lodovico) and about the ways men and women relate to each other. The bond established, Emilia leans over to "cuddle" Desdemona.

During the murder scene, Wanamaker's Emilia, who has repeatedly exuded quiet hunger for affection from her husband, rejects his advances and chooses this female bond over the marital relationship. Her outrage rises with the iteration, "My husband," until the realization of her husband's guilt (and her own) slowly dawns. When Iago places his arm around her, hoping to soothe and quiet her, she breaks away, declaring she will speak "liberal as the air" as she moves closer to Desdemona's body. As the promptbook suggests, Nunn solves the problem of what to do with Emilia's body by first having her crawl to the bed, "cover D[esdemona] with bed sheets" (5.2.247) and then cross to sit in a chair. There she dies, and when her body falls to the floor, the other actors ignore it. The stick figure of Emilia's body remains in place through the rest of the promptbook; no one rushes to see if she is dead, no one touches her, no one carries her offstage. In death she is what she has been throughout, a silent figure whose presence on the margins speaks eloquently of the breakdown in marital relations enacted at center stage.

Wanamaker's Emilia is, I believe, a battered wife. Of course, Iago doesn't beat her physically, but he exerts tremendous psychological control over her. The pain on her face shows her suffering. She speaks for herself when she exclaims:

> 'Tis not a year or two shows us a man:
> They are all but stomachs, and we all but food;
> They eat us hungerly, and when they are full,
> They belch us.   (3.4.100–03)

The animus in this speech is not just against Iago, but all men who use women for sport and profit. For Emilia, this includes Cassio, who extends his courtesy (with never a thought for the consequences) whenever he pleases with kisses and caresses that clearly discomfort a married woman with a jealous husband. Not just in the Cyprus quay scene, but also when Act 3 opens, Cassio kisses her on both cheeks. Wanamaker flinches. Cassio, who has a cavalier way with women, thinks nothing of a kiss or the gift to Desdemona of a box of sweets. But as this play demonstrates, such courtesies can be dangerous.

Cassio lies at the heart of gender relations in the RSC *Othello*. Baker plays him as a cultivated gentleman who reeks of the chivalric code of the Old South. He places the divine Desdemona on a pedestal, extolling her heavenly graces so extravagantly on the Cyprus quay that Montano and the rest of the soldiers are visibly embarrassed. But while Desdemona is one class of woman, Bianca is another, to be exploited for sexual favors but dismissed as a "customer," a "monkey," and a "bauble" (4.1.119–33). And in Nunn's production

Bianca, befitting the dark lady of easy virtue stereotype, is black. According to an interview with Nunn, this casting decision was deliberately planned to show "Cassio's double standard in sexual matters – he idealises the divine Desdemona, but relieves himself with a harlot."[11]

The whore/goddess dichotomy is also strikingly represented in blocking for Othello and Desdemona. When the pair meet on the Cyprus quay, their language is lyrical in its expression of a union of souls as well as bodies. The video shows Othello rushing onstage, where he stares at Desdemona's face, and then whisks her up on Iago's trunk where he can worship her from below. The camera uses panning shots to show him revolving around her, and reverses from his adoring gaze to her face, rapt with love and wonder. When Desdemona leaps into his arms, he spins her around, and they embrace in a deep kiss. Nunn picks up the same blocking in the brothel scene, but note the difference. The promptbook reads, "Ot[hello] grab D[esdemona]- pull her onto stool. Stand USL of her. Des[demona] try to move, Ot[hello] point + she remains" (4.2.75–80). Here the placement of Desdemona on a stool is not a gesture of adoration but contempt. The video pans around as Othello circles her, then he pulls her off the stool and casts her down. She is no longer the goddess but the whore, to be publicly displayed and humiliated.

Othello's need to categorize Desdemona as one or the other – the perfect chrysolite or the whore of Venice – is belied in this production by Imogen Stubbs's impetuous portrayal of a young girl thrust into a situation she can neither fathom nor control. In Barton's words, we see Desdemona "hurling herself prematurely into an adult world[;] she is fragile, lovely, spoilt, manipulatively aware of her charm, and very young. Self-possessed in the known world of the Senators and her father ... she goes adrift immediately in Cyprus."[12] Naive she may be, but she is no shrinking violet. Smallwood notes her poise in the Venetian Council scene: she tries to touch her father's arm on arrival, "and even after her speech of commitment to Othello and the decision for Cyprus, she was, even as he sought to evade her, still following him round the council table, first one way, then the other, trying, poignantly, to settle their quarrel with an embrace."[13] This tactic fails with Brabantio even as it will fail with Othello in Act 4.

11 Conrad, "When Less Means Moor," p. 26.   12 Barton, "Other Places."
13 Smallwood, "Shakespeare at Stratford," 112.

But it indicates Desdemona's determination to make things right and "by bad mend" (4.3.105).

Still, the Venetian Council is a man's world, where decisions are made over brandy and cigars. Once the business with her father is settled, Desdemona is relegated to a marginal seat upstage while the men discuss battle strategy. When she asks the Duke to "lend a gracious ear" to her request to follow Othello, the Duke obligingly gives her leave to speak; the promptbook directs the Duke to indicate "to Des[demona] to sit in own chair" (1.3.247). This chivalric gesture carves out a space for Desdemona to proclaim her love and desire for Othello. By speaking her mind, she succeeds in obtaining what she wants. Later, when she speaks for Cassio, her rhetoric fails.

Stubbs thus depicts a strong Desdemona who fights for what she wants with whatever weapons are available. Reminiscent of Vivien Leigh's Scarlett O'Hara, this Desdemona flirts with gusto.[14] She accepts Cassio's attentions as her due, never realizing what they might mean to her husband. In the murder scene, where her greatest desire is to live another day, she struggles forcefully. The promptbook directs her to run to the locked door after she awakens. When she finds she can't escape, she is to "turn + crouch." When Othello grabs her, she resists, breaks away "+kneels in luggage." Othello holds out his hand to her, she takes it, he pulls her onto the bed, he straddles her "+hand over her mouth." The promptbook calls for a long pause "as Ot[hello] kills her+writhes" in what seems like a final, tragic coition (5.2.64–85). Despite her aristocratic breeding, youthful exuberance, and idealistic love, in the brothel scene and in her death, Desdemona becomes – like Emilia – a battered wife who is violently murdered.

Willard White, the first black actor to play Othello at Stratford since Paul Robeson's final season in 1959, shares the qualities of Robeson's magnificent baritone voice and imposing presence. Wells describes him as "an imposing figure of great natural nobility with a resonant speaking voice of unforced power and authority."[15] An opera singer by training – White sang Porgy for Nunn at Glyndebourne – he lends Othello's lines the sort of music so often described by critics but so seldom heard in the theatre. But unlike Robeson, White downplays the racial difference between the Moor and the rest of the cast (excepting, of course, Bianca). In the final scene, he alludes

---

[14] Stubbs made the comparison to Leigh's Scarlett in her *Listener* interview with Robert Gore-Langton, p. 37.   [15] Wells, "Shakespeare Production," p. 194.

visually to Robeson by appearing in a magnificent white Moorish robe highlighted with black trim. It is as if, convinced of Desdemona's Venetian perfidy, he has rejected "passing" at last and chooses instead his native dress. The whiteness of his robe also blends with Desdemona's white nightdress. At the play's final moments, both inert bodies blend in the white space of the bed; around them is only darkness.

Iago stares blankly at the couple's silent forms. To the *Stratford Observer*, in the stage performance Iago's gaze had the detached "inquisitiveness of a schoolboy performing a biology vivisection" (31 August 1989). The video also concludes with a close-up of McKellen's far-away stare, a shot that suggests to Michael Billington "the inhuman detachment and moral vacuum of the murderer surveying his victims" (*Country Life*, 7 September 1989). According to Conrad, Iago

retreats into silence because he has no idea any more of what he should say. 'I am not what I am', the actor's creed, is a boast of power and an admission of impotence. No man can ever know himself, or be certain about where his desires and aggressions come from. What you will see on your television screen, when McKellen's Iago occupies it, is a black hole into which the illusion of human identity vanishes.[16]

So, too, with intimacy. If we cannot know ourselves, how can we ever know another? Nunn's *Othello* painfully exposes the fragility of human bonds, and particularly the difficulty men and women have in understanding each other.

The death scene in this production thus characterizes the two marriages: the display of Othello and Desdemona on the bed signifies a passionate sexual union that attains fulfillment only in death, while the isolated form of Emilia indicates the estrangement of the beaten and neglected wife.

*   *   *   *

Without "leave to speak," self-assertion entails struggle and transgression. Though each of the women in Nunn's *Othello* finds a place to speak – Desdemona from the Duke's chair, Emilia in her mistress's bedroom, Bianca resisting arrest – they are portrayed as hopelessly contained inside a military world that privileges male bonding. Nunn's military world has separate spheres for men and for women. Within the barracks, men are intimate with each other;

16 Conrad, "When Less Means Moor," p. 26.

within the boudoir, over a box of sweets, a woman relates to another woman. The relationship of man to woman and woman to man, however, is repeatedly shown to be more difficult and fragile. Through its naturalistic depiction of the small details of everyday human interaction, Nunn shows the flaws in such a world, flaws that are not confined to Iago's calculated deceptions but are embodied as well in the readiness of men and women around him to believe the deceptions.

Conclusion

Oth: But this denoted a foregone conclusion.
Iago: 'Tis a shrewd doubt, though it be but a dream.

(*Othello*, 3.3.429–30)

The *OED* demonstrates Shakespeare's influence on the English language when it explains "foregone conclusion" as "a Shaksperian phrase, variously interpreted by commentators," now commonly used to describe "A decision or opinion already formed before the case is argued or the full evidence known." This phrase, so common in our everyday conversation, is another instance of *Othello*'s continuing uses. Norman Sanders' New Cambridge edition of *Othello* glosses "foregone conclusion" as "previous consummation" (p. 131n.). The conclusion (*OED*'s "outcome" or "upshot") is foregone (*OED*'s "that has gone before or gone by"). What happened earlier is the outcome, but the outcome is also what happened earlier. To Othello, Cassio's dream denoted (not connotated or implied) that he had slept with Desdemona. Iago's response equivocates. "Doubt," according to the *OED*, had several meanings in the early seventeenth century. It could imply "a state of affairs such as to give hesitation or uncertainty." But it also suggested "apprehension, dread, fear" – characteristics readily apparent in Othello during Acts 4 and 5. While Iago rejects Othello's certainty, he still insists that the dream is just grounds for suspicion.

My conclusion is necessarily more akin to Iago's "shrewd doubt" than Othello's "foregone conclusion." *Othello*'s rich and varied acting history includes many productions and adaptations that might have been discussed just as well as those analyzed above. The lasting legacy of *Othello* is impossible to trace in full. But the preceding chapters should convey at least a small portion of the play's widespread influence.

Part I demonstrates the original text's complexity, which, in turn, encourages, if not requires, the broad range of interpretations. The centuries-old conflict between Christian Europe and the Ottomite Empire informed the dramatist's thinking about Venice and its Turkish enemy, creating the opposition between civilized Christian and barbaric Turk inherent in Othello's view of himself and his world. Within that Manichean view, the place of an increasingly professionalized military was in transition. Othello's role as mercenary general thus carried its own range of attitudes. His darkness of complexion, repeatedly emphasized in the play's linguistic opposition of black and white, foulness and fairness, problematizes the drama's social representations even further. And as we realize so often today, *Othello* presents the personal as the political. A husband's jealous suspicions against a wife from a different race and culture destroy his public role as general and his private role as an honorable man.

The four discursive formations outlined in Part I were obviously profound in Shakespeare's day and remain unresolved in today's Western culture. Recent confrontations in the Middle East and Bosnia reveal that mythologies and demonizations impede understanding between East and West and between Muslim and Christian; with the end of the Cold War, the shape of military establishments and the functions of the professional soldier are questioned anew; in the United States racial justice and equality are still elusive; backlash to the women's movement, not to mention backlash to the backlash, underscores the timelessness of gender issues. A cynic might say that in the nearly 400 years since *Othello*'s inception, each controversy has grown more poignant and confrontational. Inevitably they continue to complicate audiences' and readers' responses to *Othello*'s text.

Part II offers a chronological sampling of various ways these issues have been handled onstage and within English and American culture. From that sampling some broad conclusions can be drawn. For the Restoration, the conflict between male friendship and the hero's love for a woman, complicating factors in a military milieu, were of prime interest in *Othello*. Fear of racial difference had not yet hardened into the virulent racial Darwinism of the late nineteenth century. Despite his dusky hue, Othello could be represented as an aristocratic officer and gentleman who was deceived by a clever, manipulative villain of the lower classes. By the mid-eighteenth century, Othello could still be "one of us," though through the influence of actor Spranger Barry, he became less of a military hero and more of a romantic, exotic lover.

During the early Victorian period, Othello's relation to his wife became more important than his status as a military leader. Macready's rather pedestrian Moor was a doting husband: a model of respectability who could display violent aggression against his wife but would never talk openly about his passionate desire for her. Robbed of many of her lines, Desdemona was transformed from an outspoken heroine to a model of wifely deference, her death the pathetic stuff of melodrama.

Salvini's Othello marked a major change in racial discourse; no longer "one of us," the Moor became identified with passions antithetical to what was perceived as "Anglo-Saxon" rationality. Represented by an Italian actor speaking Italian, Salvini's tigerish Moor conjoined with English and American racial stereotypes to shape the early twentieth century's conception of Othello as a "primitive" who lacked civility and thus could not control his passion.

Turn-of-the-century assumptions about racial difference and about Othello's primitive nature were not completely negative, for they did pave the way for Paul Robeson's pathbreaking performances of 1930 and 1943. The actor who successfully portrayed the untutored primitive in Eugene O'Neill's *Emperor Jones* seemed a natural for Othello. Robeson's success in highlighting racial difference as a major factor in the play changed, in its turn, the way actors, scholars, and audiences viewed the play. In the 1990s, race is not the only issue in theatrical and filmic productions, but it is not likely to be ignored.

Race was minimized, however, in Orson Welles's 1952 film. I included this stunning film in my exploration of the uses of *Othello* because, from the middle of the twentieth century to the present, the renditions of Shakespeare's texts most influential in the larger culture have been filmic. Welles's movie of *Othello* was never widely circulated, but its treatment of Shakespeare's females was characteristic of 1940s and 1950s films. Using the camera's voyeuristic gaze, Welles shot his film from the masculine perspective, shaping his Desdemona into the object of male desire and exchange. Desdemona's visual image is seen to cause perturbations of Othello's mind, superimposing the desire to destroy onto the desire to possess.

The 1989 Trevor Nunn *Othello* problematizes gender roles even further, contrasting two marriages, one tired and dysfunctional, the other fresh and vulnerable. Nunn highlights the tremendous difficulty men and women find in creating and maintaining intimate relationships with each other, a difficulty that seems even greater when contrasted with the quick and facile male bonding of the military barracks. Whether this production will, indeed, have wide and lasting influence remains to be seen. To me, at least, Nunn's naturalistic video of *Othello* speaks profoundly to the social and sexual anxieties I see in my own culture.

Such broad generalizations simplify the materials presented in the preceding chapters, but they do indicate the parameters of a varied sample of *Othello* appropriations. They represent the ways in which the discursive formations outlined in Part I can be imbricated in production. More important, they show that while one area of concern may dominate during a particular cultural *episteme* – the military during the Restoration, for example – the other three dramatic foci are still present, even if they are minimized. At the core of racial, sexual, colonial, and military politics is power; in any given situation, their discourses are likely to overlap. When, for example, white European colonialists sent home postcards of naked African or veiled Muslim women to show the exotic appeal of conquered lands and their need for "the civilizing government only whites could bestow," their memento combined attitudes about gender, race, and "Orientals."[1] Similarly, constructs of masculine behavior, combined with racist assumptions, underly many United States government policies to bring together women of color, working as prostitutes, and service men on military bases.[2] Increasingly we recognize that we cannot understand the heritage of nineteenth-century racism without learning its effects on gender issues, colonial attitudes, and the military. With the eighteenth-century canonization of *Othello* and the spread of English culture to India, the Middle East, and Africa, these discourses, embedded in *Othello* during the early modern period, have flowed through the text and in and out of the surrounding culture. Through the processes of critical intervention and production, they have then been variously reinscribed back onto Shakespeare's text.

Though my conclusion fits one of *OED*'s standard definitions, "the last part or section of a speech or writing, in which the main

---

[1] See Cynthia Enloe, *Bananas, Beaches, and Bases: Making Feminist Sense of International Politics* (London: Pandora Press, 1989) for a fascinating account of how the discursive formations discussed above have become imbricated in international politics. Quote from p. 42.

[2] Ibid., pp. 81–84.

points are summed up," it resists another – it is not an "issue, final result," or "outcome." As should be apparent by now, there is no final result – not yet, and almost certainly never – to the uses of *Othello*. Every time the play is produced, debated in critical periodicals and conferences, taught in school, or read privately for pleasure, the text is reinscribed with a new and unique set of attitudes and values. Awareness of such multivalence will open up the text; perhaps as a result we can realize, less painfully than Othello did, that foregone conclusions and unexamined assumptions are socially and psychologically dangerous.

Index